A
Company
of Poets

Poets on Poetry

Donald Hall, General Editor

A Company of Poets

LOUIS SIMPSON

Ann Arbor   The University of Michigan Press

For James Wright, poet [1927–80]

"One light comes on in the sky."

Library of Congress Cataloging in Publication Data

Simpson, Louis Aston Marantz, 1923–
    A Company of poets.

    (Poets on poetry)
    1.   Simpson, Louis Aston Marantz, 1923–
—Aesthetics—Addresses, essays, lectures.
2.   Poetry—Addresses, essays, lectures.
3.   American poetry—20th century—History and
criticism—Addresses, essays, lectures.   I.   Title.
II.   Series.
PS3537.175C6   1981   809.1   80-24888
ISBN 0-472-06326-X

What a company of poets hath this year brought out!
. . . This April, every day some or other have
recited.

Burton, *The Anatomy of Melancholy*

Contents

I

On Being a Poet

About Jamaica

The poem is about Jamaica, the island in the West Indies where I grew up. And it is about the school I went to, from the age of nine to seventeen. The school was far from Kingston, where my family lived; situated on a barren mountain, it looked over a plain and a sea where no ships passed.

Though those years must have formed my life, I have hardly ever written about them. I have never cared to linger over childhood; and besides, my life in Jamaica was so unhappy at times, that whenever I have tried to say what was good about it, the unhappiness has come back.

This excerpt first appeared in "How I Wrote 'Returning,'" *Christian Science Monitor,* February 24, 1966.

Journeys through Bookland

1

There was a set of books called *Journeys through Bookland*. Book I was for the nursery, Book II for children learning to read, and so on, increasing in difficulty. The books were illustrated with drawings in line and color. I opened one of the middle volumes and came upon a picture that made me jump—of a skeleton sitting bolt upright, a thing of bones and ribs, wearing a suit of armor. The eyes of the skull were hollow, the jaws were open, and one fleshless hand was raised in the air.

> Speak! speak! thou fearful guest!
> Who, with thy hollow breast
> Still in rude armour drest,
>   Comest to daunt me!
> Wrapt not in Eastern balms,
> But with thy fleshless palms
> Stretched, as if asking alms,
>   Why dost thou haunt me?

This excerpt first first appeared in *North of Jamaica,* by Louis Simpson (New York: Harper & Row, 1972).

This must be poetry, for the lines on the page were short, each began with a capital letter, the ends of lines sounded alike, and the words were not the words that people used, so that I could hardly tell what they meant.

Then, starting from the page, a line that mystified me . . . speaking of the "maiden" in the story, the skeleton said, "She was a mother." Hadn't she always been a mother? Could it happen suddenly? If she hadn't always been a mother, what had she been?

The next line said: "Death closed her mild blue eyes." She was a mother and then she died.

I read through to the end. The Viking fell on his spear and his soul, "Bursting these prison bars," fled into the sky. The story ended with a frightening shout: "*Skoal!* to the Northland! *Skoal!*"

The volume exerted a dreadful fascination. Whenever I was in my father's study, where the books were kept, I knew that this book was there, with the picture of the skeleton, the maiden of whom it was said that "Death closed her mild blue eyes," and the word "*Skoal!*" that sounded like "skull."

2

There were books of adventure in [my father's] study, worm-eaten, tunneled through and through, and a powder fell out when you opened them—tales of voyages up the Orinoco and African explorations. They were illustrated with pictures of wild animals—jaguar, buffalo, crocodile—and pictures of savages and bearded men with rifles.

In his office, framed on a wall, were some lines of poetry showing that he'd once meditated on the theme of love.

> The night has a thousand eyes,
>   And the day but one;
> Yet the light of the bright world dies
>   With the dying sun.
>
> The mind has a thousand eyes,
>   And the heart but one;
> Yet the light of a whole life dies
>   When love is done.

This poem mystified me every time I saw it. It hinted at a side of my father I had never seen—sad and, had I known the word, sentimental. It haunts me to this day—I want to say to him: Don't you see what bad poetry it is? What eyes can the brain have? Or the heart? And in any case, if the brain has a thousand eyes, whatever this means, why shouldn't the heart have a thousand, too?

But he looks at me in a puzzled manner. He doesn't know what I'm talking about. It's not supposed to make sense, it's only a poem, that he hung up long ago.

3

When other boys were playing cricket I would lie under the willows, gorging on poetry and novels. Wind sighed in the leaves, and shadows of branches and clouds flitted over the page.

On Wenlock Edge the wood's in trouble;
   His forest fleece the Wrekin heaves;
The gale, it plies the saplings double,
And thick on Severn snow the leaves.

Or I would be reading *The Dynasts.*

   By degrees the fog lifts, and the Plain is disclosed. From
this elevation, gazing north, the expanse looks like the
palm of a monstrous right hand, a little hollowed, some
half-dozen miles across, wherein the ball of the thumb is
roughly represented by heights to the east, on which the
French centre has gathered . . . .

There were also poems by T. S. Eliot. I could not
make sense of them, yet I was haunted by the images
and the music of the lines.

   I will show you something different from either
Your shadow at morning striding behind you
Or your shadow at evening rising to meet you;
I will show you fear in a handful of dust.

Poetry at Columbia

I don't know how she strikes others, but Alma Mater on the steps, one hand holding a scepter, the other turned palm upward, to me seems to be saying, "Don't blame me. It's your problem." She looks right through such quarrels as I have with my education, and says, "What did you expect? Poetry?"

My first and most powerful memory of Columbia is of being overwhelmed by the Humanities. Many have praised this course, and so do I, for I have seen places where nothing like it exists. Sheep being herded into a field—that's the so-called liberal arts college today. As critics such as Robert Hutchins and William Arrowsmith have pointed out, it seems that the university, a place where you discover ideas, is vanishing, to be replaced by vocational training. But students at Columbia were exposed to ideas; in fact, some of us were encouraged not to settle down. In the Humanities, every Monday morning we were hurled into a new set of ideas, along with our instructors. Clutching one another, we tried to keep afloat. Ideas came pouring in; facts could be dealt with later.

This essay first appeared as "Ideas and Poetry," in *University on the Heights,* ed. Wesley First (New York: Doubleday, 1969).

One result of the course was that we liked ideas so well that we never got around to facts. When you had discussed the great ideas in the very best books, what could you possibly learn from experience? How could you give yourself to any one idea? And how could you ever write a research paper? In later years, the unfinished thesis was, in certain circles, a sign of the Columbia College man. In my travels I have come across the type, exiled from Columbia and condemned to live in the hinterland, because he had so many ideas that he could settle on none—at any rate, not long enough to write a thesis.

For my instructor in the Humanities I drew Lionel Trilling. Gracefully he led us from Homer to Spinoza to Fielding. His classes were chamber music in which we might be called upon to play a note or two. Then the bell rang and our conductor vanished. For me, it was like visions in a Chinese restaurant. There seemed to be an explanation, a clear reason for everything, but when I reached for it, it disappeared like a tail around a corner. I was too wrapped up in the words of the books I read to see that books are not just literature; they are part of something more important, the history of ideas, and most ideas are political. However, others saw the point, and some of my fellow students went on to become publishers, critics, and book reviewers:

hae tibi erunt artes: pacisque imponere morem, parcere subiectis, et deballare suberboe.*

I did get a crack at just literature, in a course taught by Raymond Weaver. He had a brow overhanging a

---

*[(Roman), these will be your arts: to establish peaceful ways, to spare the weak and overthrow the proud.]

glare; his voice was deep and resonant. It was said that he had lived in Japan; he had "discovered" Herman Melville; he was an amateur boxer. It was Weaver's habit to make a dramatic entrance and ask a startling question. I'm still rather proud of an answer I gave. He asked, "What is Aristotle's *Art of Poetry* about?" and I said, "How to write a play." As was his custom if the answer was correct, he ignored it.

Weaver preferred the stolid, unimaginative type of student to those who were, like himself, rather aesthetic. In his repertoire he had a trick that underlined this prejudice. He would recite "Casey at the Bat":

> Ten thousand eyes were on him as he rubbed his hands
>   with dirt,
> Five thousand tongues applauded when he wiped them
>   on his shirt;
> Then while the writhing pitcher ground the ball into his
>   hip,
> Defiance gleamed in Casey's eye, a sneer curled Casey's
>   lip.

Then he recited Dowson's poem about Cynara:

> I cried for madder music and for stronger wine,
> But when the feast is finished and the lamps expire,
> Then falls thy shadow, Cynara! the night is thine;
> And I am desolate and sick of an old passion,
>   Yea hungry for the lips of my desire:
> I have been faithful to thee, Cynara! in my fashion.

Then he would ask which was poetry. Inevitably some poor fish would bite, saying that "Cynara" was poetry and "Casey" wasn't. Whereupon, in his booming voice Weaver would explain the pretentiousness of "Cynara," its insincerity, its essential vulgarity. Some years after witnessing this performance, I met a man on Broadway who had had the misfortune to choose "Cynara." He steered our conversation back to this episode. He had been thinking about it for years, and thought he had been right, and unjustly treated, and was thinking of going to Weaver and telling him so. For all I know, he is still there, on the corner of 116th Street, telling his side of the story. But Weaver is not there. Had he lived to old age, I think he would have been one of those grand academic men of whom Wordsworth speaks, who give a university a druidic aura, who cast terror and awe before them as they walk, and leave a trail of humor in their wake. I do not see men like this coming out of the present-day graduate schools.

And I did get to poetry, with Mark Van Doren. His way of teaching was to talk about a book and express the thoughts that came into his head. He seemed to be composing the book, alongside Shakespeare, or Hardy, or Yeats. This was hardly a method, but he filled us with enthusiasm. He made us feel that we could write. Now, I am aware of the criticisms that may be made of such teaching, but more and more I place a high value on sympathy and enthusiasm in teaching, and a low value on method. For a great deal of method, when you examine it, is only another man's opinion tricked out with an apparatus. Of course, a teacher without a system must be in some way exemplary; he must have read much and be intelligent—or else his teaching is just sentimental. Van Doren was exemplary.

He put the finishing touch to my education. From then on, it was poetry that mattered. And if I have made my refusals—to be serious about scholarship, or editing, or writing criticism—it is because Van Doren encouraged me to think that poetry is more important than anything else. I have sometimes thought harshly of Columbia, because it is so conveniently near to the marketplace. As the creator of Marjorie Morningstar says, "At hand, as a quick change from the world of timeless values and hard intellectual work, was the wonderland of cynical, sophisticated New York." Cynicism and sophistication are the death of wonder, and the distance from Columbia to Madison Avenue is all too short. But whenever I am inclined to find fault with Columbia, I remember that Van Doren was part of it. There was poetry there, too, in those days.

A License to Dream

In 1943 I entered the United States Army, and after a period of training was assigned to the 101st Airborne Division. I was on the beach at Normandy on D Day, the sixth of June. My regiment was trained to use gliders, but on this occasion we came in by sea and made our way inland among the hedgerows. Our first taste of actual combat was on the outskirts of Carentan. I can see every detail of the scene as clearly as if it were present: the lane with trees among which we were pinned down by German machine guns and mortars . . . the tree a few feet away being raked by bullets.

In the weeks that followed I came to know the soil of France intimately. Moreover, as I spoke the language I was frequently required to see what some Frenchman wanted, as he came toward us. Usually it was to tell us where the Germans were, and to ask us to spare his house. The military business would end with negotiations of a different kind . . . our ciga-

This essay first appeared in a catalog, *Paris-New York: Échanges Littéraires au Vingtième Siècle,* ed. Serge Fauchereau (Paris: Centre Georges Pompidou, 1977).

rettes for their cognac. There was a great deal of friendship between the French and the Americans in those early days.

Our division was used in the unsuccessful attempt to turn the German flank at Arnhem. After that we were sent to Rheims for rest and refitting. I remember one day going for a walk by myself in order to read a book and smoke my pipe. I found a shady hollow. When I looked along it, I realized that I was sitting in a trench of the First World War. When I was a boy in Jamaica I had read about that war—to be sitting in a trench of that war, thirty years later, filled me with strange thoughts. This is the kind of thing that is important to poets, and a few years later I wrote a poem titled "I Dreamed that in a City Dark as Paris," in which I imagined myself standing in the boots of a poilu.

> I dreamed that in a city dark as Paris
> I stood alone in a deserted square.
> The night was trembling with a violet
> Expectancy. At the far edge it moved
> And rumbled; on that flickering horizon
> The guns were pumping color in the sky.

The poem evokes the image of the poilu.

> The helmet with its vestige of a crest,
> The rifle in my hands, long out of date,
> The belt I wore, the trailing overcoat
> And hobnail boots . . .

The poem ends with the thought that his life has been interchanged with mine, and that these wars, in the effect they have had on the human imagination, have disrupted the old order of history and chronology. Life has become like a dream where anything is possible.

> The violence of waking life disrupts
> The order of our death. Strange dreams occur
> For dreams are licensed as they never were.

Dogface Poetics

I got through the war all right, but afterwards, when I was back in the States, I had a nervous breakdown and was hospitalized. I had amnesia; the war was blacked out in my mind, and so were episodes of my life before the war. When I left the hospital I found that I could hardly read or write. In these circumstances I began writing poems.

Before the war I had written a few poems and some prose. Now I found that poetry was the only kind of writing in which I could express my thoughts. Through poems I could release the irrational, grotesque images I had accumulated during the war; and imposing order on these images enabled me to recover my identity. In 1948, when I was living in Paris, one night I dreamed that I was lying on the bank of a canal, under machine gun and mortar fire. The next morning I wrote it out, in the poem "Carentan O Carentan," and as I wrote I realized that it wasn't a dream, but the memory of my first time under fire. So I began piecing the war together, and wrote other poems. "Memories of a

---

This essay first appeared in *The Poetry of War*, ed. Ian Hamilton (London: Alan Ross, 1965).

Lost War" describes the early days of the fighting in Normandy; "The Battle," the fighting at Bastogne.

Twelve years after the war I wrote a long poem, "The Runner," which was devoted to the dogface soldier's war. I wanted to represent the drudgery of that life, the numbing of intellect and emotion, and the endurance of the American infantry soldier. I wanted to write a poem that would be abrasive, like a pebble in a shoe. Some readers thought this flat poem a mistake, but other readers, who were infantrymen, appreciated the details. To a footsoldier, war is almost entirely physical. That is why some men, when they think about war, fall silent. Language seems to falsify physical life and to betray those who have experienced it absolutely—the dead. As Hemingway remarked, to such men the names on a map are more significant than works of imagination.

However, in a postwar world there are limitations to the dogface way of looking at things. Love, for example, is not best written about by a man who is trying to avoid extra duty. And a country cannot be governed by silence and inertia. In recent years the closemouthed, almost sullen, manner of my early poems has given way to qualities that are quite different. Like other men of the war generation, I began with middle age; youth came later. Nowadays in my poems I try to generate mystery and excitement; I have even dealt in general ideas. But I retain the dogface's suspicion of the officer class, with their abstract language and indifference to individual, human suffering. You might say that the war made me a footsoldier for the rest of my life.

What, in these poems, was I trying to do that had not already been done? I did not wish to protest against war. Any true description of modern warfare is a protest, but many have written against war with satire or indignation, and it still goes on. My object was to remember. I wished to show the war exactly, as though I were painting a landscape or a face. I wanted people to find in my poems the truth of what it had been like to be an American infantry soldier. Now I see that I was writing a memorial of those years for the men I had known, who were silent. I was trying to write poems that I would not be ashamed to have them read—poems that would be, in their laconic and simple manner, tolerable to men who had seen a good deal of combat and had no illusions.

Postwar Years

I got back into Columbia by a rear door, by way of the School of General Studies. I could take courses there in the evenings and get a degree. It was so that I met younger students and writers who had not been in the war and whose attitudes were new to me. There were others I met at parties in the Village and in cold-water flats on the East Side. One night I gave a party of my own—I was living on West End Avenue—to which came a number of my new friends, bringing friends of their own. There was a thin, sallow young man with staring eyes and a puzzling smile, Allen Ginsberg. He'd been at Columbia while I was away. There was a burly fellow with an all-American face, Jack Kerouac. Another named Neil Cassady. The party got rough and they threw glasses out of the window to shatter on the pavement ten floors below. Ginsberg appeared from my bedroom carrying the sheet of a poem I had been trying to write, tripping rhymes about a little German girl. He read it aloud to my embarrassment. It seemed that Ginsberg, too, was trying to write poetry, and Ker-

This excerpt first appeared in *North of Jamaica,* by Louis Simpson (New York: Harper & Row, 1972).

ouac had written a novel comparing the city and the country.

The next day I found that a copy of Henry Miller's *Tropic of Cancer* that I'd picked up in Paris was missing. I've sometimes thought that, in this small way, I contributed to the growth of the Beats.

There was a man named John Hollander who seemed to know everything about poetry, especially metrics, and music. He would sit at the piano playing T. S. Eliot–that is, singing the words of "The Waste Land" to an arrangement of his own. And Ted Hoffman was living on Barrow Street in the Village; he was specializing in theater, mentioning names I'd never heard of—Bertolt Brecht and Eric Bentley.

There were a few girls who came to the parties, wild young things who had been educated at progressive schools. They were always talking about avant-garde painting and music and books. They dressed in hand-me-downs and came and went at odd hours.

I was invited to take part in a poetry reading at Columbia. The other readers were Allen Ginsberg and John Hollander. The famous English poet Stephen Spender would make the introduction. Spender's name meant a great deal to me. He was one of the so-called Oxford poets—W. H. Auden, Stephen Spender, C. Day Lewis, and Louis Mac-Neice. Many poets of the thirties and forties wrote in imitation of these men's style—a mixture of prep school flippancy and private jokes—and borrowed their Marxist and Freudian attitudes, their symbolism of images taken from machinery. Spender's poems were quite sentimental, but they were bedecked with pylons, factory chimneys, and locomotives. My own early poems had been alliterated like Auden's and brought up to date with Spenderesque references to machinery.

> Life is a winter liner, here history passes
> Like tourists on top-decks, seeing the shore through
>   sun-glasses . . .

Introducing us, Spender said a few words about the poetry of the day. The main difference between English and American poetry was that Englishmen had experienced the war and Americans hadn't. I listened to this description with some astonishment. Spender's other remarks were made with the same offhand air of authority, and for the first time I began to wonder if famous English authors knew as much as they seemed to.

Ginsberg read some poems about North Africa; he'd been there on a boat as a member of the crew. Later we walked down the Drive together talking about poetry. It was a hard life. He showed me holes in the elbows of his jacket.

Ginsberg giggled a lot, but his writing was apocalyptic.

> The land of our Forefathers has been, in history, compelled to a distinctly scatalogical habit, the fetishistic accumulation of mechanical knick-knacks, foorforaw, and plastic utilities as buttresses against reality; this, side by side with an even more patently scatalogical compulsion towards purity of convention and appearance . . . . All our healthiest citizens are at this very moment turning into hipsters, hop-heads, and poets. The state of the nation today, whether or not the proper authorities will recognize it, is one of complete anarchy, violent chaos, sado-masochistic bar-room confusion, and clinical hysteria, in which the megalopolitan mayors are continually trying to crusade against natural instincts, and unsuccessfully at-

tempting to suppress every perversion and criminality consequent in original suppression and traumatic intimidation . . . . The awful consummation of this holocaust of hysterical irresponsibility is the Atom Bomb.

Ginsberg hasn't much changed, from that day to this. I doubt that people ever do change fundamentally. They may go off in directions that seem contrary, but in a while you see that these were only digressions; the main direction is unaltered. Twenty years later, people are pretty much what you might have expected them to be; it is the ways by which they have arrived that are astonishing.

In order to be true to themselves, poets have to go far afield and discover new ways of speaking. Apollinaire says:

> Sacrifice taste and keep your sanity
> If you love your home you must make a journey
> You must cherish courage and seek adventure . . .
> Don't hope for rest risk everything you own
> Learn what is new for everything must be known . . .

The world does not see the necessity of this. But poets know that their most extravagant actions are dictated by a need to be perfectly simple.

In the postwar years poets, like everyone else, seemed exhausted. Many poets were content to write in traditional forms, taking their ideas from the critics.

T. S. Eliot had said it was an age of criticism. He meant the generation of 1910 when the imagist movement started. The imagists had original theories and wrote brilliant poems. Some of their attitudes were adopted by men who called themselves the New Critics. These men concentrated on "explication," that is, examining the "technique" of poems. They explicated the poems of Donne, but they no longer dealt with poetry as a vital, original force. They didn't ask fundamental questions—"Is this a poem?" "What is poetry?"—but knew how to explain symbols and discuss sentence structure.

Contrary to what critics said, after the imagists there had actually been a dearth of criticism. The men who grew in the shadow of Eliot and Pound were content to follow in their footsteps, imitating their opinions and even their styles. In the thirties and forties poets tried to make themselves a career in the grand manner: they knew what it was to sound like a great poet, but they had not begun, as Yeats had, by walking the roads and finding a subject of his own, or like Eliot and Pound by meeting to discuss the meaning of images.

As a result, in the fifties there were no ideas about poetry that spoke to a young man who was just beginning. Frost and Stevens were writing poems, but they said nothing to the young, and the poets of the forties, men such as Delmore Schwartz and Karl Shapiro, were imitating their elders and had no theories about what they were doing. Consequently, those who came after them were wandering about in a desert in which there were no signposts. The epigones of the New Critics were still writing textual analyses of Donne, but these were of little use to young men who had been through the war and had seen a great deal and wished to express their feelings about the contemporary world. There was no nourishment to be had. We wanted bread and were given these stones.

The New Critics—R. P. Blackmur, Cleanth Brooks,

John Crowe Ransom, Allen Tate, Robert Penn Warren, and their men in the universities—regarded the poem as an object for rigorous, empirical, objective analysis (textual criticism). The poem was treated "primarily as poetry and not another thing," without reference to the author's life or intention (the intentional fallacy), to history, to genre, or to the effect of the work on the reader's feelings (the affective fallacy). Young poets hastened to oblige the critics by writing poems that would be suitable for this kind of analysis. Above all, personality was to be omitted, except under a mask, and the speaking voice was ironic.

Dead Horses and Live Issues

In 1956, three writers met in a basement in Massachusetts and began putting together an anthology of contemporary verse. They thought of themselves as fair judges of American poetry, and one of them had an extensive knowledge of British poetry. However, though they did not know it, they were influenced by the *Zeitgeist*.

At that time the New Critics were still functioning, and many poets were writing in a manner that lent itself to so-called close reading. Let us try to remember what New Criticism stood for: the poem treated as an object complete in itself; impersonality, a distance between the poet and the poem, use of a persona, irony, et cetera. On the other hand, at that time the counterforces that have since come forward so powerfully had not begun to make themselves felt. Poets who were to become famous had not yet published a book; or if they had (Duncan), the book was not widely distributed. As the three editors turned over books and magazines, they did not discover, for example, Robert Duncan or Allen Gins-

This article first appeared in *Nation* 204, no. 17 (April 24, 1967).

berg or Robert Creeley. These poets were then writing in a manner which, contrary to the New Criticism, stressed self-expression and took Pound and William Carlos Williams as models of rhythm and diction. But in 1956, Pound and Williams were not an "influence," at least not in New England, and their disciples were practically unknown.

When it came out the anthology was titled *The New Poets of England and America*. The definite article infuriated those poets who had been left out and, in 1960, another anthology appeared which was made on principles derived, more or less, from Pound and Williams. But there was a more urgent principle: to exclude all the poets who had been in the first anthology. This was *The New American Poetry*. There were several differences between the anthologies. Most of the New Poets were Easterners; some of the New American Poets were located in San Francisco. East was East and West was West. Also, in prose statements at the back of the book, the New American Poets cocked a snoot at the "Academy," meaning the ideas of people who taught for a living (the editors of the first anthology had committed that indiscretion). To offset some domestic and uxorious poetry in the first anthology, *The New American Poetry* offered a selection of wild men, the Beats.

It has been ten years since these anthologies so neatly divided all Gall into two parts. Since then, everything has changed, though this has not been noticed by some reviewers, those deceived husbands of fashion who are always the last to know. For one thing, several of the New American Poets who were so scornful of universities have become . . . professors of English. Indeed, the only thing that looks like an establishment in American verse is the following commanded by Charles Olson, one of the poets in the second anthology. . . . .

But schools of poetry are a contradiction in terms and cannot last. For poets, who really are, want poems above everything else and will recognize good work and condemn bad, even if the praise and condemnation are not in accordance with their own aesthetic, political, or other interests. For a stunning example of this, see Pound's praise of Thomas Hardy, a poet of content and narrative power rather than style—praise that threatens to annihilate everything that Pound himself ever wrote. For a true poet, critical theory, and even friendship, must make way for the recognition of poetry when it appears, in whatever shape or voice.

Since the time of the anthologies there has been a general flight of poets of all kinds away from the sort of verse that the New Criticism was so well equipped to deal with. Though poets have not agreed on what they want to write, they have been agreeing on what they do *not* want to write. They don't want to write "low tide" verse—about finding a dead fish at low tide: or the poem about the statues in the Villa Medici: or the well-rhymed poem about picking up the kid's busted tricycle and thinking of the death of Patroclus. In fact, they don't want to write any kind of rhymed poem. Repulsions held in common—that's what we find when we look at the work of American poets today. They don't want to write the so-called well-made poem that lends itself to the little knives and formaldehyde of a graduate school.

There is an accelerating movement away from rationalistic verse toward poetry that releases the unconscious, the irrational, or, if your mind runs that way, magic. Surrealism was buried by critics of the thirties and forties as somehow irrelevant; today it is one of the most commonly used techniques of verse. The change can be measured by comparing the reputation of W. H. Auden today with what it was twenty years ago. Auden was nothing if not rational. Reading an Auden poem today is a chilling experience. Talk about snows of yesteryear!

The general movement is such as I have indicated, but within it there are poets of all varieties, and their disagreements can be sharp. Though they are, in Melville's phrase, fleeing from all havens astern, this does not mean that they are sailing for the same ports ahead. I can see very little similarity between the aesthetic principles of James Wright and Allen Ginsberg, or Robert Creeley and W. S. Merwin, or Robert Bly and Gary Snyder. Yet if these people were asked what they *dislike,* I think there'd be a surprising amount of agreement.

One common revulsion has joined American poets, at least for a while, in the common enterprise of poetry readings and protests against the war in Vietnam. They are all—or nearly all—agreed to dislike it. The occasion has not produced much good poetry—occasions hardly ever do—but it may serve to change the poets profoundly, so that in the future their poems will be political in the way that really counts—that is, by altering the angle of vision. Political poetry need not be about a political occasion; it may be about a butterfly. A poor man does not see the same glass of wine that a rich man sees, and a poet who has been deeply affected by the war may never again see the objects around him in the way he used to. Many Americans are being changed by this experience—in spite of themselves, for the experience is painful.

I think one result of the war will be that American poets will have to take their vocation seriously, as Europeans have had to take it. They are being compelled to take *themselves* seriously; they are becoming an intelligentsia.

The movement to release the unconscious, and this new political awareness, will give rise, I believe, in the next ten years, to poetry of the vatic kind. Donne is out; Blake is in. Whitman, Pound of the *Cantos,* and foreign language importations such as Neruda and Voznesensky, will be the models for young poets. At the same time, the gap between criticism and the art of poetry will grow even wider. Most critics were trained in the defunct Brooks-Warren method which didn't discuss, as I've said, anything but the poem-as-object. They have no language in which to treat the new poetry; indeed, it is increasingly obvious that they cannot see or hear, much less discuss it. New kinds of criticism will have to be developed in the coming years.

Whatever happens to poetry, we shall need poets to write it. Those who believe that poems will not have to be made, but will rise complete from the unconscious, and that the result will be poetry of a more valid and exciting kind, are having a fantasy with which poetry has little to do. We are in for some dreadful, bad writing . . . prose chopped into lines that look like verse . . . the outpourings of ignorance and vanity endlessly repeating themselves. We shall suffer through the Prophetic Book, the Whitman catalog, the Adams *Canto,* written not by Blake, Whitman, or Pound but by people without talent or humility. Yet, as we suffer these *longueurs,* let us remember, if we can, how trivial were the poems written under the direction of zanies who spoke of the "affective fallacy" as others might speak of the Whore of Babylon. And we can hope that a release of the unconscious and a larger range of concern in some poets will make for new work that has enthusiasm, imagination, vital rhythm, and original form.

For want of a better word, I have spoken of surrealism. But this is misleading, especially if we think of Breton's brand of surrealism—automatic writing. I doubt that anyone would want this back. Opposing the exaggerations of rationalism. Breton laid down the dogma that only the irrational is poetic. But the mind cannot be divided into rational and irrational sections, and the attempt to divide it is—rationalism run mad. There is nothing drearier than "pure" surrealism, a spate of disconnected images.

Contrary to Breton, poetry represents not unreason but the total mind, including both reason and unreason. (In order to explain I must use this language.) Poetic creation has been described by some poets—Wordsworth and Keats come to mind—as a heightened state of consciousness brought about, curiously, by an infusion of the unconscious. See the "Ode to a Nightingale." The images are connected in a dream; and the deeper the dream, the stronger, the more logical, are the connections.

Walt Whitman at Bear Mountain

> . . . life which does not give the preference to any other
> life, of any previous period, which therefore prefers its
> own existence . . .
>
> Ortega y Gasset

Neither on horseback nor seated,
But like himself, squarely on two feet,
The poet of death and lilacs
Loafs by the footpath. Even the bronze looks alive
Where it is folded like cloth. And he seems friendly.

"Where is the Mississsippi panorama
And the girl who played the piano?
Where are you, Walt?
The Open Road goes to the used-car lot.

"Where is the nation you promised?
These houses built of wood sustain
Colossal snows,
And the light above the street is sick to death.

"As for the people—see how they neglect you!
Only a poet pauses to read the inscription."

"I am here," he answered.

This essay first appeared in *Poet's Choice,* ed. Paul Engle and
Joseph Langland (New York: Dial Press, 1962).

"It seems you have found me out.
Yet, did I not warn you that it was Myself
I advertised? Were my words not sufficiently plain?

"I gave no prescriptions,
And those who have taken my moods for prophecies
Mistake the matter."
Then, vastly amused—"Why do you reproach me?
I freely confess I am wholly disreputable.
Yet I am happy, because you have found me out."

A crocodile in wrinkled metal loafing . . .

Then all the realtors,
Pickpockets, salesmen, and the actors performing
Official scenarios,
Turned a deaf ear, for they had contracted
American dreams.

But the man who keeps a store on a lonely road,
And the housewife who knows she's dumb,
And the earth, are relieved.

All that grave weight of America
Cancelled! Like Greece and Rome.
The future in ruins!
The castles, the prisons, the cathedrals
Unbuilding, and roses
Blossoming from the stones that are not there . . .

The clouds are lifting from the high Sierras.
The Bay mists clearing;
And the angel in the gate, the flowering plum,
Dances like Italy, imagining red.

I have chosen to be represented by "Walt Whitman
at Bear Mountain"—not because I think it the best
poem I have written, but because it marked a turn-
ing point in my work. I had recently published a
book of poems, *A Dream of Governors,* in which I had
solved to my satisfaction certain difficulties of writ-

ing "in form"—that is, in regular meter and rhyme. But now I felt that my skill was a straitjacket. Also, inevitably, the adoption of traditional forms led me into a certain way of ending a poem, polishing it off, so to speak, that sometimes distorted my real meaning. It was time, I felt, to write a new kind of poem. I wanted to write a poem that would be less "willed." I would let images speak for themselves. The poem would be a statement, of course—there really is no such thing as a poem of pure metaphor or image— but I wanted the statement to be determined by the poem itself, to let my original feeling develop, without confining it in any strict fashion.

Of course, this was a matter of degree. Even the poem that seems most free is confined in some way— if by nothing more evident than the limitations of the poet's subconscious. What I did manage to arrive at in "Walt Whitman" was a poem that presented certain images and ideas in an almost colloquial manner, in lines whose rhythm was determined by my own habits of speech. This was not absolute freedom, but the result was more satisfying to me than recent poems in which I had presented ideas in neat rhymes. In fact, whatever theory about the writing of verse enables a poet to speak the truth and fills him with energy, is good. My groping toward a poetry of significant images and spoken lines enabled me to say certain things that I had not been able to say before. This poem was followed by others in which I was able to deal with material that interested me—poems about history, my own personal life, America.

"Walt Whitman at Bear Mountain" springs from an actual experience, as do most of my poems. About three years ago I traveled up the Hudson River to Bear Mountain with my wife and the poet Robert Bly and his wife. We came upon the Jo Davidson (I believe that's the right spelling) statue of Walt Whitman. The statue was very impressive under the leaves. A few days later I started this poem. I didn't finish it for months, not until I had moved to California. The fragments of what I had attempted then cohered all at once—this is the way it happens with me, if I'm lucky.

Whitman means a great deal to me. When I came to America, at the age of seventeen, an intelligent cousin gave me a copy of *Leaves of Grass*. I recognized immediately that Whitman was a great, original poet. I now think that he is the greatest poet we have had in America. But I think that most of his prophecies have been proved wrong. It is a strange fact, when you think about it—that a poet can be great and yet be mistaken in his ideas. The Whitman who heralds an inevitable march of democracy, who praises the intelligence of the masses, is nearly always mistaken. At least, if there ever was an America like that, it no longer exists. But the Whitman who uses his own eyes and ears, who describes things, who expresses his own sly humor or pathos, is unbeatable. I tried to show the two Whitmans in my poem. I used my ideas about Whitman as a way of getting at my own ideas about America. And I think a great deal about the country I live in; indeed, it seems an inexhaustible subject, one that has hardly been tapped. By America, I mean the infinitely complex life we have. Sometimes when I look at Main Street, I feel like a stranger looking at the Via Aurelia, or the Pyramids. But our monuments are ephemeral. Poetry is the art of the ephemeral.

It is hard to talk about a poem, for talking about poetry leads you out in every direction. I do not see the art of poetry as separated from life.

On Being a Poet in America

> I swear I begin to see the meaning of these things,
> It is not the earth, it is not America who is so great,
> It is I who am great or to be great, it is You up there, or
> any one,
> It is to walk rapidly through civilizations, governments,
> theories,
> Through poems, pageants, shows, to form individuals.
>
> Whitman

A poet must have talent. No, this is not a joke—or rather, it is half a joke, like saying that one would like to be rich—but nevertheless it is true that most poets are a little short of talent. Don't ask me how the poet gets it. I am only making up a story. Ask God such questions. Talent is the one thing that cannot be bought, borrowed, or stolen. Many pretend to have it, but no one is deceived for long, least of all the man who is pretending. Give him a check and his face gets longer; give him a prize and he bursts into tears. For he knows that it is all a joke; inside himself he is standing without pants, naked, and the children are pointing.

This essay first appeared in *The Noble Savage,* no. 5, ed. Saul Bellow, Keith Botsford, and Aaron Asher (Cleveland: World Publishing, 1962).

Then maybe he ought to be not too much of his time, of his place. Perhaps he should be born in a log cabin in Ontario, where an old trapper has left the collected poems of Heine in German; and he will translate them alongside a dictionary as he grows up, in the long Canadian nights. Or he should be the third son of a realtor, embezzle his father's money, and have to emigrate to Brazil. There he will discover Rimbaud. Perhaps he should simply lie in bed in the Bronx till he is thirty, with his aunts and uncles bringing him his socks and urging him to get up, and arranging jobs for him—certainly, if he did that, jobs would be offered to him—and until he was thirty-one, he would not write a word. That would be an original start, and above all poets must be original.

He should not behave like a poet. That is, he should not pattern himself on the famous dead or the influential living. There are many kinds of reputation. Some have glossy fur, black snouts, and sharp little claws; others are like storks, tall and full of wisdom; others are striped like tigers. And they all belong in the zoo or in the museum. The poet will avoid them by all means.

He will not serve other men. That is the occupation of a valet.

●

The astonishment that anyone reads anything you write, and that anyone takes it seriously, as though it actually existed. And then, your resentment. What right do they have to read your mail?

When anyone says anything either for or against a poem you've written, you feel like saying,

"Listen, I work for a living. If I write poems that's my business."

Then, the internal writhing when anyone calls you a poet. And the look of dismay on the face of the person to whom you are introduced in this fashion.

●

"To have great poets we must have great audiences too." This tag from Whitman, which adorns or used to adorn every issue of *Poetry,* is about as close to the opposite of the truth as you can get. To have great poetry all that is needed is great talent. There can be no such thing as a great audience for poetry. An audience for bad writing—yes!

The mark of the bad writer is that he is popular, especially among people who "don't usually read poetry." To please, a writer must produce standard, name brand goods. Everything such minds produce is predictable and trite, and therefore easily recognized by the "average reader." Originality is not welcome— at least, not until years have passed, when it has been diluted and become fashionable, and is no longer original. Those who hope for a "renaissance" of verse, to be measured by gate receipts or the number of volumes sold, expect what simply cannot be. For the poet's task is to use his imagination, and imagination goes beyond what is already known—that is, beyond an audience. The poems of thirty years ago may be popular now—an audience has been prepared for them; the sentimental writing of today may be popular—for it flatters the stupidity of the audience. But real poetry cannot be popular in its own time. The poet knows this and hopes to be read by his fellow poets and a few intelligent readers.

The novelist George M. once told me, "I've been lectured on my artistic integrity by more damn people. And I meet them a few months later and they're in advertising."

True. Once at Columbia, a few minutes before I went in to take an exam in Chaucer, I met X. in the corridor. X. was a teacher in those days. I complained to him about the Chaucer requirement (I was pretty nervous). Why Chaucer? I said. Why not Tolstoy, or Sophocles?

He flew into a rage. It was people like me, he said, who were the trouble with Columbia. We expected the university to give us a degree just because we wrote poems. We didn't know the first thing about scholarship. I was astonished—in fact, he seemed slightly insane. Then I told him to go and peddle his fish.

About a year later, X. quit teaching and went into public relations where, I am told, he is making a pile of money.

Or consider Y. A few years ago he wrote a poem saying, "Where are all the young poets nowadays? They are all in the Universities." The burden of his song was that he himself was above teaching, or getting fellowships, or writing for the quarterlies. Then this apostle of the pure life proceeded to get himself a Guggenheim and a professorship.

As George said, you meet them a few months later and they're in advertising.

●

There is only one law for the poet—tell the truth!

For years you try to write, and at last you are faced with two alternatives—either write what is acceptable, or tell the truth. If you write what you really think, you will find yourself in a lonely place. But if you are serious about it—and if you're not, you aren't a poet at all—you must get to that place sooner or later. The sooner the better.

In America, success is the worst temptation for the writer, as it is for other men. At several points in my life I have seen rising clearly before me an opportunity to *belong*. I have met some of the more important literary men of my time, and they gave me to understand that they would be glad to help me in some way. But a voice within me, like Socrates' sign, said, "Flee for your life!"

I know too much about literary life. I know by what means, by what steady cultivation of his betters, by what obsequiousness in print and out of it, the mediocre writer gets himself a name. As Huxley said, fame, the last infirmity of noble mind, is the first infirmity of the ignoble. The need of fame has turned many a decent man into an envious, spiteful, vanity-ridden, self-deluding wretch. And what does he have to show for it? A handful of reviews.

The poet's task is to tell the truth. And, of course, he must have talent. His only real satisfaction is in the writing of poems—a dull-seeming procedure in which he sits down facing a blank wall, and smokes, and from time to time scratches on a sheet of paper. There have been plays about piano players and painters, but the writing of poetry is least suitable for dramatic representation.

It is getting harder and harder to write a poem. That is, I can start one well enough—but how to finish?

A few years ago I was able to begin and finish a poem. I found that the poem was directed by certain external forces toward a certain end. But one day I found that ideas were better expressed in prose. No, it was more than that. I found that I no longer wished to please. The reader has certain stock responses to ideas, and certain responses—not very strong perhaps, but operative nevertheless—to metaphor, meter, and rhyme. A poem that satisfies his stock responses is "good"; a poem that does not is "bad."

I found myself wanting to write bad poems—poems that did not depend on stock responses. I wanted to write poems that would not please. For the last three years I have been learning to write this new kind of poem. The most important change is in the content (whether one writes "in form," or "out of form," is not an essential question—it is a matter for simpletons to worry about, and of course it is the only question that reviewers usually feel competent to discuss).

Instead of statements which reassure the reader by their familiarity, or shock him by their strangeness—instead of opinions, there are only images and reverberations.

I can never finish these poems. I wrestle with them and leave off when I am exhausted. Frequently, all that remains is a handful of phrases.

The difficulty is that, to write this new kind of poem, which springs mainly from the subconscious, I must work not at technique, but at improving my character.

How easy it is to settle on a certain style, to write a certain poem over and over again! Most verse writers do just this. They publish a new book of the same poems every four years, and when they have repeated themselves often enough they win the Pulitzer.

There is this to be said for not being a professional man of letters—you can do as you like. What have you got to lose?

Work is all well and good, but what you pray for is inspiration. That is, one day when you sit down and wrestle with a poem, you find that you are wrestling with an angel. Then all the phrases flow together; the unfinished poems lying in the back of the closet rise and fly together. They are changed into something that you have not logically conceived. At such moments, which are rare enough, you are not writing but assisting at the birth of truth in beauty.

Of course, to some people this is all nonsense. To a deaf man, music does not exist; to a blind man, there are no constellations in the sky.

●

No, poetry is not dying, and verse is not a dying technique. Those who have said that it is, perhaps wishing that it might be, were writers of prose, and some of them were critics. They have congratulated themselves prematurely. A great deal of criticism is nothing to brag about, if the criticism has been an end in itself. And criticism in the last forty years has been largely an end in itself, a bastard kind of art, a kind of theatricals for shy literary men. I have known critics who were actors at heart, giving their own impersonations of Raskolnikov, or Donne, or Freud. Next week, *East Lynne*.

What is most disappointing about criticism is that when you examine the critic's method, under the appearance of sweet reasonableness there are only prejudices and taboos. The critic's art depends on an exertion of his personality, an unstable quality. Now, poets and novelists and playwrights also use their personality, but from this they extract certain definite objects—the poem, the novel, the play. They deal in facts. But the critic deals in opinions.

An age of prose? All that prose has been a symptom of culture, and the culture was not directed to any serious purpose.

New Lines for Cuscuscaraway and Mirza Murad Ali Beg

"... the particular verse we are going to get will be cheerful, dry and sophisticated."

T. E. Hulme

O amiable prospect!
O kingdom of heaven on earth!
I saw Mr. Eliot leaning over a fence
Like a cheerful embalmer,
And two little Indians with black umbrellas
Seeking admission.
And I was rapt in a song
Of so*phist*ication.
O City of God!
Let us be thoroughly dry.
Let us sing a new song unto the Lord,
A song of exclusion.
For it is not so much a matter of being chosen,
As of not being excluded.
I will sing unto the Lord
In a voice that is cheerfully dry.

●

When you are dealing with poetry itself, all these other matters—the question of an audience, fashions in criticism, the envy and malice that lie in your way like stumbling blocks—these all vanish. And the question of how to write also vanishes.

Yes. But why don't I say what poetry is, rather than what it is not?

The kind of poetry I am talking about has not existed in America for a long time. Perhaps it has not yet existed. There are starts toward it in Whitman, in Hart Crane. But mostly we have had a poetry of culture, the dry verse recommended by Hulme, or we have had sentimental verse.

What we need is the total poetic intelligence that existed in Rilke, in Yeats, in Blake. We need poetic brains. If Frost had caught fire, what a poet he would have been! But always in Frost there was a drawing back from ultimate commitment. The swung birch always carried him back safely to earth; he stopped in the woods for only a few minutes, and then he went home. This was wisdom, but it was not the greatest poetry. What we need is a poet of original, and purely poetic talent. That is, he would make up new ways of seeing things; he would push metaphor to the limit. And if such a poet were also interested in ordinary life, we would have great American poetry. Such a poet would not have to justify his existence in America; the rest of us would have to justify ourselves to him.

Rhythm

When we have understood the social and psychological conditions that affect an artist's life and form his ideas, we still have not understood the impulse and nature of art itself. After all, many people have unusual lives, but very few are artists. Why does a man choose to be a writer? And why poetry?

He doesn't choose—he is moved by the rhythms of speech. Certain people have a physical, visceral way of feeling that expresses itself in rhythm. Some people play music, others dance, and others—who are attracted to words—utter lines of verse. These are the poets.

The rhythms of poetry rise from the unconscious. This is not generally understood, even by critics who write about poetry. Before a poet writes a poem, he hears it. He knows how the lines will move before he knows what the words are.

Descriptions of poetry by men who are not poets are usually ridiculous, for they describe rational thought processes. For example, in the novel *Keep the Aspidistra Flying,* George Orwell describes a poet at

---

This excerpt first appeared in *North of Jamaica,* by Louis Simpson (New York: Harper & Row, 1972).

work—putting one idea logically after another, choosing the next word, image, and rhyme. This is completely false; prose may be written in this way, but not poetry. A poet begins by losing control; he does not choose his thoughts, they seem to be choosing him. Rhythms rise to the surface; a fraction of a moment later the necessary words fall into place.

Poets agree that rhythm is of the first importance. Paul Valéry, for example, describes the physical state of a man on the threshold of poetry:

> I had left my house to find, in walking and looking about me, relaxation from some tedious work. As I went along my street, which mounts steeply, I was *gripped* by a rhythm which took possession of me and soon gave me the impression of some force outside myself. Another rhythm overtook and combined with the first, and certain *strange transverse* relations were set up between them.

This was more strange, Valéry says, than anything he could have expected of his "rhythmic faculties"—meaning his will, his rational mind. The rhythms rising from the unconscious seem to arrive from outside. In former ages poets were often "visited" in this manner, and their utterances were regarded as divine truths. But the world has grown rational, and no head of state would consult a poet—except as a prop under the spotlights on a public occasion. Instead, it is the physicists who hand down our oracles.

When we try to explain poetry and defend it, we forget that it needs no defence, for poetry is a form of reality with certain definite powers. There is no substitute for the form and sound of a true poem. The poem is unique, therefore it exists. And the more powerfully it exists the less possible it is to explain it—that is, to replace it with prose.

Poetry is essentially mysterious. No one has ever been able to define it. Therefore we always find ourselves coming back to the poet. As Stevens said, "Poetry is a process of the personality of the poet." This personality is never finished. While he is writing the poet has in mind another self, more intelligent than he. The poet is reaching out to the person that he would be, and this is the poet's style—a sense of reaching, that can never be satisfied.

Vanishing Angel

We hope that one night when the moon has risen an angel will appear and say, "Take this down." According to Rilke this is what happened to him at Duino. An angel gave him the elegies. But with us it happens otherwise. The angel appears, dictates a few lines, looks at his watch, and vanishes. And there we are, with a handful of words. The worst of it is, these fragments don't vanish; they keep repeating themselves like a damaged record. They keep creeping into any new thing we are trying to write, where they don't belong, spoiling any new idea we may have. For example:

> I am swept in a taxi
> to the door of a friend.
> He greets me like a statue
> fixed in the position of a man
> who always marries the wrong woman.

These lines came to me three years ago, and have been returning ever since, and I can't exorcize them.

This excerpt first appeared in *North of Jamaica,* by Louis Simpson (New York: Harper & Row, 1972).

They are the beginning of a poem about New York, the comedy of Chekhov brought over to verse, that will never be written.

But how can I tell? Maybe it will be written. For I've had other fragments that managed to come together, one day when I wasn't thinking about them too hard. Also, sometimes by sheer hard work I've managed to make sense out of such things. So just waiting isn't an answer—it's necessary to try. Yet, as I've said, there's no guarantee that if you keep trying anything will come of it.

II

Reviews and Essays

W. D. Snodgrass's *Heart's Needle* and Thom Gunn's *Fighting Terms*

I wish I could find a poem in Mr. O'Gorman's book to admire but as five judges have admired it, I will pass without anxiety to W. D. Snodgrass's *Heart's Needle*. This poet, it seems, has been exposed to as much education as Mr. O'Gorman, but his poetry is not compounded of literary and classical references and striking attitudes. He is original; his ideas and language are never worked up to impress the reader; he carries his feelings as far as they can go, and no further. I think I could recognize a poem by Mr. Snodgrass anywhere, after reading only a few lines. He has managed to discover himself, and though the self is not in the grand manner, it is pervasive. He works at the other extreme from rhetoric; if anything, his tone is a little too relaxed. Now and then, from the light-moving stanzas there flashes a comment that startles by its appropriateness, and the phrasing at such moments is naturally perfect. Mr. Snodgrass recognizes the main task of the poet: to tell the truth and avoid falsifying. He has put on no fine masks to which his features must

This review first appeared in "In the Absence of Yeats," *Hudson Review* 12, no. 2 (Summer 1959).

hereafter conform; he is free to develop. The occasional thinness of his poetry may be corrected by increasing the qualities he already has.

The ending of "The Marsh" shows this poet's originality. The marsh he trudges through is a weedy, stinking place (here, as in other descriptions, Mr. Snodgrass reminds me of the author of "Peter Grimes"):

> You look up; while you walk
>   the sun bobs and is snarled
> in the enclosing weir
>   of trees, in their dead stalks.
> Stick in the mud, old heart,
>   what are you doing here?

The trick, of course, is in the last two lines; no amount of anything but talent could have invented that irrelevance. Or let us choose a stanza from "April Inventory." The argument is that the speaker, a teacher in a girls' school, is visibly decaying, while they are not; moreover, as he is not a scholar, he is falling behind his colleagues in the profession. He concludes:

> Though trees turn bare and girls turn wives,
> We shall afford our costly seasons;
> There is a gentleness survives
> That will outspeak and has its reasons.
> There is a loveliness exists,
> Preserves us, not for specialists.

The point is made lightly, yet it is vital, and it could scarcely be made more happily.

The sequence titled "Heart's Needle," on which the book is centered, recounts some emotional and practical difficulties entailed by the break up of a marriage. Divorce may be to this century what the frontier was to the last; Mr. Snodgrass's poem is a sort of American epic. Here it all is: the ordeal of "visiting," the divided child, the staring reproachful toys, the nostalgia, the sticky trip to the zoo, and the necessary, useless expense of guilt. It may not be all poetry, but it seems terribly real, and as moral as anyone could wish. The speaker ends at the zoo in front of the cages:

> If I loved you, they said, I'd leave
> and find my own affairs.
> Well, once again this April, we've
> come around to the bears;
>
> Punished and cared for, behind bars,
> the coons on bread and water
> Stretch thin black fingers after ours.
> And you are still my daughter.

Mr. Snodgrass's strength is in the language that is both ordinary and poetic, which Wordsworth recommended; in a time of much pedantry, *Heart's Needle* seems doubly original.

Thom Gunn is one of the best poets now writing in English. He has great intelligence and knowledge of the world, expressed with music and wit. I don't agree with some of his ideas—with, for example, his admiration of disciplines, and his fascination with "toughness." I prefer his imagination. By this I mean his capacity to suppose a world more interesting and enduring than that of his own experience, and his reporting that world as fact. Mr. Gunn's best work is imaginative, as when, in *Fighting Terms*, he begins:

> One night I reached a cave: I slept, my head
> Full of the air. There came about daybreak
> A red-coated soldier to the mouth, who said
> 'I am not living, in hell's pains I ache,
> > *But I regret nothing.*'

In *The Sense of Movement,* his poems "Autumn Chapter in a Novel," "The Wheel of Fortune," "The Silver Age," and "St. Martin and the Beggar," are masterpieces of imagination; on the other hand, the poems titled—and the titles point to a heavy specificity—"The Unsettled Motorcyclist's Vision of His Death," "Elvis Presley," and "Market at Turk," are more circumstantial, and less interesting. Curiously, I find Mr. Gunn most arguable where he is undertaking to report what he sees. It is when imagination flags that we search for reasons. Occasionally he is didactic:

> I think of all the toughs through history
> And thank heaven they lived, continually . . .

And he admires Mr. Yvor Winters's finely trained and caged airedales. In contradiction to Mr. Gunn's opinions, I would like to suggest these authorities. First, there is Proust's remark that people who exercise a great deal may not be so much in possession of strength as they are in need of it. There is the advice of Conrad's old butterfly-collector, to immerse in the destructive element and let it bear you up. And last, there is Yeats's warning that the will cannot do for the imagination.

"Nowadays," said Childe Roland, " . . . poetry is chiefly lyrical." Certainly, the best of it seems to be so, and Thom Gunn's lyrics are memorable. His combining of song and idea in an ominous pastoral recalls the high spirits of Auden:

> In fine simplicity
> I cry On either side
> Far as the eye can see
> These fields as green as wide
> Are my master's property.

"The Silver Age" is a deeper music:

> Do not enquire from the centurion nodding
> At the corner, with his head gentle over
> The swelling breastplate, where true Rome is found.
> Even of Livy there are volumes lost.
> All he can do is guide you through the moonlight.

There is a clarity about Mr. Gunn's mind, and precision in his use of words; to these lyric qualities he adds dramatic and narrative elements that are beyond the reach of most of his contemporaries.

A Garland for the Muse

Reviews of Books by J. V. Cunningham, Denise Levertov, and Anne Sexton

It is time for the anti-Plato to appear, the philoso-
pher of the Absolutely Bad. If there are still works
of art suspended above the earth—paintings not yet
realized; sonatas, like Vinteuil's, that tease the lis-
tener with a promise of eternal beauty—there are
also, somewhere beneath the earth, works of a bad-
ness that has not yet been realized, and these works
also have their midwives, minds prevented only by a
shadowing of intelligence and education from per-
fecting the masterpieces of dullness, misshapenness,
and folly that lurk in the Absolute. But they try, they
try, and in front of me I have sixteen books of verse
that are, if not the thing itself, certainly working
drafts of incoherence. In the upside-down cave of
the anti-Plato, these ideas also cast a light; they show
us what to avoid. We must be grateful for bad books,
and to their creators. These poems will not have to
be written again; these bats are in other people's
belfries.

Here is the deluxe edition by the master of the
"low tide" school of verse (all about clams and drift-

This review first appeared in *Hudson Review* 13, no. 2 (Summer
1960).

wood on the Maine coast in October); the new and less convincing version of the New Testament by Brother Rhinoceros; the collages of malice and obscenity by another disappointed man (they are all gone into the world of light, and he alone sits ling'ring here); the collected poems of the selected friend of a major critic; the poems dated at Fiesole, and Rapallo, and Taormina (postcards, Cecil, are not poems); an epic of the Snake Indians by an octogenarian, with a preface attacking the obscurantism of modern verse, by which he means "The Waste Land"; and the poem, no shorter than fifty lines and no longer than ten thousand, celebrating the discovery of oil in Oklahoma, which has been awarded a prize of five thousand dollars by the Oilwomen's League for the Perpetration of Culture. These works will have their meed of praise in *Time* and the *Times* and the *Saturday Review;* I will therefore discuss four books of another kind, which have been mixed in with the lot, seemingly by accident.

The first is J. V. Cunningham's *The Exclusions of a Rhyme.* There are not so many serious poets in America that we can afford to neglect the collected poems of a talent like this, yet I am afraid that present neglect is what Mr. Cunningham must have—and, to some extent, he has courted it. By reaction, it appears, he has particularly cultivated just those qualities that are likely to repel the publicists of the age. I sympathize with his attitude, for there is no general public worth having, yet I regret that his attitude has constricted his poetry; it is too much in reaction. But before I go into this, I would like to show his advantages.

First, he is a master, in his way. His tight, short,

rhymed lines could hardly be improved. They have, as he writes:

> The classic indignation,
> The sullen clarity
> Of passions in their station,
> Moved by propriety.

A further concentration produces this:

> You wonder why *Drab* sells her love for gold?
> To have the means to buy it when she's old.

The word, of course, is *hard*. The forms and tone of Mr. Cunningham's verse are neoclassic; as far as his style goes, no poet since Swift need have written, and the vernacular does not exist. Exclusions with a vengeance! Now and then an image is admitted, as in "The Dog-Days":

> Nothing alive will stir for hours,
> Dispassion will leave love unsaid,
> While through the window masked with flowers
> A lone wasp staggers from the dead.
>
> Watch now, bereft of coming days,
> The Wasp in the darkened chamber fly,
> Whirring ever in an airy maze,
> Lost in the light he entered by.

But there are entire poems which contain no image; they are written as *sententiae*. What are they about? The discipline of the will . . . love, pride, anger . . . the work of art. Dispassion and diffidence are key words. His poems are demonstrations of ideas, and are themselves the ideas they demonstrate. Moreover, there is much grace in his method, and those who have an ear for verse will enjoy his poems for that reason alone. It is odd to have to praise a poet for being talented as a writer, but nowadays when every other botched novelist, peevish Ph.D. candidate, or rabbit-spirited junky sets down the wanderings of his brain in separate lines and calls it verse, it seems necessary to remark that the ability to write poetry is a rare gift, as rare as the talent of a first-rate violinist, and not to be simulated by mere energy or mere intelligence. This is a dismaying truth to some, and the reason that verse is often distrusted and sometimes hated. Nothing infuriates mediocrity so much as talent. Besides, it is profoundly unconventional to spend time perfecting the form and meaning of words, in a society increasingly run by admen. I hope you will not think I am just being paradoxical if I say that Mr. Cunningham's poetry is revolutionary—for what is revolution but opposition to the status quo? And it is the eccentricity of such minds, expending themselves in a search for perfection, that will save us at last, if we are to be saved.

Yes, I admire Mr. Cunningham, as you see, and I am glad that there is one of him in America. But there are other ways of poetry which, I am afraid, Mr. Cunningham would exclude, and this brings me to my main criticism of his verse. It is simply that you cannot show the triumph of discipline over disorder unless you also show the disorder. You cannot produce *Lear* without the storm scene, nor bring Oedipus to Colonus without passing through Thebes. The poet must always fear his own wisdom, the self-examination which says, Why write anything at all? Is not the perfection of understanding perfect silence? Is not the best poem a blank page?

When one comes to this resignation, one is abnegating the task that poets, if not philosophers, have, which is to translate the world. The task was not beneath Shakespeare, nor Dante, nor Sophocles; they did not merely give you the epilogue; they also made you see and feel their experience, and so you were able to participate in their wisdom. You had earned the right to be resigned. But Mr. Cunningham's poems do not often give you the opportunity to earn that right. You may see how he justifies himself in the poem, and yet have no joy in it.

Again—can you turn your back so entirely on the language of your own time and place, neglect the traditions of your own country, without marring your perceptions? In his adherence to English traditions of verse, Mr. Cunningham is excluding—of course, deliberately—all that is specifically American, the traditions of Twain and Whitman and Hart Crane, for example. I wonder if this is not a serious error. For can you really revive antique ways of thought? Can an American writing like a sixteenth- or eighteenth-century Englishman avoid seeming to be only an American et cetera? Poetry is not all a matter of idea and technique; it is also in the air we breathe. I miss in Mr. Cunningham's poetry a local habitation and a name. Sometimes, when Americans try to be like Europeans, their native twang creeps in willy-nilly, producing a slightly ludicrous juxtaposition; or their precision reveals their discomfort. I find it difficult to imagine any Englishman's verse being quite as impeccably formal as Mr. Cunningham's. He has an excruciated sense of poetic manners. But here I find my argument turning against itself, for no one is as pure as the American. No Englishman was ever as proper as Henry James; and

Mr. Cunningham, in the excess of his severity, is our old friend the American Puritan.

And like the Puritan he has a sardonic side. The poems, and more strikingly the epigrams, exhibit a standard, old-fashioned way of treating love and lust. It is in these places particularly that I feel the deficiency of the neoclassic, or neoclassic-Puritan, way of dealing with experience. Why is it that triumphs of the will, so often, seem to induce despondency—at least in the spectator? I would like these poems better if I felt that fun had been had, at some point, by somebody. Looking back at love, or looking at it from the outside, no doubt there is little to be said for it. The postures, as Chesterfield remarked, are ridiculous, and you cannot argue reasonably for an action that requires, for its consummation, a loss of control. But if you are involved in it, that is another matter. The art of reason also has its inadequacies, and the romantics, who tried to recreate and heighten experience in their poems, though they might arrive at no explicit conclusion, were not so foolish after all. They made you see again that the world is a delightful place, that the whole is more interesting than the sum of its parts. The pleasures of the reasonable man are always such a little thing— pipe-smoking, or sipping wine, or handling first editions. If I were the friend addressed by Mr. Cunningham in his poem, "To a Friend, on Her Examination for the Doctorate in English":

> What have you gained?
> A learned grace
> And lines of knowledge on the face,
> A spirit weary but composed
> By true perceptions well-disposed,
> A soft voice and historic phrase

Sounding the speech of Tudor days,
What ignorance cannot assail
Or daily novelty amaze,
Knowledge enforced by firm detail.

if I were that friend, I'd go out and get drunk! So much trouble, and such small satisfaction!

In putting down some of the matters that the poems brought to my mind, I have hardly done justice to Mr. Cunningham's. I will end, therefore, by letting one of his poems, in its entirety, speak for itself:

Envoi

Hear me, whom I betrayed
While in this spell I stayed,
Anger, cathartic aid,
Hear and approve my song!

See from this sheltered cove
The symbol of my spell
Calm for adventure move,
Wild in repose of love,
Sea-going on a shell
In a moist dream. How long—
Time to which years are vain—
I on this coastal plain,
Rain and rank weed, raw air,
Served that fey despair,
Far from the lands I knew!

Winds of my country blew
Not with such motion—keen,
Stinging, and I as lean,
Savage, direct, and bitten,
Not pitying and unclean.

Anger, my ode is written.

Denise Levertov's *With Eyes at the Back of Our Heads* is a very real book; the poems are carefully worked, and each has moments of perception. Miss Levertov's mind is curious; it delights in itself—a little too much for my taste, but not perhaps for that of others. She cultivates a stillness in which any freak of sight, sound, touch, may suggest its meaning. Her poems are all in "free" form, depending for their effect upon your willingness to let your mind go straying with hers. There is always an assumption that what comes into her mind is important, a total seriousness of self-examination, warmed here and there by a surrender of affection toward some object vividly glimpsed, or more rarely toward a human situation. Hers is essentially a poetry of meditation, a little static in its descriptiveness; but if one has to choose between extremes, the inward-turning poem has possibilities, while the poem that is all action and surface ends by disgusting you with the whole fiddling process. Of the several good poems in the book I prefer "February Evening in New York." At one point the poem seems to lose control in an outpouring of sympathy; the dramatization, rare in Miss Levertov's work, gives the description significance:

> As the lights brighten, as the sky darkens,
>   a woman with crooked heels says to another woman
>   while they step along at a fair pace,
>   *"You know, I'm telling you, what I love best*
>   *is life. I love life! Even if I ever get*
>   *to be old and wheezy—or limp! You know?*
>   *Limping along?—I'd still . . ."* Out of hearing.
> To the multiple disordered tones
>   of gears shifting, a dance
>   to the compass points, out, four-way river. . . .

Miss Levertov's casual phrasing permits much of natural and domestic life, lilies and paper bags, to appear without embarrassment; she gets her more exotic effects not by using rhetoric but by placing you in an out-of-the-way corner of the world, or her mind—for example, the apparently Mexican scenes of "Triple Feature" and "Xochipilli." Her adaptation of Gautier's famous poem:

> The best work is made
> from hard, strong materials,
>   obstinately precise—
> the line of the poem, onyx, steel.

shows that there is nothing accidental about her method, and suggests a determination that, if the range of her interests can be expanded, may produce a body of first-rate work.

I had completed this review when I received Anne Sexton's *To Bedlam and Part Way Back*. For once the blurbs don't lie. The book is an experience—original, moving, and delightful. Above all, delightful—for though Mrs. Sexton's poems sometimes deal with Bedlam, that is, scenes in a mental hospital, and often with anguish, yet the mind at work is so keen and the technique is so excellent that her book is an uninterrupted joy. It is a *book,* as so few collections of verse are, everywhere infused with the character of the author. From the jacket I learn that she has been writing poems for only three years. This then is a phenomenon, like Rimbaud, to remind us, when we have forgotten in the weariness of literature, that poetry can happen.

The poems are lyrical structures; the movement of the lines and the ease of rhyme provide an impetus, an aesthetic pleasure, that balances the almost, at times, intolerable reality she deals with. But the more poetry succeeds, the less it can be described; here then is the poem titled "Her Kind":

I have gone out, a possessed witch,
haunting the black air, braver at night;
dreaming evil, I have done my hitch
over the plain houses, light by light:
lonely thing, twelve-fingered, out of mind.
A woman like that is not a woman, quite.
I have been her kind.

I have found the warm caves in the woods,
filled them with skillets, carvings, shelves,
closets, silks, innumerable goods;
fixed the suppers for the worms and the elves:
whining, rearranging the disaligned.
A woman like that is misunderstood.
I have been her kind.

I have ridden in your cart, driver,
waved my nude arms at villages going by,
learning the last bright routes, survivor
where your flames still bite my thigh
and my ribs crack where your wheels wind.
A woman like that is not ashamed to die.
I have been her kind.

Mrs. Sexton has an eye for ordinary life too, like W. D. Snodgrass, whose *Heart's Needle* was so welcome last year. For example, there is a description in her "Funnel" of a house in Maine that seems like all the old seaside houses that ever were:

It is rented cheap in the summer musted air
to sneaker-footed families who pad through
its rooms and sometimes finger the yellow keys
of an old piano that wheezes bells of mildew.

Yet this descriptive gift does not restrict her imagination. I have read many descriptions of war, yet have seen none truer than this:

> This was the first beach of assault;
> the odor of death hung in the air
> like rotting potatoes; the junkyard
> of landing craft waited open and rusting.
> The bodies were strung out as if they were
> still reaching for each other . . .

The point is, her poetry is much more than a recreation of facts, though apparently it draws largely on experience; it is a power of imagination also. Maybe Mrs. Sexton really *is* a witch. And this imaginative power can be sustained over long stretches, as in her story of a woman who, in 1890, traveled in Europe, and was loved by a man who was already married, and returned to wither in New England—ending with these extraordinary strokes of fiction:

> I tell you, you will come
> here, to the suburbs of Boston, to see the blue-nose
> world go drunk each night, to see the handsome
> children jitterbug, to feel your left ear close
> one Friday at Symphony. And I tell you,
> you will tip your boot feet out of that hall,
> rocking from its sour sound, out onto
> the crowded street, letting your spectacles fall
> and your hair net tangle as you stop passers-by
> to mumble your guilty love while your ears die.

I won't try to predict Mrs. Sexton's future. There is always an air of apology in the forecasts with which reviewers are so free. But she has a present, and it is great.

Important and Unimportant Poems

Reviews of Books by William Stafford, David Ignatow,
Robert Duncan, W. S. Merwin, John Betjeman,
and Maxine W. Kumin

Readers of verse, particularly the young, are becoming more and more dissatisfied with the status quo, and are turning away from the official standards with disgust. The award of the Pulitzer Prize to Phyllis McGinley, a writer of light suburban verse, shows that their dissatisfaction is right; if this state of things is perpetuated by the old men who hold the strings, there will be a complete break between the young and the old. It is all very well for a Tate, a Blackmur, a Bogan, to consult their own tastes and ignore what is being done now in this country. (These were not, as far as I know, the dispensers of the Pulitzer; the judges are shrouded in anonymity—I list these names only as a representative selection of poetry officials, poet-critics, arbiters of prestige.) But the result of their indifference will surely be that, in about five years or so, their opinions will seem completely irrelevant. Wherever the young may look for direction, it is certainly not to them; and in poetry the young are always right. The universities have

---

This review first appeared in *Hudson Review* 14, no. 3 (Autumn 1961).

established Brooks-and-Warren as the official way of reading poetry exactly at the point where Brooks-and-Warren are of no further use to poets. As usual, the old are talking about matters that happened thirty years ago. The good poetry being written in America today is turning its back upon the taste of Eliot's generation, just as Eliot turned away from the standards of J. C. Squire. Thirty years from now, the universities will be reading Whitman, Rilke, Neruda, and other poets of imagination—and they will again be out of touch. The Pulitzer prize that should have been awarded in 1961 will be awarded in 1991.

The present disparity between performance and reputation is appalling. Take William Stafford, for example. Is Stafford really so far inferior to Robert Lowell that Lowell should be treated as a classic, and Stafford virtually unknown? I have the greatest respect for the author of *Lord Weary's Castle*—clearly he is one of the few significant poets of the age—but when I read the poems of Stafford, I must respect him also, and yet who, outside of a few readers, is aware of Stafford? What a concatenation of critics, what sheer ignorance, must control the American literary scene, for such a disparity to exist!

This is a poem from Stafford's *West of Your City:*

At the Bomb Testing Site

At noon in the desert a panting lizard
waited for history, its elbows tense,
watching the curve of a particular road
as if something might happen.

It was looking at something farther off
than people could see, an important scene

acted in stone for little selves
at the flute end of consequences.

There was just a continent without much on it
under a sky that never cared less.
Ready for a change, the elbows waited.
The hands gripped hard on the desert.

Stafford's subject matter is usually important in itself. (The theory that subject matter is nothing, the treatment everything, was invented to comfort little minds.) Also, he deals with his subject directly; that is to say, he has a personal voice. Contrary to what many poets believe nowadays, it is not necessary to spill your guts on the table in order to be "personal," nor to relate the details of your aunt's insanity. What is necessary is originality of imagination and at least a few ideas of your own. Another point in favor of Stafford is that he actually writes about the country he is living in; all sorts of ordinary places, people, and animals appear in his poems, and not as subjects of satire, but with the full weight of their own existence. As we read Stafford we are aware of how much has been omitted from modern American poetry only because it is not literary, or because it springs from the life of ordinary, rather than "alienated" people. An observer from another country would be struck by the absence from American poetry of the American landscape; he would find, also, that the language of our poetry is not the language of our real thoughts; and he might wonder at the psychic disorder this indicates. As for history—it seems we are trying to forget it. But Stafford is one of the few poets who are able to use the landscape and to feel the mystery and imagination in American life.

Light wind at Grand Prairie, drifting snow.
Low at Vermilion, forty degrees of frost.
Lost in the Barrens, hunting over spines of ice,
the great sled dog Shadow is running for his life.

He is a poet of the people, in the deepest and most meaningful sense. And a poet of nature—in a time when poets claim our attention because they are unnatural, pitiable, demoralized. His poems are strong and true; rightly understood, they will enrich our lives.

David Ignatow, who in *Say Pardon* writes mainly about New York City, is also original, and of course, equally ignored. For years I have read his poems with exasperation because they so stubbornly refused to fall into happy patterns. Should a poem really begin like this?

I'm in New York covered by a layer of soap foam.

And if the following is a poem, what are most of the verses taught in schoolrooms?

The Dream

Someone approaches to say his life is ruined
and to fall down at your feet
and pound his head upon the sidewalk.
Blood spreads in a puddle.
And you, in a weak voice, plead
with those nearby for help;
your life takes on his desperation.
He keeps pounding his head.
It is you who are fated;
and you fall down beside him.
It is then you are awakened,

the body gone, the blood washed from the ground,
the stores lit up with their goods.

Resistance to this kind of poem, I believe, is not merely on literary grounds—it is also a social matter. Some critic ought to consider the influence of social snobbery upon our literary judgments. Mr. Ignatow's poems, because they deal with ordinary life—the confined, sweating, hallucinatory life of a city—will not be liked by those who prefer genteel, literary poems. And such readers will miss the charity and tenderness that illuminate his work. It is as though Mr. Ignatow, like some odd angel, has come down to live among machines and bills of lading, in order to change them into poetry and enable men to endure them:

The Errand Boy II

It was the way he went to pick up the carton
fallen to the gutter from his handtruck,
his arms outstretched, his body stooping
to the ground. I wondered at his smile,
weary and amused and so gentle withal,
as if this was what he had expected,
not for the first time and not
for the last time either.

And this is the poet of whom a reviewer, who shall surely be nameless, said that he needed to "grow some wings!"

In spite of the fragments of in-group talk and theory that litter Robert Duncan's *The Opening of the Field*, the reader is soon aware that he is in the presence of an extraordinary lyrical talent. I call it lyrical because, like Pound, Mr. Duncan is strongest when he is expressing his joy—and weakest when he is compounding mythology or history. It is not that he cannot present general ideas coherently—"A Poem Beginning with a Line by Pindar" is a magnificent play of ideas, with a striking, directly stated discussion of history in the second part; but too often he utters gnomic fragments, literary references, dates, names, as though their lodgement in his mind were enough to make them poetic. On the other hand, he has a wonderful quality of light—like Blake's, his words are permeated with light; these are visionary lyrics. The lines advance with suppleness, pause to digest some intractable matter, and advance again. Always, in even the most reluctant of his poems, one finds a delight in the act of poetry itself—these are really poems about being a poet; only in an age of prose would this be considered a limited subject.

The light and movement are in these lines:

> *The light foot hears you and the brightness begins*
> god-step at the margins of thought,
> quick adulterous tread at the heart.
> Who is it that goes there?
> Where I see your quick face
> notes of an old music pace the air,
> torso-reverberations of a Grecian lyre.

Here is Mr. Duncan's startling, prophetic turning of a phrase:

> He wrestled with Sleep like a man reading a strong sentence.

And here, unfortunately, is the detritus of his reading:

> honord by verse that preserves
> Hippokleas, first of the boys
> in the double course at Delphi;
>
> Ford Madox Ford as well; or
>
> Mr. W. H., half in half out of ground . . .

The most important poems in W. S. Merwin's *The Drunk in the Furnace* are those that deal with ancestors, country characters, and landscapes. There are good poems too, in an earlier manner; poems about the sea in which natural objects gather emblematic significance—but I have always found these poems rather contrived, and not sufficiently differentiated in form, one from the other. The new poems, however, show a decision on Merwin's part to change, if not his lines, at least his preoccupations. It is a strange movement, when you think about it, from the extraordinary literary brilliance of his first book, to this simplicity. He has never lacked imagination; it is good to see this imagination applied to the American scene. His new poems are rather like short stories—their effect does not depend on individual lines but on the whole; I will therefore not attempt to quote them. He is certainly one of the most intelligent, and one of the least obsequious, of the younger poets; I wish he would become astonishing as soon as possible.

John Betjeman's poems seem a special English taste, but as part of his *Summoned by Bells* has been published in the *New Yorker*, some Americans must also like them. A hundred years ago a poet, in a long book of blank verse, described the growth of a poet's mind; the poetic process, he said, took its origin from emotion recollected in tranquillity. Mr. Betjeman, in the same medium, celebrates the comforts of the middle class; his poetry originates in bath water:

> Luxuriating backwards in the bath
> I swish the warmer water round my legs
> Toward my shoulders, and the waves of heat
> Bring those five years of Marlborough through to me
> In comfortable retrospect . . . .

It is tempting to think that the difference between *The Prelude* and Mr. Betjeman's book measures the decline of imagination in English poetry over the last hundred years. Yet there are good poets still in England—Ted Hughes, for example.

Mr. Betjeman's popularity is not hard to explain. His verse appeals to those—both English and American—who wish to return to the world-before-taxes. Their hearts are with Winnie-the-Pooh; for them the church clock stands at ten to three, and there *is* honey still for tea. It is only fair to say that Mr. Betjeman makes no great claims for his verse. He takes part in the charade with good taste and smiling self-deprecation. Poetry, he seems to say, is really no more important than tiddlywinks.

I find it hard to evaluate the poems of Maxine W. Kumin, for what I want from poetry is something altogether different from this—yet her verse is intelligent, skillful, and perceptive. There is a poem to her son, a poem to a dead friend; there is a poem about the movie "Casablanca"; there is a poem on "Crib biting, n., a vice/ of horses"; there is poetry about many things that might occur in a civilized, reasonable life. Here is a specimen which shows her sharp vision and authentic feeling:

> For lunch we shared a coconut.
> Not twenty yards away
> a terrible white heron fished
> in an absent jerky fashion.
> He was anything but fierce
> or facile; I had never seen
> an awkward bird till then.
> This shamed me.
> Only when he turned to us I saw
> his upper bill was eaten away
> by pellet or disease, and pity
> soured in my gut.

The trouble with this verse—well done though it is—is that it is almost entirely a verse of statement. There is no mystery in it. That is to say, once more we are confronted with the attitudes and tone of prose, in the form of verse. Is it unfair to ask for something more? It depends on what you expect from poetry; how important you think it is.

Silence in the Snowy Fields

Recently in this magazine Mr. John Simon compared a specimen of contemporary verse with a "poem" he had made simply by putting together the titles of books of verse. The point of this funny experiment was that nowadays it is impossible to tell the difference between verse and nonsense. But as Mr. Simon showed when he got down to cases, it is quite possible to discriminate. If criticism can't tell the difference, surely it isn't poetry that is at fault, but criticism.

The trouble with modern poetry is criticism—rather, the lack of it. For years in America there has been no serious criticism of verse. It is said that this is an age of criticism, but what is meant, I suppose, is that articles about Marvell and Melville appear in the quarterlies; you will look in vain for any discussion of verse that could help contemporary poets. As Mr. Blackmur said in "A Critic's Job of Work," criticism has become an end in itself, a kind of art form. Of course, there have been essays by Mr. Jarrell, Mr. Ciardi, and others, in which they have talked about

This essay first appeared as "Poetry Chronicle," *Hudson Review* 16, no.1 (Spring 1963).

their contemporaries, but these essays were so whimsical, so unfertile in general ideas, that however amusing they might be, they could hardly encourage poets to write. And without criticism—contrary to what some writers say, who are always complaining that criticism stifles their powers, as well it may—without criticism there can be no important art.

The poets of the twenties—Eliot, Pound, Stevens, Williams—learned to write in an atmosphere of controversy. They were in revolt. But the poets who came to maturity in the late thirties and forties—Schwartz, Shapiro, Ciardi, et al.—did not examine received ideas or revolt against anything. They seemed—perhaps it was the Depression and the war—to have been stunned. Instead of criticizing they did a rather curious thing: each in his own way settled down to imitating a master—Yeats, or Rilke, or Auden, or Eliot—and what they imitated was not the nerve that had made these men masters, but their style. Though the Depression poets—to give them a name—wrote some good poems, much of their work now seems imitative. They themselves have come to see this, witness the belated attempts of these poets—Shapiro and Lowell, for example—to break with their past and break through to some kind of revelation.

In the fifties appeared the university poets (*The New Poets of England and America*) and the Beats (*The New American Poets*). . . . If the Depression poets were hardly aware of criticism, these were even less so. . . .

Meanwhile, the positions of authority were filled by minor poets of the twenties—people such as Miss Bogan and Mr. Untermeyer. Though they had no ideas about poetry, no authority, they reviewed and judged and anthologized. So we have the situation today, in which the old and the young confront each other across an abyss—in the *Times* or *Saturday Review,* or at some table where prizes are given—with nothing to say to each other. The middle generation, the poets who came after Eliot, simply are not there as a critical force. One would be willing to be judged by Mr. Roethke—who doesn't; instead, one is judged by Miss Moore.

It is any wonder that the new poets seem to be making a complete break with the past, and that their poems are strange? There are many different kinds of poetry being written today, and ideas are flying about—as they were when Eliot and Williams began to publish. At least this is preferable to the silence of the Depression and postwar years. One of the younger poets goes off to study Arabic poetry; another is translating Jimenez; another is in Japan. This may look like confusion, but it is intelligent confusion. And it is no use complaining that traditions are being violated. In America we have no traditions. Writing pseudo-Elizabethan or seventeenth- or eighteenth-century English verse in America is not a tradition; it is merely an amusement. In America tradition is another name for laziness. . . .

But let us talk about poetry. What is it? To see what it is we must rid ourselves of delusions, and above all, the Puritan delusions.

When the Puritan looks within himself he sees darkness and serpents. All hell is waiting to break loose. So the Puritan artist refuses to look within, and adheres to conventional forms. This he calls the life of reason.

Or he plunges into the hell he imagines. To this Puritan, feeling is a criminal activity. He wants to be through with feeling; he wants to confess; he wants to cease to exist. Like the accused in a Moscow purge, he hastens to rid himself of the last vestiges of human dignity. He hands himself over to his nightmares. He looks at himself in the mirror and sees *Naked Lunch*. And there's your American avant-garde. It is nothing if not masochistic.

If you were to suggest that instinctive life can be good; that the self is not necessarily evil; in short, that the kingdom of God is within—well, you can imagine the letters of protest to the *Village Voice*. We know what life really is. It is horrible, and we want to get through with it as soon as possible. Please Do Not Disturb.

But poetry is from within, from that share of instinctive life which is glad. The life we share with animals and saints is the source of poetry.

Mr. Bly's poems are from the inward man, from the ground of pleasure. And this pleasure is by no means simple:

> Inside me there is a confusion of swallows,
> Birds flying through the smoke,
> And horses galloping excitedly on fields of short grass.

There has been very little poetry in English that represents states of being. Wordsworth's is the only great poetry in English to have done so. Mr. Bly in his poems shows states of being. To do this, he must abandon rhetoric, bringing the poem close to the words we actually use:

> When we are in love, we love the grass,
> And the barn, and the lightpoles,
> And the small mainstreets abandoned all night.

Now this kind of writing will strike you either as totally poetic, or not poetry at all. If you are sold on the English department, then this poetry is not for you. You would have a devil of a time trying to explicate it according to the principles of Brooks-and-Warren. But if you are bored with the status quo and hope for new poetry, then you will find Mr. Bly's *Silence in the Snowy Fields* one of the few original and stimulating books of poetry published in recent years. I do not know any better way to show this than to quote. Here is his "Poem in Three Parts":

I

Oh, on an early morning I think I shall live forever!
I am wrapped in my joyful flesh,
As the grass is wrapped in its cloud of green.

II

Rising from a bed, where I dreamt
Of long rides past castles and hot coals,
The sun lies happily on my knees;
I have suffered and survived the night
Bathed in dark water, like any blade of grass.

III

The strong leaves of the box-elder tree,
Plunging in the wind, call us to disappear
Into the wilds of the universe,
Where we shall sit at the foot of a plant,
And live forever, like the dust.

Demons All Along

Here are all the poems Lawrence wrote (*The Complete Poems of D. H. Lawrence,* edited by Vivian de Sola and F. Warren Roberts), including poems that until now have been available only in manuscript or in obscure publications; also, for the curious, there are variant drafts. Apart from its usefulness to readers of Lawrence, the collection should interest anyone who is looking for poetry. This poem, for example, is discovered in Appendix II (juvenilia):

> I have sat in the recreation ground
> Under an oak tree whose yellow buds dotted the pale
>   blue sky:
> The young grass twinkled in the wind, and the sound
> Of the wind hung round the knotted buds like a canopy.

He thinks about Dostoevsky's St. Petersburg, and thinks again of his surroundings:

> Now to the Recreation Ground
> I am come back a foreigner, wondering and shrinking
>   from the scene
> From the noise of children playing around

This review appeared in *Book Week,* December 13, 1964.

From the tulips coloured with chalk, and the dull grass'
  evening green.
How lonely in the wide world is this playground.
How lonely, under the tree; unnoticed

As Lawrence said, his demon was there from the beginning. Yet there is a division between his writings up to 1912, and his writings after. The early poems are about nature in the Midlands, and little dramas of rustic love in the manner of Hardy. And they rhyme. The influences of his mother, and Miriam, and one or two other women, spill over from the novels into the poems.

Lawrence went from Nottingham to London, to teach in a "big, new red school . . . . Then starts the rupture with home, with Miriam, away there in Nottinghamshire. And gradually the long illness, and then the death of my mother. . . ."

Why does the thin grey strand
Floating up from the forgotten
Cigarette between my fingers,
Why does it trouble me?

Ah, you will understand;
When I carried my mother downstairs,
A few times only, at the beginning
Of her soft-foot malady,

I should find, for a reprimand
To my gaiety, a few long hairs
On the breast of my coat; and one by one
I watched them float up the dark chimney.

When his mother died, "everything collapsed, save the mystery of death. . . . I almost dissolved myself, and was very ill." In 1912 he recuperated, and "the other phase" commenced. "I left teaching, and left England, and and left many other things, and the demon had a new run for his money."

The new demon expressed himself in free verse. For Lawrence this was the form of poetry of the present, in contrast to poetry of the past. There was nothing wrong with the old, rhymed, stanzaic poetry—Keats was perfect—but the new age demanded poetry that "does not want to get anywhere. It just takes place." For this poetry of the present, "any externally-applied law would be mere shackles and death."

R. P. Blackmur has attacked Lawrence's principles in a well-known essay. Lawrence, he said, suffered from "the fallacy of the faith in expressive form," the belief that "if a thing is only intensely enough felt its mere expression in words will give it satisfactory form." The effect of the fallacy, in Blackmur's view, was to ruin much of Lawrence's work, to give us frenetic outbursts of personal feeling and few realized poems. But Blackmur was not doing justice to Lawrence, as the editors of the *Complete Poems* suggest in their introduction. Lawrence was not against craftsmanship; he wanted a new form for each new experience, lines that would represent "the quality of life itself, without denouement or close . . . the rapid momentous association of things which meet and pass. . . ." This was harder work than counting tummty-tum on his fingers; and also, it is a fallacy to think that because you write in traditional forms you are writing poetry. When Lawrence wrote bad poems it was the subject or his mood that failed. But you cannot fault a technique that produced poems of the quality of Lawrence's best.

His best subjects were landscapes, plants, and the

life that runs, plods, or slithers on the surface of the earth or swims in the sea. He was not interested in particular men or women. He hated intellectuals, all smarmy with culture; he hated women who were always poking into his soul and asking to be *loved;* he hated the money-making, hand-rubbing, or the beer-drinking Englishman. He hated Americans with their machines for washing and machines for running about in. But nearly always he was able to feel what ordinary people are conscious of only in flashes—the few feet of plant life and soil underfoot, the earth we really live on. Men he saw only dimly, as trees walking. But he shared in the nature of flowers:

> Not every man has gentians in his house
> in Soft September, at slow, sad Michaelmas.
> Bavarian gentians, big and dark, only dark
> darkening the day-time torch-like with the smoking
> blueness of Pluto's gloom . . . .

He could slip into the skin of an animal, or bird, or reptile, mimicking it in a kind of tribal dance. In "Snake" it is Lawrence, hunching his shoulders, who glides away through a cranny. He is the turkey-cock with wattles:

> the colour of steel-slag which has been red-hot
> And is going cold,
> Cooking to a powdery, pale-oxydized blue.

To those who knew Lawrence and were targets for his spite, "The Mosquito" may have seemed familiar:

> It is your hateful little trump,
> You pointed fiend,
> Which shakes my sudden blood to hatred of you:
> It is your small, high hateful bugle in my ear.

And last, in "Kangaroo," a portrait of the Nottingham Madonna:

> Her little loose hands, and drooping Victorian shoulders.
> And then her great weight below the waist, her vast pale
>   belly
> With a thin young yellow little paw hanging out, and
>   straggle of a long thin ear, like ribbon,
> Like a funny trimming to the middle of her belly, thin
>   little dangle of an immature paw and one thin ear.

Though Lawrence didn't care much for individuals, he generalized vividly about people. When he had digested the animals and rocks of a new continent, America or Australia, he had visions of the kind of people who must live there. His intuitions are startling; all that is omitted is the life of every day, with which Lawrence had no patience. He had, especially, an eye for collective guilt, which is more visible to the stranger than the native. In "O! Americans"—a poem spoiled, as many of his poems are, by prose statements—he put his finger on our original sin and the cause of our troubles:

> The American Indian is, basically, a savage.
> But be careful how you destroy him.
> Because he is so *absolutely* in your power, that, before God,
>   you must be careful.

Much of Lawrence's poetry is peevish, private stuff. Nearly all the book called *Nettles* is doggerel—Lawrence castigating the censors and the dirty-minded public who rejected his paintings and his novels. Throughout his works he could not help ranting:

Humanity needs pruning
It is like a vast great tree with a great lot of sterile, dead,
   rotting wood
And an amount of fungoid and parasitic growth.

This is a voice that turns us off. Most of the harm to humanity is done by people who want to prune it and remove the fungus. And when it has been pruned, what then? We get very little from Lawrence's opinions. They are an attempt to convert every one into himself—like a nursing child. Yet, having said this, I am reminded of Lawrence's awareness of this also; his insistence on "otherness," the need to be separate in order to be oneself. There is no denying his intelligence and honesty. At the worst he was a poet and could do no harm; at the best, he wrote the strongest English in this century.

A Swift Kick in the Rhetoric

In 1907, when Pound arrived in London, there had been no serious thinking about poetry in English for a hundred years. Symons had introduced Yeats to the French symbolists, but that was all. Those who published and reviewed poetry used Palgrave's *Golden Treasury* as the touchstone of verse. There was no criticism, only a genteel agreement between such men as Walter Raleigh at Oxford and J. C. Squire in Fleet Street that rhymed lines about nature in the home counties were poetic. For deep thinkers there was A. E. Housman. The romantic tradition in England had sunk to banalities from which it has not fully recovered.

Then Pound with his red hair began haunting the environs of the British Museum, carrying imagist poems and the manuscripts of foreign poets in translation. He proceeded to insult the "tradition": "Here are a list of facts on which I and 9,000,000 other poets have spieled endlessly: (1.) Spring is a pleasant season. (2.) The flowers, etc. etc. sprout, bloom etc. etc. (3.) Love, a delightsome tickling. Indefinable

This review first appeared in the *New York Herald Tribune,* January 2, 1966.

etc. . . . (4.) Trees, hills etc. are by a provident nature arranged diversely, in diverse places. . . ."

To anyone who would listen, unknown beginning writers such as Hemingway, and authors of reputation such as Yeats, he explained what writing was:

> Poetry must be *as well written as prose*. Its language must be a fine language, departing in no way from speech save by a heightened intensity (i.e. simplicity). There must be no book words, no periphrases, no inversions. . . . There must be no interjections. No words flying off to nothing. . . . Rhythm *must* have meaning . . . . There must be no cliches, set phrases, stereotyped journalese. The only escape from such is by precision, a result of concentrated attention to what is writing.

Pound's ideas are responsible for much of the good writing in verse in the twentieth century, and for a good deal of the prose too. But at the time they were not ingratiating. As he went about London, cajoling or bullying people into writing better, showing his manuscripts from the Provençal or Chinese and poems by his friends, including a ridiculous American thing about someone named Prufrock, Pound made himself hated. He was attacking the "tradition." Now as we look back, it is easy to see that it was Pound who was the traditionalist; his enemies were merely ignorant.

As the public does not read poetry but reads newspapers knows, Pound made some radio broadcasts during World War II under the auspices of Mussolini. After the war he was arrested for treason, found insane, and confined for years in an American hospital. And, while his indiscretions were still fresh, he was given a Bollingen award for "American" poetry.

This was a scandal. At that time I attended a dinner of some society poets, at which the master of ceremonies impugned the motives of the Bollingen judges. Another speaker compared Pound's *Cantos* to the ravings of a maniac. In those circles, it seemed, Pound could be vilified. They didn't mind his political ideas, but they still hated him for what he had done to the "tradition," their kind of junk. If Pound has had enemies, however, he has also had friends. In the next moment a young poet took the microphone, said that he was ashamed to be present, and walked off the platform. Then a very famous poet indeed, who was sitting at the end of the guest table, had a coughing fit in his handkerchief and slipped away behind a screen, not to reappear. Sensation! At the table where I was, a gentleman-poet rose to his feet in anguish and exclaimed, "And with Mrs. — here! What will she say!" Mrs. — was one of the rich people who supported poetry in America, or rather, retarded it.

Whenever I am tempted to criticize Pound harshly, as I am whenever I have to read the *Cantos*, I think of that dinner and what poetry would be like today if Pound had not existed. Above all, he gave us a language to write in. Poetry contains ideas, but unless the language of verse has a relation to the language in which men really think in their own time, then the best ideas are stillborn. Pound made poets look at things as they were, and say what they truly saw and felt. He gave us "something to read in normal circumstances." He revitalized poetry as Wordsworth had a hundred years before. And his teaching is still urgent, for the ignoramuses, society-poets, and misusers of language always come creeping back. And some of them take strange shapes, for they have read the *Cantos* and wear the costume of the avant-garde—1910. But you can be sure that if Pound were a young man today, he would not write like his imitators.

The poet of the *Cantos* was always "making it new." He had ideas, he had an excellent gift of mimicry—at one moment he has caught the voice of Browning, at another, that of a condottiere—but, and this may be inseparable from his virtues, he never had a center of his own. And he was oddly naive, unable to think beyond appearances. He could not see that his famous usury was not a cause, but a symptom. He thought that men go to war because of a conspiracy of arms manufacturers. The so-called difficulties of the *Cantos* are all on the surface, in the references; underneath there is emptiness. Here and there, especially in the anthology piece on vanity, perhaps because Pound himself was vain, he experiences an idea:

> What thou lovest well remains,
> > the rest is dross
> What thou lov'st well shall not be reft from thee
> What thou lov'st well is thy true heritage
> Whose world, or mine or theirs
> > or is it of none? . . .
> The ant's a centaur in his dragon world.
> Pull down thy vanity, it is not man
> Made courage, or made order, or made grace,
> > Pull down thy vanity, I say pull down.
> Learn of the green world what can be thy place
> In scaled invention or true artistry,
> Pull down thy vanity,
> > Paquin pull down!
> The green casque has outdone your elegance.

Pound is now eighty years old. In *Ezra Pound: Perspectives: Essays in Honor of His Eightieth Birthday*, a number of poets and critics bear witness to his influence and their loyalty. Collections like this can be embarrassing, but this collection is refreshingly honest. There is, for example, Herbert Read's remark: "A man who sets out (1908) with the idea that 'no art ever yet grew by looking into the eyes of the public' is bound to find himself increasingly isolated from the social matrix that ensures 'sanity' (which admittedly may be no more than an accepted code of conduct)."

This has been Pound's tragedy, and the tragedy of all serious writers in the modern world. One does not want to hate society, but society being what it is, how can one stomach it? So the artist—Eliot, Joyce, Hemingway—the list goes on—creates a world of his own. It may be a very fine world indeed—as Proust's or Yeats's is—but it is invisible to the public at large, and the cost to the creator, in isolation, is terrific.

As you might expect, the contributions to *Perspectives* by A. Alvarez and Hugh Kenner are careful examinations of Pound's method. Allen Tate has an essay that discourses in a dignified manner, but as is the case with most of Mr. Tate's writings, I am not sure what the dignity consists of. And there is a tribute by Hugh MacDiarmid, the poet of Scotland, who happens to be a Communist. I do not know which to admire more, the teaching of Pound or the agreement of these disciples.

New Books of Poems, 1

It used to be easier to write poems than it is now. In the time of the New Criticism an idea or anecdote rendered in conventional literary language would serve as a poem. There was a sense of form, I suppose you could call it traditional, that is absent from the work of many poets nowadays, who write as though their lives depended on it. For readers who want reasonable ideas expressed in verse, the poems of Robert Penn Warren in *Selected Poems: New and Old, 1923–1966,* are just the thing. He can write convincing narrative, as in "The Day Dr. Knox Did It," and when he writes about country life seen through the eyes of a boy he sounds accurate:

> A thousand times you've seen that scene;
>> Oak grove, bare ground, little white church there,
> Bone-white in that light, and through dust-pale green
>> Of oak leaf, the steeple pokes up in the bright air.

For my taste there is too much imitation in these poems; besides I am not sure that Warren knows

---

This review first appeared in *Harper's* 235, no. 1407 (August 1967).

that he is imitating—in his "Infant Boy at Midcentury," Thomas Hardy; in his "Ballad of Billie Potts," T. S. Eliot.

Exception! It wasn't easy for Kenneth Rexroth to write poems. Rexroth has been excluded from the front ranks of fame, not by the establishment—an establishment is a thing that wants to include everybody—but by his own temperament. In California's affluent society Rexroth is a *memento mori,* remembering the Depression. Like the American in *Martin Chuzzlewit* who dared the British lion to personal combat, he challenges the Academy. His least thoughtful side is shown by his poem on the death of Dylan Thomas: "They are murdering all the young men. . . ." Too often he brags about his integrity; too often his thoughts are flat, end-stopped, void of rhythm. But in *The Collected Shorter Poems of Kenneth Rexroth,* there remain a number of lively irascible poems and a few poems with real feeling about nature and a handful of people. The following lines show him at his best:

I think of you in *Gas,*
The heroine on the eve of explosion;
Or angry, white, and still,
Arguing with me about Sasha's tragic book.
Here in the empty night,
I light the lamp and hunt for pad and pencil.
A million sleepers turn,
While bombs fall in their dreams. The storm goes away,
Muttering in the hills.
The veering wind brings the cold, organic smell
Of the flowing ocean.

Another exception—Hugh MacDiarmid, whose real name is Christopher Grieve. He is a Scottish Nationalist and a Communist. Almost single-handed MacDiarmid invented the Scottish Renaissance, a poetry of the vernacular together with old Scottish words and synthetic combinations of Scots and English. He has devoted his life to reviving the culture of Scotland, depressed ever since the Union with England. Some people think MacDiarmid a better poet than Burns; certainly he has a range of reference that has not been in Scottish poetry since Dunbar. He has written fine lyrics and discursive poems, in English as well as Scots, gathered in the *Collected Poems of Hugh MacDiarmid*. But MacDiarmid has alienated many of his followers by writing didactic poems which he frankly admits are propaganda. There is a great biography of this man waiting to be written, which would involve much of the culture of modern Scotland.

This has been a year of collected poems: the *Collected Poems* of Louis MacNeice; yet another collection by Robert Graves. These are standard authors, they don't need my recommendation, but I would like to praise the *Collected Poems of Theodore Roethke*. Here, for the first time, his development can be seen from beginning to end: an ear for sounds, a talent like an animal, expanding and deepening, in the great inheritance of symbolism, ruminating the plants, birds, beasts, and women of his psyche. When he died he was one of the few poets capable of conferring happiness rather than asking for it. We know that the good die young; it is hard to be reconciled to their dying in middle age.

In ways James Dickey resembles Roethke. In *Poems 1957–1967* time and again Dickey creates a poem that enlarges our experience. The mind in these poems is original and even inhuman. I can think of no one else who could have imagined, as

Dickey does in "The Sheep Child," what it might be like to be half-sheep and half-human. Nor can I think of any other poet, given the idea, who would have had the inventiveness to bring it off:

> My hoof and my hand clasped each other.
> I ate my one meal
> Of milk, and died
> Staring . . .

There is genius, Elizabethan energy in the ways Dickey hurls himself into strange modes of being. In early poems such as "Listening to Foxhounds" and "The Owl King," we see him, by turning inward, transforming himself into a bird, or animal, or another human being. Sometimes these poems fade in conventional symbols, stock words such as "light." But his vision focuses, he discovers unusual narrative power—almost alone among contemporary American poets he can tell a story—and in works such as "Cherrylog Road" and "Kudzu" this power realizes itself fully.

In "Cherrylog Road" a boy and girl are compelled to meet in an automobile junkyard for their love-making. Her excuse to her parents for going there is that she collects junk; so she approaches

> Through the acres of wrecks . . .
> With a wrench in her hand.

This idyll takes place in an inferno of blistering paint, spark plugs, bumpers. Then,

> We left by separate doors . . .

an affectionate parody of illicit assignations. In the poem titled "Kudzu," vines grow over the fields;

snakes thrive among the vines; hogs are driven in to kill the snakes. The surface of the earth is a heaving mass of horror. Then the vines and snakes fuse with the narrator's arm, strengthening it. How this leap occurs—somehow by way of the veins in his arm—I don't know, for Dickey's empathies are peculiar. He is certainly not, in spite of his jacket copy, representative.

In later poems there is a fabrication of emotions. For example, "Slave Quarters" is thoroughly unconvincing. A white man speaks as he lurks around the slave quarters at night; he is sweating with . . . I suppose the word is lust; at the same time he is ridden with modern, liberal guilt. It's like a bad movie. Sometimes Dickey seems to be writing in a panic. He seems to be faced with a choice: either to inflate and lose himself, like Thomas Wolfe, in volumes of pseudo-writing, or to tell the truth. When he does the latter he is a magnificent poet.

Robert Creeley is not gifted like Dickey with narrative power, actions to write about. In his new book, *Words,* everything is style; there is no subject but the poem talking to itself. Such visible objects as were present in his early poems are missing here. These are syllables, breathing pauses, whispers. As he says,

> It is all a rhythm,
> from the shutting
> door, to the window
> opening,
>
> the seasons, the sun's
> light, the moon,
> the ocean, the
> growing of things . . .

Creeley is trying to purify the dialect of the tribe by writing in purely colloquial rhythms and phrases:

> What
> has happened
> makes
>
> the world
> live
> on the edge,
>
> looking.

The words are impeccable, the voice is refined. But, as Aristotle said, there is nothing in the intellect that was not first in the senses, and in *Words* there is little for the senses to work on. Louis Zukofsky's *All the Collected Short Poems, 1956–1964* comes, with a blurb by Creeley, from the same finishing school:

> We breakfast
> facing a mountain:
>
> a yellow—wild!
> a yellow leaf–
> not fall
> the yellow leaf a thought–
> is yellow bird. . . .

These mutterings escape me.

I'd like to turn up an astonishing new poet, but most of the new poems are written by people who've been writing for some time. Only publishers are always discovering a new poet; readers are less fortunate. It is rare to come across a poem as good as this in a first book—*Cold Water,* by Lou Lipsitz:

Reading Walt Whitman I find he compares his soul
     to a spider.
    Fantastic!
    Who could know he would?

And suddenly my life tips over! a bed in a rat-infested
    apartment with scared kids jumping on one end.

My head can take it—
like a cheap flowerpot with hyacinths,
uncracked after a four-story drop
from the window sill.

My heart, that was just a heart,
begins to fit everywhere, like newspapers
stuffed into the broken ceilings of Harlem.

Many are angry, but few are poets.

"I shall say 'I'," said Montherlant, "for that is the way to be natural." Many poets nowadays would agree with this. And free verse is their medium. At the worst, this makes for flat, confessional writing. Anne Sexton's *Live or Die,* which won the Pulitzer Prize, shows the limit of the method when it isn't strengthened by ideas. Her previous books were interesting, but now mere self-dramatization has grown a habit. A poem titled "Menstruation at Forty" was the straw that broke this camel's back.

Denise Levertov writes just as persistently about herself, but also she is full of the thought that poetry needs. Writing such as this, in *The Sorrow Dance,* is a joy to discover:

        Arbor vitae, whose grooved bole
        reveals so many broken
        intentions, branches

lopped or
wizened off,

in the grass near you
your scions are uprising
fernlike, trustful.

Katherine Hoskins is not read widely, but if there is any justice, someday she will be. Not, I am sure, that it matters a great deal, for a talent so painstaking is not hunting after acclaim. *Excursions: New and Selected Poems* contains twenty-five new poems, as well as selections from three previous books. Incidentally, it is a beautifully made book; the publishers are to be congratulated. Hoskins has a quiet voice, an exquisite sense of forms, delicacy of language. But this is misleading. With some apprehension I started reading "Pity and Power," which begins:

With us, everybody (albeit well known
For a bastard and son of a bitch) is 'a great feller.' . . .

Uhuh, I said to myself, now she's going to be tough, in the prevailing mode. Tough she was, and a great deal more. She sustained the narrative for three pages, a hair-raising story about a man named Louis Guevin, a sadist, and his daughter. The thing developed into a ghost story; when it came to an end I thought Katherine Hoskins could write anything, if she had a mind to.

For a book of poems to sell in America today it must speak to our city-bred anxieties. William Stafford's *The Rescued Year* isn't going to start a rush on the bookstores. He is a habitant of nature, and his thoughts run deep.

At the Bomb Testing Site

At noon in the desert a panting lizard
waited for history, its elbows tense,
watching the curve of a particular road
as if something might happen.

It was looking for something farther off
than people could see, an important scene
acted in stone for little selves
at the flute end of consequences.

There was just a continent without much on it
under a sky that never cared less.
Ready for a change, the elbows waited.
The hands gripped hard on the desert.

This isn't nature writing in the usual sense: his nature is a mask through which thought works. Stafford has only one fault: at times he falls into plodding meter. He is a true poet; if ever this country is to have a sense of itself, it will be through work like Stafford's.

How does work become "classic"? What makes it so? Roethke is a classic; Stafford may become one. The *Collected Poems* of Keith Douglas, last on my list, is a classic . . . I'm sure of it. Douglas wrote poems about World War II; many poets today are writing poems against the war in Vietnam. What are the qualities that, in Douglas, strike deep, while much of what we write sounds like a newspaper? I think it was because Douglas was there in flesh as well as spirit:

I am the man, I suffered, I was there . . .

Having experienced suffering gives a poet assurance. He knows what to leave out. He is not hysterical with continuous fantasies. Having suffered, he is rid of guilt; he may even be happy. Douglas recorded what he saw, and had pity for it:

> Peter was unfortunately killed by an 88:
> it took his leg away, he died in the ambulance.
> I saw him crawling on the sand; he said
> It's most unfair; they've shot my foot off.

But, at the same time, he kept a sense of joy, the reality of his own life. He wrote:

> Remember me when I am dead
> and simplify me when I'm dead.

As time passes, real men and real books are simplified. Intelligence, feeling, rhythm, the poet's mystery, become clear. While poems that are only words soon fade.

New Books of Poems, 2

We have been having a romantic revival and nowadays poets look and act the part. It was different fifteen years ago when the New Critics were still in the ascendant; then poets looked like graduate students and wrote accordingly. But now, once more, poets are reading their works in public, attacking the Administration, and justifying the idea that the lunatic, the lover, and the poet "are of imagination all compact." This is a famous tradition and maybe it will produce poetry. At any rate, it is a more interesting scene than that of the 1950s. The temper of that time is represented by W. H. Auden's remark that the aim of poetry is "by telling the truth, to disenchant and disintoxicate." Such views of poetry accounted for the rise, for want of a better word, of the English "small beer" school of verse, of which Philip Larkin was an example. Larkin seemed unable to write of anything more important than his bicycle and his trouser clips. If I must have either the romantic, with its attendant absurdities on display in the Haight-Ashbury district in San Francisco

This review first appeared in *Harper's* 237, no. 1419 (August 1968).

and the East Village in New York, or trivialities uttered by a merely reasonable mind, I will choose the romantic.

My only objection to the present madness of the arts is that I do not think they are mad enough. Too frequently the madness is assumed. Is there an "alienated" poet who does not hope that he will have a fellowship? Is there a painter now raging against the establishment who does not hope that he will have a grant? These suspicions prevent my taking the frenzies of the Now generation as seriously as, maybe, I should. I do not think that all the kids are wonderful geniuses, to use the language of Hollywood and their mothers. I think that many of them will be big wheels in advertising when some poor fool will still be trying to write a poem or paint a picture.

Think of Friedrich Hölderlin, who lived in the romantic period and died in 1843. Hölderlin was really mad, and did not wish to be. He wished that the gods would stop observing him and coming to the door disguised as apprentices on their way to the village. He wished to be allowed to have a share in nature, the normal world, where smoke rises above the rooftops and a housewife hangs out her sheets on the line. But if Hölderlin only went for a walk it was soon clear that something was wrong:

> You wayside woods, well painted
> On the green and sloping glade . . .

He had no share in nature. He was eternally detached.

> How beautiful, clear from the distance
> These glorious pictures shine . . .

Hölderlin did not hate the world; he loved it. But he could not discover his own place in it. This is the difference between genius and madness and the store-window figures of genius and madness, triumphs of the art of decorating, which pass for "alienation" today. Moreover, as Hölderlin was inescapably himself, he discovered the modern, a new way of writing that was not to be heard again until the First World War, when Ezra Pound again expressed it. I mean a consciousness that has been fragmented:

> So Mahommed,* Rinaldo,
> Barbarossa, as a liberal spirit,
> The Emperor Heinrich.
> But we are mixing up
> the periods
> > Demetrius Poliorcetes
> Peter the Great
> > Heinrich's
> crossing the Alps, and that
> with his own hand he gave the people food
> and drink and his son Conrad died of poison
> Example of one who changes an age
> reformer
> Conradin etc.
> all as representative
> of conditions.
>
> *Hear the horn of the watchman by night
> After midnight it is, at the fifth hour.

The *Poems and Fragments* of Hölderlin have at last been translated, with German on one side and English on the other, by Michael Hamburger, who has devoted years and his own talent as a poet to the task. The translation is as magnificent in its way as the Scott Moncrieff version of Proust. Those who do not read German have been given a great poet, and this alone would make it a memorable year.

A few American poets have the genuine accent of romanticism. Robert Duncan, in *Bending the Bow*, seems inspired for whole paragraphs and sometimes for whole pages. He too has created his own system of belief, and invokes irrational powers:

> as the poet takes up
> measures of an old intoxication that leads into poetry,
> not "square" dancing, but moving figures,
> the ages and various personae of an old drama . . .

There are a few poems in his book that are completely realized: "An Interlude," a poem about dancing from which I have taken the lines above; a totally unexpected poem titled "My Mother Would Be a Falconress"; a poem called "God-spell." There are lines of considerable beauty in other poems, and passages which are incoherent. Duncan reminds me of the French Revolution; he is both the best and the worst of times. I know that it is useless to wish that a poet of this kind would try to be clearer, for his poems are the result of his confusions. Nevertheless, it is a fact that William Blake, by persisting in his follies, did not become wise; he merely became tedious. In an age without critical intelligences, when true artists are not recognized, they are left entirely to their own resources. They have only their own thoughts to support them, and therefore they must believe that all their thoughts are good. So Duncan is able to write as badly as this:

> Chancellor Strong, the dragon claw
>
> biting his bowels, his bile
>
> raging against the lawful demand
>
> for right reason.

The subject of these lines is the former Chancellor of the University of California at Berkeley. Now, I find it impossible to visualize Chancellor Strong in the claws of a dragon. This picturesque writing makes me think only of Disneyland. Duncan is inspired, but those who live by inspiration also fade with inspiration, and then they are as likely to write a dead language as anyone else. Usually, however, Duncan's imagination and lyric talent are far beyond what passes for great poetry nowadays on publishers' blurbs. He is capable of delight:

> What we hold to is no more than
> words. Yes, it is hard to assay
> the worth we hold to.
>
> We said it was gold. The soul
>
> weighed against Maat's feather.
>
> Our treasure the light in the dandylion
> head shining,
> they wld blow out. "See, your heart
> hold to
> a lost cause."

Reading Bert Meyers' first book, *The Dark Birds,* I am ashamed, for I remember writing a letter to the author complaining that he wrote merely images, and did not put them together to make larger poems. I think I advised him to read Keats and Rilke. Now it is true that these are small poems in that they do not run on. But poetry does not depend on length, and the idea of a man's spending years to perfect a few lines is a great enough thing to remind me that we should not grow impatient. We must not forget how to read, though McLuhan and Legion howl on the other side. Bert Meyers is doing an unusual and, I believe, the one necessary thing. He is trying to find images for ordinary life that will at the same time reveal depths. We have had little writing of this kind in America. Satire we have had in plenty—but who needs satire? It is truth and poetry that are in short supply. I hope that Meyers will continue to provide them, as he does in "The Family":

> The boy will grow and be a man,
> He'll have no father then.
>
> The girl, assuming womanhood,
> will burn herself in bed.
>
> The father leaves the house at dawn.
> The mother turns her dream-world on.
>
> Still, night brings them all together,
> to shriek and shudder.

The contrast between what I have called romanticism and what may be called traditional verse—meaning verse that makes its first appeal to order and tradition—is suggested by the books that won the National Book Award and the Pulitzer Prize for poetry. Robert Bly's *Light Around the Body,* that won the NBA, shows a debt to surrealism and recent European and Spanish modes; Anthony Hecht's *The Hard Hours* includes poems that hark back to the 1950s, when an English tradition was the only one we knew. This, however, is far from being a complete description. In recent poems Hecht has developed direct ways of speaking and let his feelings come to the surface, dropping those masks of irony which made his early poems seem too much like exercises.

In Bly's poems I am always conscious of an arranging intelligence. Bly's ideas are clear. It is his method that is extraordinary:

> I hear voices praising Tshombe, and the Portuguese
> In Angola, these are the men who skinned Little Crow!
> We are all their sons, skulking
> In back rooms, selling nails with trembling hands!

He has developed his own landscapes, inhabited by murdered Indians and Vietnamese; visions in which moles are significant and shop windows are filled with terrifying objects:

> . . . a branch painted white.
> A stuffed baby alligator grips that branch tightly
> To keep away from the dry leaves on the floor.

What is true of surrealists in general is true also of Bly; his poems are moving when they are moved by a central flow, one feeling which holds all the parts together. I am aware that this can be argued against; André Breton thought that surrealism that was not automatic writing was not surrealism at all. But this made only for juxtapositions of objects, and shock became a mannerism. When surrealist poetry has been effective, as in the poems of Neruda, the images have been in the grip of that logic of the irrational which we perceive also in dreams. In certain poems by Bly I perceive a flow, and it is powerful; in other poems I do not. "The Busy Man Speaks," "After the Industrial Revolution," "Counting Small-Boned Bodies," and "Melancholia," cohere; but I do not know what connection the following images have:

> Floating in turtle blood, going backward and forward,
> We wake up like a mad sea-urchin
> On the bloody fields near the secret pass—
> There the dead sleep in jars . . .

On the other hand, these lines seem to rise out of a consciousness that is beyond the personal:

> How strange to awake in a city,
> And hear grown men shouting in the night!
> On the farm the darkness wins,
> And the small ones nestle in their graves of cold:
> Here is a boiling that only exhaustion subdues,
> A bitter moiling of muddy waters
> At which the voices of white men feed!

Bly is one of the few poets in America from whom greatness can be expected. He has original talent, and what is more rare, integrity. I think he should forget about images for a while and concentrate on music, the way things move together.

I find Anthony Hecht's early poems precious; the voice is not convincing:

> Though learned men have been at some dispute
> Touching the taste and color, nature, name
> And properties of the Original Fruit . . .

This kind of thing went well enough once, when all poetry was divided into two parts, one of which was named Lowell and the other Wilbur. I do not blame Hecht for having written elegantly, but wonder that he has seen fit to reprint these poems. The front half of *The Hard Hours* is, however, a new book. Poems such as "The End of the Weekend" which smack of that early elegance have been deepened by suffering. "Rites and Ceremonies," Hecht's most ambitious poem, is a departure—about being a Jew, which is likely to make anyone serious. Hecht has always known the music of verse; it is seriousness he has lacked.

I am not, however, confident of Hecht's change of heart being permanent, when I read his endorsement of W. D. Snodgrass's *After Experience:* "not merely . . . as good as his extraordinary . . . *Heart's Needle*, but distinctly better." To the contrary, Snodgrass's new book is distinctly not better; it is more of the same, and—as with most books by so-called confessional poets—a dilution of his first. Snodgrass deserves our gratitude for the fine writing in *Heart's Needle*, but surely in the years since that book was published he might have changed a little and taken a few risks.

Here is the same tone of mild desperation, the same suburban landscape, and the resignation typical of the 1950s:

> We'll try to live with evils that we choose,
> Try not to envy someone else's vices,
> But make the most of ours. We picked our crisis;
> We'll lose the things we can afford to lose . . .

Snodgrass's book is impassioned, however, in comparison with Howard Nemerov's new offering, *The Blue Swallows*. This is weary work that justifies all the attacks on "academic verse" that have been launched in the past decade.

But poetry is not a matter of attitudes, and Gary Snyder, one of the heroes of the "antiacademic," in his new book demonstrates that there is no security anywhere, not even in bohemia. *The Back Country* describes Japan and the Sierras, not suburbia, yet this book too is conventional. Snyder is content to describe the great outdoors and sentimental moments; his poems are snapshots taken on the road, bits of quaint information:

> In the rucksack I've got three *nata*
> Handaxes from central Japan;
> The square blade found in China all the way back to
> Stone . . .

So what? There are all sorts of things, old and new, lying about everywhere. The question is, what happens in the poem? Snyder's new book, most of it, just moseys along. There is a fallacy in his idea of poetry—I think going back to W. C. Williams—that the poet is a holy man who has only to point to an object; the initiate will perceive its significance. What actually results, however, is a lack of tension, an absence of drama. This may be the peace of the Orient, but I doubt it. I think it is just monotony.

In recent years poets have been driven more and more to tear their poems apart, rip their rhythm to tatters, smash their sentences to bits, and inhabit distant landscapes. I think this is because the taste of the reading public is so bad. How can any poet compete with Rod McKuen (*Listen to the Warm*), who sells a hundred thousand copies of lines such as these:

> I live alone.
> It hasn't always been that way.
> It's nice sometimes
>   to open up the heart a little
> and let some hurt come in . . .

But it is not only the taste of the public that causes poets to move away. There has been taking place also a "treason of the clerks"—critics who have no talent or character and who therefore are suckers for any opinion, particularly the opinion that art does not require character and talent. These are the men who say that objects in themselves are artistic, and chance is artistic; in short, that art does not exist. These people would like to eliminate intelligence in poetry, painting, and music as it has been eliminated on the assembly line. So there is Pop or "found" poetry, as in Ronald Gross's *Pop Poems:*

> Pay
> Toilet.
> 10¢
> Each
> Patron
> Insert
> One
> Dime
> in
> Slot . . .

The assembly line moves fast, and Pop is already passé; the latest thing is concrete poetry, patterns of letters on the page.

Confronted with so much folly and treason, poets are going underground or far out. In *The Lice* W. S. Merwin has turned away from the wit and profusion of adjectives that made him known, toward a weird simplicity:

> Every year without knowing it I have passed the day
> When the latest fires will wave to me
> And the silence will set out

Tireless traveller
Like the beam of a lightless star . . .

For years David Ignatow has been drilling down
through asphalt. In his new book, *Rescue the Dead,* he
wanders in a labyrinth of dreams and self-analysis:

> down is where I want to go,
> these stairs were built to lead somewhere
> and I would find out

In *Body Rags* Galway Kinnell puts on the skins of
wild animals. He kills the bear, climbs into its body,
and becomes the bear. Kinnell's poems are matted
with blood and hair and blinking at the light.

Arnold Adoff has edited and Macmillan has
published an anthology of "modern poems by Ne-
gro Americans" titled *I Am the Darker Brother.* The
book is attractive; the poems are surrounded with
space and there are line drawings by Benny An-
drews. The anthology seems aimed at an audience
of young people. It would certainly be of great use
in schools, but is just as useful to the general
reader.

I do not think there has been a conspiracy to
"keep the Negro out of poetry" in America, but
there has been indifference to the poetry of the Ne-
gro, which is just as bad. I have never read half the
poets in this collection. The poetry of Robert Hay-
den, for example, is new to me though in quality and
ambition it is superior to the work of white poets
who have been much anthologized. Hayden's "Mid-
dle Passage," a collage of slaving-ship documents
and his own commentary, and "Runagate Run-
agate," are strong, sustained poems:

> Shuttles in the rocking loom of history,
> the dark ships move, the dark ships move,
> their bright ironical names
> like jests of kindness on a murderer's mouth;
> plough through thrashing glister toward
> fata morgana's lucent melting shore,
> weave toward New World littorals that are
> mirage and myth and actual shore.

Langston Hughes is here, of course, and Gwendolyn Brooks, and LeRoi Jones, who seems to be a representative poet for American Negroes today, as Hughes was in the 1930s. Jones's "Each Morning" is already well known:

> Each morning
> I go down
> to Gansevoort St.
> and stand on the docks.
> I stare out
> at the horizon
> until it gets up
> and comes to embrace
> me. I
> make believe
> it is my father.
> This is known
> as genealogy.

But there is a streak of hatred in Jones that will destroy his talent if he cannot control it; I mean the kind of thing that appears at the end of "A Poem for Black Hearts":

> For Great Malcolm, a prince of the earth, let nothing in
>   us rest
> until we avenge ourselves for his death, stupid animals
> that killed him, let us never breathe a pure breath if

we fail, and white men call us faggots till the end of
the earth.

The poems of Conrad Kent Rivers, particularly
his "Four Sheets to the Wind," are delightful. There
are a number of poems by Negroes who have used
the language and forms of traditional verse. They
would have written better had they written less care-
fully. The anthology ranges from original living
speech to literary imitation. But it is all valuable, for
all the poems tell something of Negro history and
culture.

Apollinaire! The Perfect Romantic

Fifty years after his death a prophet is being honored—in another country. The life and works of Guillaume Apollinaire, French poet, art critic, editor, writer of erotic novels, lover, soldier, patriot and, above all, spokesman for modernism—or as they called it in those days, *L'Esprit Nouveau*—this phenomenon is being honored with an exhibition in London, at the Institute of Contemporary Arts. On the other hand, though Apollinaire is a hero of modern French letters, and a street has been named after him in Paris, the anniversary is not being celebrated in France. It may be that Apollinaire has remained so continuously present to the French that it has not been thought necessary to revive him. Or it may be that Apollinaire's Bohemian life and attitudes do not appeal to General de Gaulle and André Malraux, guardians of the national monuments.

Though in his own time he was known also as an art critic and writer of prose tales, Apollinaire's reputation today rests on his poetry. The earlier poems are somewhat old-fashioned, with symbolist echoes:

This essay first appeared in the *New York Times Magazine*, January 19, 1969.

> The days pass and the weeks together flow
> > None none return
> > Nor loves of long ago
> The Seine runs under the Pont Mirabeau . . .

Then, with "Zone," he leaped into modernism:

> And you drink this alcohol that burns like life
> Your life that you are drinking like a brandy
> Toward Auteuil bedward you home on foot
> To fetishes of Oceana Guinea
> Christs of another form and other culture . . .

It is to the later, experimental poems that men turn these days. They look to the Apollinaire who hailed a fusion of science and metaphysics; who, in *Calligrammes,* found images for a new poetry in airplanes, submarine cables, bombs, the telephone, and the phonograph; who placed images in sudden, illogical juxtapositions, thereby achieving "simultaneity"—representing several points of view at the same time, the actual flow and confusion of sense perceptions. After Apollinaire's death André Breton, leader of the surrealist movement, called him the "re-inventor" of poetry and pointed to the apparent disorder of his writings as the major characteristic of modern poetry in France.

"Each of my poems," said Apollinaire, "commemorates an event in my life," and the reader of the poems is immediately involved in the atmosphere of the pre-1914 years and the "mystifications" of Apollinaire's existence. His life was a series of misfortunes—especially in love—that were not tragic only because he had an appetite for further misfortunes and the ability to transform them into poetry. Apollinaire was romantic. "He seemed always to be playing the parts of several characters simultane-

117

ously," said a man who knew him. "Even his handwriting was affected by this, and his bank required him to supply five or six specimens of his signature." This suggests the "criminal" tendency of the artist's life in the twentieth century, described by Thomas Mann and others. I do not mean that Apollinaire was a criminal—though in fact he was arrested "and dragged to justice like a criminal." I mean that he had a confidence man's charm and was always decamping from one role to another. On the one hand, a Bohemian; on the other, a man who joins the colors in order to establish himself as a French citizen and, moreover, writes happy poems about the front:

> In the days when I was in the artillery
> On the northern front commanding my battery
> One night when the gazing of the stars in heaven
> Pulsated like the eyes of the newborn
> A thousand rockets that rose from the opposite trench . . .

It is clear that we are dealing with a perfect romantic specimen. If we consider, also, that Apollinaire hinted that he was descended from Napoleon and his father was a Cardinal; that he called himself *mal-aimé,* unlucky in love, yet was always chasing women—we are dealing with a romantic who is not entirely responsible for his actions and not strictly accountable for his ideas, leaving us to discover the truth and put everything in order. The type is especially sympathetic nowadays, for we suspect that the opposite type, the man who is in control of his life, is intending to control ours. The Apollinairean life is permissive, and at the center of the permissive life there is a child.

The child, in this case, was illegitimate. There

were two children, born of a woman named Angelica Alexandrine Kostrowitzky. Her parents were Poles who had taken part in an anti-Russian insurrection and had been forced to leave Poland. They settled in Rome, where Angelica's father was appointed papal chamberlain. Angelica was placed at school in the French Convent of the Sacred Heart. At sixteen she was expelled. She would not be obedient; one biographer speaks of "precocious sensuality." Six years later, in 1880, Angelica gave birth—out of wedlock—to a male child, listed in the register as being of a "father N. N." (*non noto*, unknown). This child would be Apollinaire the poet.

Biographers think that one Francesco Flugi d'Aspermont has the best claim to being Apollinaire's father, but this is uncertain. Two years later Angelica bore another son, also listed as being "of father N. N." Then we find Angelica—who has changed her name to Olga—living with her two children in Monaco, where she is employed as an *entraîneuse*—we call them B-girls. She is invited by the police to leave, but manages to hang on. Then we find her in a more stable relationship, being protected by a man named Jules Weil. It is worth considering Olga, for her way of life determines that of her son Guillaume. Having cut herself off from bourgeois society, she assumes the extravagant manners of a royal personage, a dragon, ridiculous but formidable. It is she who teaches the poet how to decamp, moving from one place to another.

When Apollinaire was nineteen he and his brother stayed with Jules Weil at Stavelot, in eastern Belgium. Weil went away, and then, after running up a long bill, the brothers slipped off, too, without paying it. Throughout this episode Guillaume told people that their mother was coming to pay the bill. When he was brought before a magistrate in Paris, Olga came to his defense with a great deal of aristocratic hauteur. But though she acknowledged him, it is clear that all her life Olga thought him a nonentity. After Apollinaire's death, having learned from the newspapers that he was a famous poet, Olga Kostrowitzky appeared at the offices of the *Mercure de France* and asked for an explanation. Paul Léautaud told her about Apollinaire's works. Olga listened, then she remarked, "My other son is a writer, too. He writes financial articles for an important paper in New York."

Apollinaire's illegitimacy and Olga's influence may account for his Bohemian life, his womanizing, his pursuit of novelty in art. On the other hand, it could just as well be argued that his doubtful origins account for Apollinaire's sporadic attempts to be respectable. Psychoanalysis can tell us some of the reasons that men act as they do, but psychoanalysis cannot analyze or evaluate the work of art itself, and it is a relief to turn from explanations of Apollinaire's behavior to the poetry that he made out of it.

The poet began with a good education—enrolled in 1889 at the College of Saint Charles in Monaco. Guillaume had a strong religious and mystical side to his nature, and at Saint Charles he was instructed by nuns. He developed a taste for literature and planned to write a novel in the manner of Jules Verne. In 1891 he took seven prizes and received five honorable mentions at the prize distribution presided over by the Bishop of Monaco. Then the college was closed, and the schoolboy commuted every day by train along the Côte d'Azur to the Stanislas College at Cannes. In February, 1897, he transferred to the lycée at Nice.

By this time he was reading the poets Henri de

Régnier and Mallarmé and the prose of Remy de Gourmont. He was fond of bizarre anecdotes. He delved into rare texts and collected esoteric information, particularly Gothic mythology, with which he impressed his companions. He was taking note of the fabulous creatures that would later flash into his poems, along with the planes and submarine cables:

> . . . the pihis, long and supple,
> They each have one wing only and fly in a couple.

For some reason the student failed his *baccalauréat*. In June, 1897, he returned to Monaco, and from then on he studied or idled as he wished. He had already tried writing verse in classical Alexandrines. The themes, too, were traditional:

> Flora and warm Phoebus were returning to earth
> And the murmuring waves were breaking on Cytherea
> And the golden Venus, adored in those places
> In her temple listened . . .

Soon, however, he tried his hand at free verse, describing the carnival at Nice:

> Songs! Bengal fires!
> Champagne! Dithyramb!
> The Carnival King is burning! . . .
> And the cannon down there tolling,
> And the moon, pale golden watcher,
> Lighting the sky starred with pale gems
> (Ruby, emerald, opal)
> Seems the wonderful lamp
> Of gigantic Aladdins . . . .

In April, 1899, the Kostrowitzky ménage, including Jules Weil, moved to Paris, where they settled in the Avenue MacMahon. Apollinaire delighted in Paris. He rummaged every day in the booksellers' boxes along the quays. "I imagined myself meeting one or another of the poets I loved, a prose writer I admired, a pedant I hated."

It was then, when Apollinaire was nineteen, that he traveled with his brother and their "uncle" Weil to Stavelot, in Belgium, with the result we have seen. But there was another, happier result. At Stavelot, Apollinaire began writing seriously. He walked the roads, talking to the peasants and observing Walloon customs. He rambled about the heath and rocks and fell in love with an innkeeper's daughter. Out of these experiences he wrote poems—love poems, of course—and stocked his mind with images and legends of the Ardennes countryside. He wrote the greater part of a prose story, "L'Enchanteur Pourrissant"—"The Putrefying Wizard"—a medieval tale about Merlin, depicted as the son of a virgin and a devil, who esteems man above Christ.

After Stavelot the next milestone for Apollinaire, both as man and poet, was his love for Annie Playden. She was an English girl employed as governess by a German family. After one look at the governess, Apollinaire took a position as tutor with the family and accompanied them to Oberpleis in the Rhineland. But it didn't work out. Annie Playden was straitlaced, and "Kostro's" manner of wooing terrified her. On one occasion he proposed marriage to her on a mountain top, the Drachenfels, where Siegfried was reputed to have slain the dragon. He offered to make her a countess—"he came of a noble Russian family, full of generals and heaven knows what." He offered her his huge fortune. The governess declined. Whereupon Kostro pointed to the precipice at their feet and said that he could easily explain the accident when her body was discovered.

A year later he came to see Annie in London. This muse lived in Landor Road, Clapham. While renewing his attentions Apollinaire stayed with an Albanian friend, Faïk beg Konitza, and he rang the Playden doorbell late at night, and flew into rages. The courtship was not a success. Annie escaped by the desperate expedient of going to America. Out of this, however, Kostro made a ballad, "La Chanson du Mal-Aimé," and some poems about the Rhine.

In 1951 a lady named Mrs. Annie Playden Postings was interviewed in New York by LeRoy Breunig. She remembered Kostro, but in those days on the Rhine she had not known that he wrote verse. For fifty years she had not heard his name; she had been living in Texas; only recently had she discovered that he had become a famous poet named Apollinaire. She thought, in retrospect, that she had been prudish; it was the result of her puritan upbringing. But, she said, if she had been more generous maybe Kostro wouldn't have written the poems. During the interview she gave the impression that if she had to do it all over she would have been more romantic.

In the years when Apollinaire was writing the poems that would appear in *Alcools* and make him famous, he supported himself by writing for magazines and editing. He was the editor of his own magazine, *Le Festin d'Esope* (Aesop's Feast), from November, 1903, to August, 1904. In order to make money he wrote two erotic novels, *Les onze mille verges* and *Les exploits d'un jeune don Juan*.

The first—*The Eleven Thousand Strokes*—has been described by Francis Steegmuller as a "high-spirited parody of a holocaust by the Marquis de Sade . . . and indeed Picasso once owlishly pronounced it Apollinaire's masterpiece." *The Exploits of a Young*

Don Juan is "limpidly perverse . . . fragrant with young private perfumes." These novels are finding new readers today, for what used to be called pornography and read for its aphrodisiac effect is now being taken seriously, and there are even courses in it.

Apollinaire made a more conventional bid for fame in 1910, when he published a collection of short stories, *L'Hérésiarche et Cie.* "The author of all these inventions," said the jacket blurb, which Apollinaire wrote himself, "is intoxicated by a charming erudition, which he makes use of to charm his readers as well." This was one of the books voted on for the Prix Goncourt that year.

Besides his poetry and stories Apollinaire was also busy with art criticism. He wrote about exhibitions and painters in magazines and newspapers; from 1910 to 1914 he occasionally wrote about art for the newspaper, *L'Intransigeant.* Today this second string of his reputation is somewhat frayed. To appreciate Apollinaire's role in modern painting we must concentrate not on what he wrote about painting, but his activity, buzzing about in the ateliers of Montmartre, bringing one artist to meet another, issuing manifestoes:

L'Antitradition Futuriste

Manifeste-synthèse . . . ce moteur à toutes tendances impressionisme fauvisme cubisme expressionisme pathétisme dramatisme orphisme paroxysme . . . . "Mer . . . de,"

he says, accompanying the word with notes of music, "to critics, pedagogues, professors. A rose to . . . Marinetti, Picasso, Boccioni, Apollinaire . . . . "

It was a significant moment in both modern painting and poetry when the young Apollinaire, walking along the Seine, stopped to observe a man dabbing at a canvas. This was André Derain. They became friends, and then Apollinaire met the *fauve* Vlaminck. From these friendships Apollinaire emerged as an art critic. Then one day "Baron" Mollet—Jean Mollet, managing editor of *Le Festin d'Esope*, nicknamed "Baron" by Apollinaire because he was so elegant—brought his friend Picasso to the Criterion bar to meet Apollinaire, who at that moment was holding forth on the comparative merits of English and German beer. In his turn Picasso brought the poet Max Jacob—and the character of artistic and poetic life in Paris was established for the following decade. It was a time for cross-fertilization of the arts—painting affecting poetry (the painters were insistent on this point—they had changed the poets, not vice versa), a time of conversation, theorizing, innovation, and hard work.

Apollinaire was also enjoying himself vastly. Who would not, in Paris and with friends such as Picasso and Max Jacob, whose specialty was a dance called "the barefoot dancing girl"? Jacob, who had once actually seen Christ . . . Jacob was hairy all over, except his head, which was bald, and he never took off his glasses. He would dance "with airs and graces that made it impossible not to laugh and that were a perfect burlesque—his steps, his manipulations on tip-toe." (At about the same time by my calculations, in another street James Joyce might have been doing his "spider dance" for *his* friends.)

These Bohemian types would gather in the bars opposite the Gare Saint-Lazare. There Apollinaire ate and drank large quantities. Photographs of him at that time show a stout man with a pear-shaped head; he needed quantities to sustain this frame. Sometimes the painters and poets gathered to feast (these, as Roger Shattuck has said, were the "banquet years"). One night they held a banquet in honor of the painting of the *Douanier* Rousseau. It was half a joke; some of the celebrants thought Rousseau an old idiot who had tried to draw correctly, like an academy painter, and had failed. So much for primitivism! But they celebrated nevertheless, and the old man sat above it all with tears running down his cheeks, delighted as a child.

As a critic of art Apollinaire has been harshly criticized. "It is difficult," says Steegmuller, "to discover in all of Apollinaire's art writings, a mention of a picture that has been seen—let alone seen as an artist's image." When we turn to Apollinaire's book, *The Cubist Painters,* the harshness seems justified. Here is Apollinaire on some precubist paintings by Picasso: "Picasso's predilection for the fugitive line changes and penetrates and produces almost unique examples of linear etchings in which the general aspect of the world is unaltered by the light which modifies its form by changing its colors."

Apollinaire uses paintings as a point of departure for his own lyrical flights. In this, however, he strikes me as no better or worse than other art critics, for most art criticism is nonsense—attempting to represent paintings and sculpture in the medium of language. Finally, one can forgive Apollinaire his shortcomings as an art critic when one considers his usefulness as a publicist. He knew them all—Pablo Picasso, Georges Braque, Juan Gris, Jean Metzinger, Albert Gleizes, Marie Laurencin, Fernand Léger, Francis Picabia, Marcel Duchamp, Robert

Delaunay, Henri Matisse, André Derain, Maurice de Vlaminck, Raoul Dufy, Henri Rousseau, Marc Chagall, Giorgio de Chirico . . . . The list stretches on; in fact, it is difficult to think of an important artist living in Paris before World War I whose later fame does not owe something to Apollinaire's friendship and his writings about art. Cubists, Orphists, fauvists, independents—Apollinaire had something to say in praise of them all. The recipients of his publicity were grateful, though a few of them sniggered. It was evident that their torchbearer didn't know a damned thing about art, really.

This is true if we look at Apollinaire's ideas about art as only art criticism. But if we regard them as ideas for poetry they are a great deal more important. Out of his studies of the new painting Apollinaire envisioned techniques that could be applied to poetry. Reality has nothing to do with "realism." Chronology, logic, rational connections are not important. What matters is to seize a feeling and get it across. The artist must be bold—audacity above all!—reducing experience to the essential elements and representing them according to the importance they have in his mind. Today, these ideas are a cliché in poetry, and in art they are a doctrine—excluding Pop Art—of the academy, but in 1913 they were new.

He deduced an idea of cubist poetry. "Cubist poetry?" said Pierre Reverdy. "A ridiculous term!" What Apollinaire meant, however, was not ridiculous—it was simultaneity of points of view, juxtaposition of images, the stream of consciousness. Applying this technique in his poem "Lundi Rue Christine" and elsewhere, Apollinaire anticipated Pound's *Cantos*, and by about fifty years anticipated the theories of Marshall McLuhan.

Three gas lamps lighted
The boss has T. B.
When you've finished we'll play backgammon
A conductor who has a sore throat
When you come to Tunis I'll show you how to smoke kief
That seems to make sense . . .

Above all, in Apollinaire's art criticism, and then in his statements about poetry, he insists on innovation. Here he is certainly up-to-date. Modernism could be defined as the belief that novelty is a virtue. "Make it new," says Ezra Pound, and in most serious art and writing of the twentieth century the asumption is made that if a thing is new it is good. This belief would have astonished artists of former periods, and a hundred years from now it may again seem unfounded, but today the creed is everywhere, and no one promulgated it more forcefully than Apollinaire, or demonstrated it more clearly than he in his pleadings for the new painters and in his own works.

In 1913, when *Alcools* finally was going to press, Apollinaire wrote a new poem, "Zone," to introduce the book and give the whole of it a modernist cast and emphasize the importance originality had assumed in his mind. (At the same time he struck out all the punctuation in the galleys.) "Zone" was one of the seminal poems of the new century—worthy to stand beside the poems of Eliot and Pound and Rilke—though the influence of "Zone" is only now beginning to be apparent. In the free flow of images "Zone" anticipates surrealism:

Christ surpasses pilots in his flight
He holds the record of the world for height
Christ apple of the eye
Fruit of twenty centuries he can fly
And changed to a bird this age like Jesus rises

> The devils look up at him from the abysses
> They say he imitates Simon Mage in Judea
> They cry since he is stellar call him stealer
> The angels stunt around the pretty stunter
> Icare Enoch Elie Apollonius of Thyane
> Float around the first aeroplane . . .

And fifty years in advance, "Zone" anticipated the confessional poetry of the 1960s. The poem is a promenade through the splendors and glooms of cities. In every place there rises the lament of the "ill-beloved":

> Today you walk in Paris the women are bloodstained
> It was and I would wish to forget it was then beauty waned
> Surrounded with leaping flames Notre Dame at Chartes looked down on me
> The blood of your Sacré Coeur at Montmartre drowned me
> I'm sick of hearing the windy pieties
> The love from which I suffer is a shameful disease
> The image possessing you makes life a sleepless woe
> This fugitive image is with you wherever you go.

In "Zone," Apollinaire has fulfilled his own prescription of a new form, "a supple line, based on rhythm, subject matter, and breathing." Even in translation Apollinaire's audacity comes through. The opening line is a clarion call; the young men of 1913 went around repeating these words like a charm:

> Finally you're tired of this ancient world

The poem proceeds:

> O Eiffel Shepherdess the flock of bridges bawls this morning

"O Eiffel Shepherdess . . . . " Apollinaire is never free of tradition; indeed, he believes that it is necessary to incorporate "the classical heritage" if anything new is to be done—and, like Eliot, he has been criticized for being too knowledgeable.

> You're tired of living in Greek and Roman styles

> Antiquity has touched the automobiles
> Only religion is still new Religion
> Still simple as the hangars at the airport . . . .

In this poem about his wandering years Apollinaire speaks of "a picture hanging in a somber museum," and no account of his life would be complete without the episode of the Mona Lisa. On August 23, 1911, the *Paris-Journal* revealed that the Mona Lisa had been stolen from the Louvre. A reward was offered for the return of the painting. Then the newspaper received a letter from a young man who offered to return, not the Mona Lisa, but a "Phoenician statuette" he had stolen from the Louvre. Sensation! "An edifying story—our Museum is a supply center for unscrupulous individuals."

It turned out that the man who lifted the statue had been Apollinaire's secretary. Moreover, on a previous occasion he had stolen two other statuettes. These he had given to Apollinaire, who had passed them on to Picasso, who still had them. (If you look at Picasso's "Les Demoiselles d'Avignon," the ears of the two central figures are modeled on these stolen statuettes.) Threatened with exposure, Picasso and Apollinaire debated throwing the statuettes in the Seine, but thought better of it, and turned them in at the offices of the *Paris-Journal.*

Then Apollinaire was arrested and taken to prison. He was interrogated by a magistrate who evidently enjoyed humiliating the Bohemian poet and friend of artists. It was clear, however, that Apollinaire had been guilty only of harboring a thief, and he was released. But he was profoundly disturbed—his photograph, in handcuffs, had appeared in the papers. He was shaken by the treachery of Picasso. Brought to the prison to confront Apollinaire, Picasso had denied knowing him. Apollinaire was disturbed, also, by the outcry of the rightists, who demanded his expulsion as an undesirable alien. Some of these people were anti-Semites who supposed that, being a Pole, Apollinaire must be a Jew. Six brief, agonized poems in *Alcools* record the experience:

> Before I entered my cell
> I had to strip myself naked
> What sinister voice resounding
> Guillaume, what has become of you?
>
> Lazarus entering the tomb
> Instead of emerging . . .
> Adieu adieu . . .
> O my life O young women

The Mona Lisa, as it turned out, had been taken back to Italy by a patriotic Italian, and of course was safely recovered. The sadness of the episode for Apollinaire was that this was how he became famous. Louise Faure Favier remarks: 'Guillaume Apollinaire abruptly became famous throughout the entire world. He was thought of as the man who had stolen the Mona Lisa. Even today there are Parisians who believe it, and who are a little disappointed to learn that Apollinaire had nothing to do with the theft."

"O my life O young women. . . ." I believe it is Camus who, writing about life in prison, has a character remark that when we say freedom has been lost we mean sexual freedom. The imprisonment in La Santé, for Apollinaire, presented itself immediately as a kind of castration, reinforcing his history of sexual failure. Not incapacity—he was always trying to seduce some woman and frequently succeeding—but he never could attach a woman permanently.

After Annie Playden his next major love was Marie Laurencin. It is hard to discover the right and wrong of this affair, which ended in bitterness on his side. My impression is that, although Apollinaire was possessive and even violent, and was not faithful, yet he seems ingenuous, while Marie Laurencin was a nasty, calculating type. She met Apollinaire when he was making a name for himself as an art critic, and then when she had made a little name for herself as a painter she broke the connection. She strikes me as an all-too-familiar type of young woman, with a little talent and less sincerity. The portraits of Marie Laurencin give me a bad feeling—those beady eyes . . . .

Apollinaire's third passion was "Lou"—Louise de Coligny-Chatillon, a member of the aristocracy whom he picked up at an opium party in Nice. She kept him dangling for a while. He enlisted, in the fashion of rejected lovers, to ride off to war. Then she threw herself at him, and for a week Apollinaire was swept beyond his depth by a woman of considerable sexual inventiveness, with pronounced sado-masochistic tastes.

From the front he wrote her letters; Lou answered. Then she stopped answering; she had taken another lover. Apollinaire wrote her erotic letters, and she wrote back describing her new affair—

more erotica. The thing becomes a case history, reminiscent of Aldous Huxley's bitch, Lucy Tantamount. A further complication—returning from a visit with Lou, Apollinaire had met a young lady on a train. Out of his reminiscences and masochistic fantasies of Lou he was writing erotic poems—it is terribly chaste at the front—and copies of these poems he sent also to his new friend, Madeleine.

The end of Apollinaire's life is melancholy, from one point of view. In the trenches, having been transferred at his own request from the artillery to the infantry, he was wounded by a shell fragment in the head. At first the wound seemed superficial; then it was found necessary to trepan—to cut into the bone. He was discharged from the hospital to a desk job, censoring mail, which he did with a scrupulous sense of his patriotic obligations.

The wound had changed him physically; he was more corpulent, drowsy, given to irrational outbursts of anger. In 1918 he married Jacqueline Kolb (the "pretty redhead" of a poem). Then, a few days before the Armistice, he contracted influenza and died. His body was laid out. His friends tiptoed in to gaze at the decomposing modernist. His mother, the dragon Olga, arrived and began a furious quarrel with his widow. Final touch of the ridiculous: outside in the streets people were shouting, "*A bas Guillaume!*"—meaning down with Kaiser Wilhelm, but dreadfully ironic in these circumstances.

On the other hand, toward the end of his life Apollinaire was writing with increasing gaiety and freedom, and moving into a new field, the theater. He invented the word surrealism, and in his play *The Breasts of Tiresias* and in statements about esthetics he made at this time—urgently, as though he sensed his approaching death—he was predicting new forms of art.

In *Calligrammes,* a collection of poems published in the last year of his life, he discovered what could be done with typography, making the poem on the page look like an object. So he anticipated the present fashion of concrete poetry. Recently in the *New Republic,* a writer said that Apollinaire "invented a new poetic form . . . a mixed-media type of poem where letters, words and images were graphically intermingled." Actually, the form is as old as the hills, but Apollinaire deserves credit for reinventing it.

He welcomed the phonograph and the cinema, and predicted and wrote for a theater in which several media would be used simultaneously to achieve astounding effects. Indeed, Apollinaire went beyond theater in his prediction of a "new art . . . an orchestra that will include the entire world, its sights and sounds, human thought and language, song, dance, all the arts and all the artifices—more mirages than Morgan le Fay conjured up on Mongibel to compose the book seen and heard by the future." He sounds positively psychedelic as he foresees:

> The full unfolding of our modern art
> Often connecting in unseen ways as in life
> Sounds gestures colors cries tumults
> Music dancing acrobatics poetry painting
> Choruses actions and multiple sets

In one respect, Apollinaire is not typical of modern times. He is full of enthusiasm. He would not have felt at home in the Waste Land of the twenties, nor would he be happy in the present circles where paranoia reigns. Apollinaire was fundamentally innocent. Under the masks—melancholy being only another mask—there is a childlike confidence in love and in art. I think that as we get bored with pessimistic poetry, novels, painting, and theater—and surely the creators of boredom must be beginning to bore themselves, as well as the public—Apollinaire's writings will flourish and his influence will increase. In every generation there will be those who respond to his appeal for "a new spirit":

A joyfulness voluptuousness virtue
Instead of that pessimism more than a hundred years old
And that's pretty old for such a boring thing . . . .

The Failure of a Poet

Poets have been destroyed by neglect, and drink, and love. There is another cause that is hardly ever mentioned: the failure of an idea. Yet I think that this may account for more deaths than all the other reasons together. A case in point: the suicide in 1932 of the American poet Hart Crane, whose life is presented for the first time in detail in John Unterecker's biography. I think Crane killed himself because he felt that he had failed as a poet, rather than for any reason connected with drinking or homosexuality, though I do not think that Mr. Unterecker would hold with my view. In fact it is hard to tell from this book what Crane really thought about anything. Even when dealing with Crane's homosexuality Unterecker is unsure. On the one hand he says that too much has been made of it; on the other, he documents it, in episodes which obviously caused Crane great anguish and at times great satisfaction.

Mr. Unterecker discusses the poet's family, traces his movements, quotes his letters, and tells us what he has been reading. This has the appearance of a

This review first appeared in the Washington Post *Book World* 3, no. 28 (July 13, 1969).

definitive biography; all that the book fails to do is provide us with a reason for reading it. The writing is undistinguished, and there is little selectivity, hardly any penetration beneath the surface to give us Crane's feelings and his mind. Repeatedly we are told about Crane's parents and about their quarrels, and how they pulled their child to and fro. But Unterecker seems unable to present what is typical and let the rest go; or if he does strike on a significant moment, he is unable to convey it. For example, when Crane was an adolescent he went with a friend, male, to the friend's house. The friend had a sister who collected dolls. Crane and his friend put the dolls, one by one, under a rocking horse and proceeded to decapitate them. Unterecker's only comment on this is, "pure deviltry."

In recent years we have had pudding biographies of novelists: Mark Schorer's *Sinclair Lewis,* for example. Now poets are getting the treatment. Last year it was Seager's biography of Theodore Roethke, from which I learned that Ted could cook and his wife was intelligent. Now it is Hart Crane's turn:

> Most of his things were at Fitzi's country house, still closed for the winter. Peter Blume and his wife were, however, staying nearby and invited Hart, Malcolm Cowley, and Muriel Maurier to spend the weekend with them.

There are pages of this kind of writing, and you rise from Unterecker—you always rise—thinking: How could anyone make Hart Crane seem so dull? I don't want to be unfair to the author; the research is thorough, and the biography is informative, but surely there must be many people who are as fed up as I am with nonwriting, the unselective, repetitive chronicling of trivia that you meet with in so-called biographies. It is as though what has long been thought of novels is now thought of biographies: anyone can write one. All you need is access to the estate and permission to quote. Then, damn the torpedoes! If it runs to 700 pages (*Voyager:* 787) you are sure of two inches on every library shelf. Consider, in contrast, what Johnson did with the life of the poet Savage in a mere handful of pages . . . how much sympathy and intelligence, what insight into the splendors and miseries of bohemia! The difference is that Johnson had ideas of his own, principles, and a style; but the men who write biographies of our writers have neither and so they must put everything in, and nothing. The method is excused as being impersonal and objective, presenting just the facts. And twenty facts make a truth. But this is a delusion. Dullness is not impersonal; dullness has a personality of her own:

> Laborious, heavy, busy, bold, and blind,
> She rules, in native Anarchy, the mind.

Important things remain to be said about Crane's work. Several of the short poems are brilliant and worth a line-by-line reading. In spite of shaky syntax they present new images and at moments new cadences. Crane's poetry is to be tested, as Keats recommended, on the pulse; reading him at his best is a sensory experience. In "Chaplinesque" he writes:

> We will sidestep, and to the final smirk
> Dally the doom of that inevitable thumb
> That slowly chafes its puckered index toward us . . .

One critic sees the thumb as Moby Dick, and he may be right; but there is something else, too, which I discovered by rubbing my thumb (chafing) and index finger together. It is the American sign meaning "Gimme!" It means hard cash.

And *The Bridge* remains to be dealt with. Crane undertook to write a "major" poem; and failed. I don't see how anyone who reads *The Bridge* without prejudice can find a real structure or meaning in it. Crane's failure was suggested by Yvor Winters and Allen Tate while Crane was alive, and I think in this matter they were correct. Rather than repeat their criticisms, which were muffled by their friendship for Crane, I'll subsume them in my own. Crane had been reading *The Waste Land,* as had everyone. Moreover, as had nearly everyone, he misread it. He thought that Eliot's poem was nihilistic. At the same time he was haunted and compelled by the images in the poem. Now, whatever else *The Waste Land* may be, it is not nihilistic; to the contrary, it is a poem of religious faith. But Crane went along with the common misunderstanding of the poem; he thought it was just about rats and stones . . . a footnote to Spengler. Then, for reasons that are obvious in the description of Crane's life that Unterecker provides, he felt that he had to counteract Eliot's "nihilism." He had to write a great, big, healthy, optimistic American poem. He saw himself as contending with Eliot. In this he was, indeed, very American, for here our writers, too, are competitive; they see themselves as contending for first place: Hemingway versus Anderson, Mailer versus Hemingway, Roethke versus Lowell, and so on. It's a sad spectacle. In order to get and hold first place they must write big things. So Crane got hold of the Brooklyn Bridge, which is not a subject; it's a pile of incipient junk.

Then he went off in descriptions of landscape, more dead things, trying to tie the lyrical passages together with a "myth." But Pocahontas and Columbus are no myth; they have nothing to say to this century. The flashes of poetry were there, but there was no structure to it all, only his own desperation, trying to pull things together, a pressure to be great. For a work of art to have structure there must be, first of all, an organization of the artist's feelings. And as Unterecker shows, Crane's personality was extremely disorganized. A writer may write out of anguish and despair, and many do, but he cannot pretend to be happy. This is truly self-destructive. And Crane was pretending. He had bought a booster's idea of poetry. He wrote like an advertising man about the triumph of America, that is, machinery, while in himself he was wretched. The result is a poem with no central thought, no sincerity; lyrical fragments tortured out on a Procrustean bed.

The true poems of America, and China, have been created out of necessity, the real feelings of the poet, though it be only a few lines. But the curse to be big and to beat all others—as though art ever beats anything—ruined Crane and, with the speedup of advertising, it is ruining writers faster than ever. Crane was no fool. He knew that *The Bridge* was a failure and, unlike his critics, he lived by poetry. So he jumped off the boat on his way back from Mexico. He was destroyed not by drink or homosexuality, but by his failure to think clearly. And by ambition and the consequence of ambition: an inability to wait. It is painful to wait for poems, but it is necessary, and this is the real work that poets do.

The Heart of the Cabbage

One June I flew to Scotland to see Hugh MacDiar-
mid. I had been reading the *Collected Poems* and
everything else by MacDiarmid I could find in the
New York libraries. But I could find no critical study
of his works. Then I had the idea of writing one
myself. I wrote a letter to Robin Lorimer in Edin-
burgh, who had edited my study of James Hogg,
asking his advice. Lorimer answered that a great
deal had been written about MacDiarmid, but most
of it was superficial, and he proposed that I come to
Edinburgh and "get to know Chris, who is always
very receptive to people who are genuinely inter-
ested in him and his work."

There is a society in New York that gives money to
poor scholars. I went to their offices and told the
director that I must go to Scotland at once. MacDiar-
mid was a great poet, neglected in America, and I
wanted to gather materials for a book. The director
said that it was late to apply. Wouldn't next year do?
No, I said, I must set off at once. The director told
me to put my application in writing and also to get a

This essay first appeared in *Memoirs of a Modern Scotland,* ed.
Karl Miller (London: Faber and Faber, 1970).

letter from MacDiarmid saying that he would see me. In answer to the letter I wrote, MacDiarmid said that he would be "available—and delighted."

So, at a height of 37,000 feet and a cruising speed of 520 to 580 m.p.h., I approached MacDiarmid's Scotland. The night was dark with a few diamond-hard stars. This paled to blue green and a red line with a long streak of cloud.

> Mars is braw in crammasy,
> Venus in a green silk goun,
> The auld mune shak's her gowden feathers . . .

Two hours later I woke in bright sunlight, above a surface of ridged, gray clouds. Then there were breaks, abysses, where the blue sea was. I turned to MacDiarmid's later poems in English. They seemed appropriate to this flying:

> Sound shrinks to nothingness and musical composition
> Becomes an abstract philosophical activity.

When I got to Edinburgh Robin Lorimer was absent in London, so I spent a few days wandering about, renewing my acquaintance with the town. The King's Theater was playing "Five-Past Eight '63, the Fast-Moving, Song, Dance and Laughter Show." I bought a ticket and watched a spectacle MacDiarmid would have detested. It was all a parody of movies: dancers in "western" costume against a background of hanging wagonwheels and fence rails. A woman bawled a song, "I've got your number," the words and gestures heavily Americanized. Then, God help us, there were songs "that had been awarded American Oscars," with appropriate scenery and chorus routines. I escaped during the intermission. On the way back to my lodging house as I passed the gardens between the Castle and Princes Street there was a lighted platform on which kilted dancers were dancing to the pipes. I was no judge of piping and dancing, but I could see the difference between this and what was going on at the King's Theater. This was pleasure; the other a Paradise of Fools, whirling to the gusts blown out of Tin Pan Alley.

> We have no use for the great music.
> All we need is a few good-going tunes.

One evening I met Sydney Goodsir Smith in the Paper Bookshop off George Square. We talked about poetry and he said: "American poets are lucky. You can get published." We talked about prose, and he said that the American tradition was the "fiction of space," as in Mark Twain, Whitman, and Wolfe. I told Smith that I didn't find American "expansiveness" in his own poems, but wildness, as in his "Meth-Drinker" poem, a wildness strictly controlled. Smith said he was a classicist: he wanted "the concentration of feeling that explodes and goes straight upward." I said he seemed more lyrical than MacDiarmid was nowadays. "Don't compare me with MacDiarmid," he said. "I look at a man's shoes—MacDiarmid, at a man's dreams in the air." By this time we had moved on to a bar where Smith bought whisky for both of us and also three strangers. These people, good middle-class Scots, looked at Smith with a mixture of curiosity and some other feeling I could not place.

The next day Robin Lorimer was back from London. We went together to Milne's pub in Hanover

Street, and there we met MacDiarmid. He was on his way to a wedding reception. I had an impression of white hair, a wide brow, clear eyes, a white complexion. He talked Scots-English and he was in a twinkling mood. Robin and I had come into the middle of a conversation about Christine Keeler and the current Tory scandal. "Sexual promiscuity," said MacDiarmid, "I'm all for it, but I've never encountered it myself." A little later he told me, looking around the pub: "I've been a caterpillar crawling on the edge, but this is the heart of the cabbage." I told MacDiarmid that when I was in New York I had met a man who knew him. He had a collection of MacDiarmid's works, and offered to let me look at them and also to give me an introduction. But on my next meeting with the man he had become very secretive. Oh yes, MacDiarmid said, he had known the man in the thirties; he had gone to Spain. As for his unwillingness to help me, "people have a sort of proprietary interest in me, you know." Robin asked if it would be all right if we brought out a tape recorder when we had our interview, and MacDiarmid said yes. "I'm all for publicity—but Christine Keeler, I wouldn't like that sort of thing."

On July 2 in the morning Robin and I drove to MacDiarmid's cottage at Candymill. The "haar" was over the country and the road, and there was a light drizzle. Chris answered the door. He said that his wife Valda was absent, having made a previous appointment. He let us into the small living-room and offered me a chair near the fire, from which he ejected his dog. Its name, he said, was Janey. A neighboring farmer had a dog of the same species, and Chris had thought he'd be getting "a pound a pup," but this dog turned out to be "a pure hermaphrodite." It was a friendly creature, though frustrated.

We settled down facing each other. Robin put the tape recorder on a table to my left and the microphone on another table to Chris's right. We began to talk. I started with a sentence from MacDiarmid's autobiography, *Lucky Poet,* and asked him to explain it: "The true poet never merely articulates a preconception of his tribe, but starts rather from an inner fact of his individual consciousness." Chris talked of his boyhood in Langholm, his beginnings as a poet, his parents, his attitude to religion, his service in World War I, the Scottish Renaissance, and other matters. I asked him to read from his early poems in "Synthetic Scots." He put on his glasses and read with enjoyment and feeling. I said I was afraid of wearing him out. "No chance of that," he answered, and laughed. Then we talked about his years as a journalist, his communism, his life in the Shetlands, his experiences as a shipyard worker in World War II, his pacifism, and his anglophobia. I asked him to read also from his poems in English, and he did, with a long extract from "Direadh III." He stopped reading because his mouth was "filling with spit." He had his false teeth out and he said that without his teeth he could not cut off his words as clearly as he'd wish to.

He was solicitous; he offered to make tea and was sorry Valda was absent. He said that there were six visitors the day before, and if he had a telephone he would be answering all the time. He had a slight and winning vanity—rather, it was as though he were not quite sure that I knew how important he was. When I showed him a review of his *Collected Poems* in an American magazine he told me there had been forty or fifty reviews that he had copies of, but there were few intelligent reviewers.

As he talked I tried to memorize his features. His face, as in the good photographs, was wide with a great brow and prominent jaw, the whole face receding from the jaw. The eyes were gentle among their wrinkles. When I asked him a question he attended carefully, looking into my eyes. He cupped a hand to his left ear to hear better. Sometimes he turned to Robin for him to explain what I meant. He would answer to the point, then digress. He talked about the people who, hearing that his cottage was in need of repair, had come out to Candymill with tools and materials and worked on the cottage and made it habitable. For a man who had once written "I have had to get rid of all my friends," Chris seemed better provided with friends than anyone I had ever met.

During our conversation he rose to get a book, one of his own, entitled *The Islands of Scotland*. He couldn't find it. "If *I* put the books somewhere, I can find them," he said. But Valda, it seemed, had put it somewhere. Was it in one of the boxes under the couch? We pulled out two boxes, bumping our heads together, but couldn't find the book.

Late in the afternoon I asked him if he would like to come to the States. I had talked of this with Elizabeth Kray of the Academy of American Poets, and she was interested. Chris said he would very much like to come to America, but—and he looked serious—Mrs. Grieve would not like his coming. She would be afraid of the same thing happening to him that happened to Dylan Thomas. "I was a close friend of Thomas." I told him that an effort would be made to bring Mrs. Grieve over too. "Then it would be all right," he said, "but would I be able to get in?"—meaning his communism and the attitude of the American State Department. I said that if Mrs. Grieve and he were willing, and if Betty Kray could arrange for a reading, then an effort would be made to clear the matter with the United States government. He asked me to come back whenever I felt like it. He was quite free for a few weeks.

Robin and I had some trouble getting the car started on the grassy verge of the road, about fifty feet from the house. Chris walked out and got behind the car to push. He was seventy-one years old, the ground was muddy, and I had a feeling that a disaster might occur. I did not want to be the American who had come all the way to Scotland to disable a poet. I asked him to stand aside. Finally the car got going and Chris waved us off.

Robin and Priscilla Lorimer had invited me to move from my lodgings to their house in Sciennes Gardens. There I wrote home my first impressions of Christopher Grieve: "I had the impression of being in the presence of a truly great man and poet—the first, in my experience, to combine both qualities."

In the days that followed I tried to buy MacDiarmid's works. But it was impossible to find copies of the early books. I left my name with the booksellers and a message for Kulgin Duval who, I had been told, was collecting MacDiarmid material. Then Robin arranged for me to have an interview with the poet Helen B. Cruickshank, who had been for many years a friend of MacDiarmid. She invited me to spend a day with her looking through her correspondence. On the fifth of July I went out to her house and was received warmly by a handsome woman in her seventies. We talked about my plan to write a book. As we were talking I saw on a shelf behind her a line of first editions of MacDiarmid. I began shaking with buck fever, the nervousness felt by hunters who sight a deer and are afraid that some precipitate movement on their part will cause it to dash off. I asked Helen Cruickshank if she would sell me any of the books, for I needed them desperately for my work. She said yes and lifted down the volumes I named. She looked at the price marked on a book jacket and asked if I were willing to pay that much. I pointed out that the book in her hand, *Lucky Poet,* for which she was asking $3.50, was worth at least $25, and I could not pay less. She said that she was not interested in making money, that when she died her possessions would be dispersed, and, besides, she liked me. Then we sat in the garden and had tea and the birds came. The garden was full of flowers, foxgloves, and roses: there was a birch tree like the birches outside my cabin in California.

She brought out a box containing seventy-five letters from MacDiarmid or relating to MacDiarmid that she had collected over the years from 1922 to 1962. I asked if I might make copies. She said yes, and I set about it, writing as fast as I could. I was trying to get everything down—the facts about his early struggles as a writer and his poverty when he lived on the island of Whalsay in the Shetlands: "The core of the problem . . . is the difficulty in maintaining our credit accounts here for such daily essentials as milk, bread, and paraffin oil, until such time as I can get my books—or some of them—finished and sent in to the publishers."

Then I began getting writer's cramp. I asked Helen Cruickshank, again with apprehension that it might be refused, if I might take away all the letters and have photostats made of them. She had said that just a few days ago a man had visited her and gone through the letters and taken away the ones he wanted. I told her that the collection was valuable and copies should be made immediately and placed in the National Library before other visitors helped themselves. She said I might borrow the collection for this purpose.

I took the letters away, and had two sets of photostats made. I asked Robin Lorimer to place one set in the National Library, kept the other set myself, and returned the originals to Helen Cruickshank.

At my second interview with Chris, Valda was present. She was, as we say, loaded for bear. She told me that she did not approve of people who came to see Chris, interviewed him and made him record his poems, and made promises which they did not keep. I told her that my intentions were honest and that my main reason for seeing Chris was that I admired his poetry. Then she tore into Americans. Referring to the crisis during which the United States had brought pressure on the Soviet Union to withdraw their rockets from Cuba, she said that in her opinion the rockets should have been launched against the United States. I said that such a course of action would have entailed the destruction not only of the United States which she detested, but also of the USSR which she admired.

I knew something about Valda's life with Chris, particularly their years of isolation in the Shetlands, and I could understand her resentment of a visitor coming from America. Communism had not been just a theory to the Grieves. They had lived it. For many years it had been difficult for Chris to find a market for his poems, articles, and books. His opinions offended many people. His pleading for Scotland offended "the English Ascendancy, the hideous khaki Empire." His dogmatic Marxism offended others. Naturally both Chris and Valda were anti-American. In the Marxist fable the United States is a capitalist state inhabited by only two kinds of people, the oppressors and the oppressed. But I was not here to explain the United States, and in any case people who have a fixed system of belief do not wish to hear anything to the contrary.

Valda gave us lunch, and then we stopped trying to make a businesslike recording of poems and a series of questions and answers. The conversation degenerated, or perhaps it rose, to the level of gossip. Weeks later, back in America, when I had the interviews transcribed by a stenographer and looked them over, I realized they were almost entirely worthless. I had not got from Chris anything that he had not already expressed more vividly in his books. I wished that instead of trying to be a reporter I had just spent my time talking to him about poetry. Nevertheless, I submitted the manuscript to the *Paris Review,* at the editors' invitation. They did not publish it. Then I asked them to return the manuscript, but I never received it.

There was a great book waiting to be written about Christopher Grieve—a study of his life and works. It would have to be, also, a study of Scottish culture over half a century, for Grieve had been involved in several movements of that culture. But I realized that I did not have the knowledge to undertake the task, nor was I tempermentally suited. To write such a book what was needed was a *Scottish* Boswell.

Then why not forget the man and just write about

the poetry? The trouble was MacDiarmid's didacticism. Once he had written:

> Better a'e gowden lyric
> Than a social problem solved.

But in later years he turned sharply against this attitude. He spoke with contempt of readers who wished that he would write lyrics as he used to; they were "seductive voices" that he must not heed. As time passed he became more devoted to communism, and the dialectic could not be separated from his poetry. As he told me, "if the communist dialectic gets thoroughly into you, into your blood and bones, as it is in mine. . . ." Long stretches of his poems were political tracts. I would have thought them tedious no matter what kind of opinion they were propagating, but communism was a belief I found singularly unattractive. Whatever communism might be in theory, I could not sympathize with MacDiarmid's praise of its manifestation in the Soviet Union. Under that system of government men who spoke out were silenced. And when MacDiarmid approved of this—

> What maitter't wha we kill
> To lessen that foulest murder that deprives
> Maist men of real lives?

—my sympathy failed. I could not stomach opinions such as this, and in MacDiarmid's poems they were not translated into narrative or song—they were preached straight at the reader.

I thought MacDiarmid had mistaken the source of his strength. Instead of echoing communist dogma he should have stuck to Scotland, the heart of the cabbage. It was Scotland that made him and would understand him at the last. His best writing was about the places where he lived and the friends and enemies he had. It was Scottish ways of thinking that gave his poems their vigor. What on earth did the working-class poet from Langholm have in common with the politicians in the Kremlin? MacDiarmid had undertaken to support a totalitarian system of government that was a means of enslaving men. But the Scotland in his poems was true and would endure forever—at least while men loved freedom and had the heart for a song. MacDiarmid's strength was in the fusion of his personality with the pride and despair of Scotland. When this fusion occurred, his poetry was powerful, wild, ranging in thought; he combined lyrical and argumentative powers. At the end of "Lament for the Great Music" he had the force, and by his devotion to Scotland he had earned the right, to summon the great pipers:

> standing shoulder to shoulder
> With Patrick Mor MacCrimmon and Duncan Ban
>   MacCrimmon in the centre
> In the hollow at Boreraig or in front of Dunvegan Castle
> Or on the lip of the broken graves in Kilmuir Kirkyard
> While, the living stricken ghastly in the eternal light
> And the rest of the dead all risen blue-faced from their
>   graves
> (Though, the pipes to your hand, you will be once more
> Perfectly at ease, and as you were in your prime)
> All ever born crowd the islands and the West Coast of
>   Scotland
> Which has standing room for them all, and the air
>   curdled with angels . . .

Poetry in the Sixties—
Long Live Blake!
Down with Donne!

In the 1960s poetry got off the page and onto the platform.

In the previous decade poetry, together with other forms of self-expression and political expression, had been mute. Dylan Thomas made his American tours and boomed out his lyrics, and audiences were stunned; but Thomas disappeared, and again there was silence in the land. Then, in the late fifties, Allen Ginsberg did his readings of "Howl," and the fashion of listening to poetry was upon us.

It made a considerable difference. For years, under the New Criticism, we had been told that a poem was a construction rather than a performance. The perfect poem talked to itself, and the reader's reactions to it were a kind of eavesdropping. The poem was born of tension and irony, and consequently, in a kind of rage, it "disdained to have parents." If you were fond of a poem—watch out! This was probably the "affective fallacy." If you were curious about the man who wrote it, or the "meaning" of

---

This essay first appeared in the *New York Times Book Review,* December 28, 1969.

the poem—watch out again! This was the "intentional fallacy."

Being a poet in those days, or a reader of poetry—but were there any readers?—was like being in hell. Every step was surrounded with Thou Shalt Not's, and the only guide through the difficult task of reading a poem was the critic, an Empson, Richards, or Blackmur, who might keep you from making a sentimental fool of yourself.

As for reading poetry aloud—it was understood that, as the poem was a self-contained object, the sound of the human voice had little to do with it. If you were compelled through some unfortunate circumstance to read a poem aloud, the only way was to read it as flatly as possible. To give the words any sort of expression would be cheating. For example, there is the recording of Elizabeth Bishop reading her poem "The Fish"; in speaking the final words, "rainbow, rainbow, rainbow!" she manages to suggest that seeing colors has been a distasteful experience.

It was Ginsberg almost single-handed who changed things. This is giving a great deal of credit to one man, and I suppose that my crediting Ginsberg with so much will be resented, for instance, in San Francisco, where poets had been reading in coffee shops before he came along. But it is one thing to read foolish poems aloud, and another to read poems such as "Sunflower Sutra" and "America." Or "Kaddish" (1961).

> . . . She reads the Bible, thinks beautiful thoughts all days.
> "Yesterday I saw God. What did he look like? Well, in the afternoon I climbed up a ladder—he has a cheap cabin in the country, like Monroe, NY the chicken farms in the wood. He was a lonely old man with a white beard.

"I cooked supper for him. I made him a nice supper—lentil soup, vegetables, bread & butter—miltz—he sat down at the table and ate, he was sad.

"I told him, Look at all those fightings and killings down there. What's the matter? Why don't you put a stop to it?

"I try, he said—That's all he could do, he looked tired. He's a bachelor so long, and he likes lentil soup."

Ginsberg was humorous; and he'd learned—from William Carlos Williams—to write of common American things in plain language. Ginsberg's original contribution, however, was a note of hysteria that hit the taste of the young exactly. He spoke for the spiritually disenfranchised, numbers of wretched young people from middle-class homes, who had grown up after World War II—weeds of an affluent society. They flocked to his readings; they had found someone who spoke aloud for them; more than this, someone who gave them a way to live—ragged and bearded—without feeling ashamed, and even with pride. Hemingway created the life-style of the Lost Generation; Ginsberg created that of the Beat. It was a spectacular achievement.

Ginsberg's success brought wider recognition for the writings of his teacher. In the 1960s William Carlos Williams would be the prime model for younger poets. For years Williams had lived a poetic credo that was not fashionable. He had done much of his writing according to the principles of objectivism, which stated that the poem should be taken from nature—and by nature the objectivists meant broken bottles and garbage cans, as well as flowers.*

---

*My ideas about Williams have changed considerably since this article was written. For a later view, see "William Carlos William's Idea of Poetry," beginning on page 339 of this book [Author].

The objectivist poem was an imagist poem carried one step further. The personality of the author was to be excluded; subjectivity was tolerable only in so far as it reflected a mood of the external world. Poetry was a kind of lens, selecting and concentrating reality, which was external to the mind.* Williams derived his thinking from painters of the thirties, Demuth and Sheeler, as well as from his own solitary thoughts in the dismal landscape of New Jersey.† His poems were like Sheeler's paintings of gray wood and sandy stone. Williams looked with a depersonalized gaze, not far from insanity, at the objects produced by an industrial, commercial society, which he loathed. By gazing long and hard he compelled himself to love them—or at least, to draw forth their essence. Or, if objects do not have an essence, they are manifestations of America, the great unknown. And he loved America.

> Plaster saints, glass jewels
> and those apt paper flowers, bafflingly
> complex—have here
> their forthright beauty, beside:
>
> Things, things unmentionable,
> the sink with the waste farina in it and
> lumps of rancid meat, milk-bottle-tops: have
> here a tranquillity and loveliness . . .

There were others besides Ginsberg who had learned from Williams. Williams searched for

---

*No. The poet's "subjective" response is part of the process that produces the "objective" poem [Author].

†No again. Williams, Deemuth, and Sheeler shared certain points of view—Williams did not "derive his thinking" from the painters [Author].

American speech-rhythms and he claimed to have found the "variable foot." Now the Black Mountain poets began to be heard from. They were mad about technique; they had discovered a way for the poet to write verse lines in the rhythm of his breathing. Charles Olson has explained the way in which Black Mountain poets wrote, but as I cannot understand Olson's prose, I shall quote an explanation of it by Robert Creeley, another member of the school:

> He [Olson] outlines . . . the premise of "composition by field" (the value of which William Carlos Williams was to emphasize by reprinting it in part in his own "Autobiography"); and defines a basis for structure in the poem in terms of its "kinetics" ("the poem itself must, at all points, be a high energy-construct and, at all points, an energy discharge . . . "), the *principle* of its writing (form is never more than an extension of content), and the "process" ("ONE PERCEPTION MUST IMMEDIATELY AND DIRECTLY LEAD TO A FURTHER PERCEPTION . . ."). He equally distinguishes between breathing and hearing, as these relate to the line: "And the line comes (I swear it) from the breath, from the breathing of the man who writes, at that moment that he writes. . . ."

This was projective verse. In coffee shops all over the country young poets read aloud, breathing hard and pausing significantly at the end of each line, and as some of them had short breaths their poems were long and skinny. There was an owlish solemnity about these proceedings; if you were trapped in a corner and couldn't get out, you would be in for a bad night. Perhaps a theory of any kind is better than no theory at all—for people who must have a theory. But what dreariness, and what a dismal lack of humor!

Next to Williams, Ezra Pound was the master most spoken of. Many of the people who knew that

Pound's *Cantos* were sacred had never taken the trouble to read them. But every age has its cant, and Pound is not responsible for the sycophancy of his admirers. There was, indeed, an element in the *Cantos* which, when it was added to the elements derived from Williams, would produce the typical "avant-garde" poem of the 1960s. That is, a poem that would let in the author's opinions of history, myth, anthropology—you name it—as well as describe the visible objects in the poet's pad. Williams himself in *Paterson* had moved away from objectivism toward a poetry that would include everything that came into his mind; but it was Pound who was the master of the method. The *Cantos* were a stream of consciousness; everything seemed to be happening at once—poetic images, facts, prose documents were jumbled together. To what purpose? Just live in the poem, and don't ask silly questions! The poem is like life itself, "open" and interminable. There is no such thing as form, anyway not as it has been understood, with a beginning, a middle, and an end. The "well-made poem" is dead. Ask not whether a poem is good or bad. Ask, rather, if it is interesting. Anything that comes into the mind of a real poet, i.e., a bard, is interesting.

Long live William Blake! Down with Donne!

The better poets who subscribed to this theory were a lot better than the theory. Robert Duncan and Gary Snyder were better. One reason for their excellence was that, like Ginsberg, they had a sense of humor, and this indeed made their poems interesting. I have just read a new poem by Snyder. It's a funny, curiously touching poem, a mixture of mystical Asian words and realistic descriptions, all subsumed in an epiphany to Smokey the Bear.

And if anyone is threatened
by advertising, air pollution,
or the police, they should
chant SMOKEY THE BEAR'S
WAR SPELL:
DROWN THEIR BUTTS
CRUSH THEIR BUTTS
DROWN THEIR BUTTS
CRUSH THEIR BUTTS
And SMOKEY THE BEAR will
surely appear to put the enemy
out with his vajra-shovel.

Ecology, the study of relations between different forms of life and between life and environment, is beginning to be a subject for poems. At the present time a manifesto by poets is going the rounds; it urges the necessity for preventing mankind from exterminating the other species.

The poets I have been talking about were those most admired by younger poets. This is not to say that these were the most widely read poets of the time. For every reader of Ginsberg or Snyder there have been twenty of Rod McKuen. He has sold two million copies. His publishers say that he is the leading poet of the age—just as Jacqueline Susann, by the same measure, is the leading novelist. There is a beautiful simplicity about judging literature by the number of books sold. As Dr. Johnson said, a man is seldom so innocently employed as when he is making money, and Rod McKuen is certainly innocent.

Come with me, then, and *Listen to the Warm:*

On this Tuesday away from you
I wonder if the time will ever pass
till we're together
even for a while again.

> But yesterday you touched me
> and we drove to the toll beach
> and ran in the sand.
> Sorry no one could see
> how beautifully happy we were.

Well, what's wrong with it? It's simple, it makes lots of people happy. Only an effete intellectual snob would find fault with it.

Right you are. The world is like a sandpile with lots of nice gooey wet blobs to play with. It's a soda pop, a weenie roast, a sticky, marshmallow kiss. The world is the province of Youth.

If only Youth were as happy to be ignorant as middle-aged losers say it should be! But Youth, alas, has brains, and these days Youth is having a pretty hard time. Even if Youth does not read Dante, Youth will learn about life—in the slums or the rice-paddies—and Youth sooner or later will want to have poetry. Not this slop.

Which brings me to poetry and politics. The 1960s were different from previous years in that poets began talking from the platform about political matters. There were poetry readings against the war in Vietnam, and readings of black poetry. Poems were read at meetings to help the children of Biafra, and poems were read during sit-ins.

Some of the poets who read against the war traveled from place to place and exposed themselves to a great deal of discomfort and to some abuse. The names of Galway Kinnell, Robert Bly, Denise Levertov are respected today not only because they are fine poets, but because they have shown qualities of self-sacrifice and courage. It may be said that these qualities, however admirable, have little to do with the quality of poems. I don't agree. In the hands of a poor writer, a cause is likely to produce bad art; he would have produced bad art anyway. But if the writer has intelligence, his political activity is an extension of his awareness, and, if it does not produce masterpieces at once, in the long run it is bound to add to his writing—as will everything he does. Or does *not* do. Many writers have become empty vessels simply because they stopped living with any interest. Eliot's prayer, "Teach us to sit still," is dangerous stuff; to use it properly you had better have, as did Eliot, spiritual resources.

The bad poem about the war, or about the Negro, was bad for the reasons that poems are usually bad; there was a statement, sure enough, but the ideas could have been had from a newspaper, and the subject was not connected to the writer personally. You did not feel that this man was compelled to write this poem and that the poem was therefore original—for anything that a man does out of the necessity of his own unique being must be original.

Among the black poets LeRoi Jones spoke most vehemently for revolutionary attitudes. But there were other poets who had something to say and who were now beginning to be heard, thanks to the waking consciousness of America in regard to the Negro. Robert Hayden, Mari Evans, Dudley Randall, and black poets whose works are in anthologies but not yet published in books, were being read seriously for the first time. It made a great difference to black children in schools to be able to read poems by black writers that had something to say to them personally.

Looking back at the poetical-political sixties, what Senator Eugene McCarthy says in *The Year of the People* rings true, and it is so well said that I won't try to paraphrase it.

As a general rule, I believe that the artist should remain somewhat detached and independent of politics, but when the issues are as crucial as they were in 1968, no citizen, no matter what his vocation or profession may be, can remain completely aloof. It was a year in which artists had to be, as Albert Camus has said, both artists and men even to the point of being prepared to neglect their special work or calling in order to involve their person, their time, and their art in the country's problems. "If we intervene as men," wrote Camus, "that experience will have an effect upon our language. And if we are not artists in our language first of all, what sort of artists are we?"

In 1968, the artists served their land and language well.

I have left till last a discussion of individual poets whose work has struck me as particularly fine, no matter what group they belong to, or no group at all. It all comes down to talent, after all. This has not always been remembered, and in recent years the art of criticism—following the collapse of the New Criticism—has practically ceased to exist. Instead we have had literary politics and polemics. It is easy to know beforehand what attitude the *New York Review of Books* or *Evergreen Review* will take toward a poet. The question is not, "What is he?" but "Is he one of us?" Reputations are made, invested in, and upheld. But who cares for poetry? Who pays attention to the individual?

One recent poet and critic has paid attention, and though he has committed some absurdities (for example, he does not consider Robert Duncan or Donald Hall)—yet in *Alone With America* Richard Howard has undertaken to criticize forty-one poets for what they are, ignoring what schools they may belong to. Forty-one! There is something ridiculous about such charity. Yet this is a fault on the side of the angels. Time and again Howard is able to find something to praise, and he treats everyone's poem as though it were important. Which, of course, it is—but we have almost forgotten how to think so. Does this book herald the beginning of a new era, when poems will be read instead of being either ballyhooed or ignored? I hope so.

I too have a list, of poets who have recently published excellent books. These poets have one thing in common—they write in free form. I am of Whitman's opinion: "The poetic quality is not marshalled in rhyme or uniformity." When the free-form poem works, it is as wonderfully irregular as a lilac or rosebush.

First, George Oppen, whose *Of Being Numerous* was awarded a Pulitzer prize. Oppen shows how Pound's *Cantos* can be used as a basis from which to develop. Oppen's language has been stripped clean of references to things outside the poem itself. Yet, as in Pound,

> The context is history
> Moving toward the light of the conscious

Reading Oppen I am aware of all that has been excluded by a very discriminating mind in order to arrive at significant life. The mind, moving toward clarity, sheds those matters that are, as Gatsby said, "just personal." As it begins to know itself, the mind moves, and thought is felt as movement, along the line. We experience the life of the mind in its physical reality, the movement of verse:

> What is or is true as
> Happiness

> Windows opening on the sea,
> The green painted railings of the balcony
> Against the rock, the bushes and the sea running

Unfortunately, as there is not an automatic forward propulsion by meter, poets who write in free form have difficulty sustaining a mood, or train of thought, or narrative. Jim Harrison, author of *Locations*, has tackled the problem by writing "suites," longer poems in sections which are really short poems related not by a logical narrative but by association. He has gone to Rilke and Apollinaire for models—and sometimes, most noticeably in "Suite to Fathers," the model sticks out:

> From Duino, beneath the mist,
> the green is so dark and green it cannot bear itself. . . .

Harrison writes about landscapes, birds, and beasts, a hunter's wandering. His poetry moves heavily, convulsively, as though burrowing through quantities of psychic material—turning it over, sniffing around it. This poet seems determined to experience much and not make up his mind. It is as though he wishes to lose himself in the life he is describing:

> My mouth stuffed up with snow,
> nothing in me moves,
> Earth nudges all things this month.
> I've outgrown this shell
> I found in a sea of ice—
> its drunken convolutions—
> something should call me to another life.

Inside the Blood Factory, by Diane Wakoski, has its limitations—one reader spoke to me of her "absence of music"; by music I think he meant the resonance we get from the images of poets who are not so engrossed in their personal lives. Wakoski's poems are confessional, and we have had so many confessions. But there is a difference between Wakoski's confessions and those of other writers; she takes you, in the poem itself, through the experience she is talking about—whereas others just complain about their feelings. Wakoski's poems are a struggle, sometimes gay, sometimes desperate; always there is the hard work of actually thinking on the page.

And last, *The Naomi Poems,* by Bill Knott, who publishes under the name Saint-Geraud. Here we have entered a strange world where anything at all may happen. The images are astonishing. Whatever you may think of Knott's poems, they have not been written before by anyone else. This is a passage from "Prosepoem":

> Ringed by starfish gasping for their element, we joined to create ours. All night they inhaled the sweat from thrusting limbs, and lived. Often she cried out: Your hand!—It was a starfish, caressing her with my low fire.

This is called "Hair Poem":

> Hair is heaven's water flowing eerily over us
> Often a woman drifts off down her long hair and is lost

Poetry such as this strikes me as extending our awareness. And with poets such as these we have come a long way from the timid, silent fifties.

An American Shape

There are certain shapes American poems make. I have never been able to buy the idea that there is a distinctive American meter—what Williams called "measure"—because Americans speak in many accents and rhythms. Insofar as they speak alike they are speaking English. They speak with local words and phrases, of course, but this does not produce a standard foot or time-measure that is different from the rhythms, regular and irregular, of English spoken in Birmingham and Sidney. The idea of an "American Measure" is propaganda, springing from the old national bragging and feeling of inferiority. But I would certainly argue that American poets make shapes on the page that look different from, on the one hand, sonnets, and, on the other hand, free verse. These poems are unrhymed, written in short lines, and divided in paragraphs balanced against each other. The writing seems to have been carved in cadences out of blocks of rhythm. The carving is as careful as the old work in rhyme and stanza. The poet is making

This review first appeared in "Four Poets," *Ohio Review* 16, no. 1 (Fall, 1974).

his own shape, but at the same time he is following the grain of the materials—sculpture, not clay modelling, not merely carrying out a preconceived idea. The poet as sculptor, as Davie says in his book on Pound. The poem looks natural, but it has been crafted, like a canoe. This may go back to the peculiar shape of American democracy: license but not liberty.

There are poets, of course, who think that any kind of shape is immoral. They see a policeman under every bed. So they just put down whatever comes into their heads, the way it comes. Usually they write about themselves, for they have never been able to be interested in anything else. But some poets avoid falling into that swamp; they discover material and write in the shapes I have been describing. Not invariably, but often enough for me to think that, contrary to what we hear these days (that there are no longer any standards, that there is no common way of writing verse), in fact there is a great similarity between one book of American poems and another, if we look at the shape of the poem.

If I had to show a foreigner in a few moments what American poetry looks and sounds like, I'd give him *Giraffe* by Stanley Plumly. It is beautifully crafted; he seems able to say whatever he thinks, which is freedom, yet to say it so that it is interesting, which is craft. In one place he comes too close to Wallace Stevens:

> The clumsy children should be dancing on the lawn
> or the women without underwear;
>
> there should be barns at the edge of the town
> and one light in the kitchen window . . .

But in general he shares some of Stevens's preoccupations without echoing his sentences. Plumly is concerned with the nature of poetry, what the imagination is, the process of writing poetry. This is not popular these days; we are supposed to be writing about "real life," which is usually what someone else thinks it should be. To be a poet in the United States, and not lend oneself to the service of one pressure group or another, is as difficult as it ever was. American poets tend to have a moral purpose—even when morality has been stood on its head—and that is why they can be such solemn bores. But Plumly's poems are obviously written with enjoyment—for the sound, the hovering sense of the words, about nothing and everything. Here's "One Line of Light:"

> Six across. The windows give away
> everything. Some nights
> I'm the only one up
> in Athens, Ohio,
> all the lights on,
> the music loud enough
> to leak, like water,
> out of every seam,
> each soft spot.
>
> I think of my house as a ship
> lit up like a birthday.
> I would walk around inside it
> with the page of a poem—
> the day's log,
> the night's psalm.
> The dark is my ocean.
> I know the water's rising
> in the next town.

I don't know what is meant by the rising water, and poets should stay away from the idea of darkness as an ocean—in fact the word "dark" has become a cliché of the past few years, the way "light" used to be. But this poem in its shape exemplifies the carving of poetry out of speech, phrase by phrase, and balancing it in verse-paragraphs, the American shape I've been describing. Also, Plumly's poem is interesting for its language. If you look at the words they become transparent and you are able to see straight through to the thought. I'd call this sincerity, except that the word has been so abused: let's say credibility instead. I believe it when he says that he's the only one up in Athens, Ohio, because the language tells me so. He doesn't try to make a big thing out of it. But it's not a little thing either; if you're up late at night in America, true, you can get a feeling of exultation, that the house is leaking music and light. For many people it's the only chance they get to feel alone. The only chance to feel

> the day's log,
> the night's psalm. . . .

This signifies something. I wonder how many readers there are who can see that it does? Neglect of poets seems inevitable . . . but perhaps it's not a bad thing. Think what you would have to write in order to please the public, Emily's "admiring bog," and be thankful for small audiences.

"Silence" is another cliché of the period. Plumly says:

> I would walk out of this flesh,
> leave the whole body of my bones.
> If I could I would undress utterly.
>
> I would be silence. . . .

Poets who keep hoping for silence had better watch out—they may get it. The silence of those infinite spaces is not, as Pascal tells us, a delight. We have heard enough about silence for a while—the purity of American poets is getting to be a scandal. What we are short of is a sense of human life. As Plumly says in another mood:

> back to the sun,
> a bottle of beer
> in one hand,
> your hat in the other. . . .

The Ghost of Delmore Schwartz

Reviews have pointed out that the character Humboldt in Saul Bellow's new novel, *Humboldt's Gift,* is based on the life of the poet Delmore Schwartz. Like Humboldt, Schwartz had paranoid fantasies that involved him in farcical, humiliating situations. Schwartz's career started brilliantly; at the end he could no longer write; he drank heavily and quarreled with his friends. The end came in a seedy hotel in mid-Manhattan—a heart attack in the middle of the night while taking out the garbage. For days the body of the poet lay unclaimed.

Bellow has chosen to make a character out of Delmore Schwartz because Schwartz's life illustrated the difficulty of being an artist in America, a problem that affects Bellow himself.

Moreover, Schwartz was a Jew, and Bellow is committed to Jewish traditions. Schwartz was born in Brooklyn in 1913, the son of Harry and Rose (Nathanson) Schwartz. He was educated at the University of Wisconsin, at New York University where he distinguished himself in philosophy, and at Harvard.

This essay first appeared in the *New York Times Magazine,* December 7, 1975.

While a student he edited a little magazine, *Mosaic*, and earned a reputation for "precocity." At the age of twenty-four he published a short story, "In Dreams Begin Responsibilities," that made him famous—at least in literary circles.

Dwight Macdonald, who began editing *Partisan Review* in 1937 as a "revolutionary socialist magazine," recalls the impact of "Responsibilities." It was an astounding story, in Macdonald's opinion, better than anything by Hemingway or Fitzgerald, and other critics have agreed on the merit of this particular work. In its conception, from the first line to the end, "Responsibilities" has the appearance of a myth or fable, an idea that has leaped full-formed into the mind, a situation that strikes us as perfectly obvious once we have seen it. The story begins in 1909. "I feel," says the narrator, "as if I were in a motion picture theatre." He is watching an old silent picture. "It is Sunday afternoon, June 12th, 1909, and my father is walking down the quiet streets of Brooklyn on his way to visit my mother."

His father is thinking as he walks, how nice it will be to introduce her to his family. But he is not sure that he wants to marry, "and once in a while he becomes panicky about the bond already established." He reassures himself by thinking about the important men he admires who are married: "William Randolph Hearst, and William Howard Taft, who has just become President of the United States."

Immigrant dreams! Watching this movie as it unrolls we share the apprehensions and bewilderment of the narrator. When his father proposes to his mother she begins to cry; his father is puzzled: getting married is not what he thought it would be like when he strolled on Brooklyn Bridge "in the revery of a fine cigar." At this point the narrator stands up and shouts, "Don't do it. It's not too late to change your minds, both of you. Nothing good will come of it, only remorse, hatred, scandal and two children whose characters are monstrous." At the end of the story, when the father and mother quarrel and the father goes away, the narrator rises again and shouts, "What are they doing? Don't they know what they are doing? Why doesn't my mother go after my father?" Then the usher drags him out of the theater. The usher says, "What are you doing? Don't you know that you can't do whatever you want to do?"

"A Freudian movie," Dwight Macdonald calls it. I would add that in this story Schwartz was the first to have a vision of Jewish life in America that would be picked up by other writers. Everyone said that Delmore Schwartz was brilliant, and he was praised by T. S. Eliot, which was like being canonized by an archibishop. But this was more success than Delmore knew how to handle. He became involved in literary politics, trying to preserve the fame he had won so early. He was terribly self-conscious. He knew he was expected to turn out masterpieces and that the critics were laying for him. Literary life in America is as competitive as any other kind of business, and no writer who has been praised fails to arouse envy. Schwartz's second book, *Genesis,* was rather disappointing. People said so. And it wasn't just that people were out to get Delmore—there seemed to be a flaw in his character. He did a translation of Rimbaud's *A Season in Hell* and it was evident that he didn't know French—the translation was full of schoolboy howlers. What made him think that he could translate from a language he did not know?

He had delusions of grandeur. These were followed by a train of suspicions. In later years Schwartz was convinced, like Humboldt in the novel, that Rockefeller was plotting against him, damaging his brain by sending out rays from the Empire State Building. Between the two extremes, the mind that could see the lives of its parents as clearly as if it were watching a movie, and the mind clouded with suspicion, there were many stages—windings, losses, returns to itself, new beginnings, and new failures. The stages are described or suggested by Bellow in the novel based on Schwartz's life.

There are aspects of Schwartz, however, that are not represented by Bellow. Schwartz had a reverence for tradition, especially literary traditions. When he taught at Harvard—the first of a series of academic appointments—he would take visitors on a tour of Mt. Auburn Cemetery where the James family is buried. And the reader of Schwartz's critical essays will discover that when he is thinking as a critic and not as a poet he is fair-minded. Philip Rahv speaks of Schwartz's "rare precision of statement and shrewdness of insight." Schwartz as a critic was the antithesis of the wild ranter in *Humboldt's Gift*. It is possible that Schwartz was primarily a critic, an appreciator of literature. But a poet was what he wished to be or thought he should be. He loved poetry so much! It may have been straining to rise to the heights of imaginative writing he admired and others had predicted for him that destroyed his sanity.

It is dangerous to make generalizations about the life of the poet in America. Every individual is a special case, and the psychological reasons for Delmore Schwartz's destruction are not those that apply to Randall Jarrell, Sylvia Plath, John Berryman, or Anne Sexton. Nevertheless, some cultures do encourage art while others don't. America has not been kind to poets; it offers them neglect and obscurity. Very few American poets are known to the public, even the public that reads. What Wordsworth says of poets everywhere seems particularly true of poets in America.

> We Poets in our youths begin in gladness
> But thereof come in the end despondency and madness.

The ideas a man chooses to live by can make a difference to his well-being even though he may have a psychological weakness. Samuel Johnson trusted his religion to keep him sane. Delmore Schwartz, like other literary people in an age of unbelief, had nothing to trust but literature. When we look back at the generation that began to publish around the time of World War II, we see that they had no sense of community, only an image of fame. It was every man for himself. The masters of modern art were solitary figures, each ruling a world he had created and to which he alone held the key.

If you were an American poet just down from Harvard you were conscious of the overwhelming influence of T. S. Eliot. Delmore Schwartz had a comic routine in which he played the roles of T. S. Eliot and Delmore Schwartz. He was an excellent mimic, not just capturing a mannerism but seeming to enter the skin, the very mind of the one he was imitating. He also admired Joyce enormously—he thought of him as Apollo. Yeats, too, was a model. And there was the current fashion of writing like Auden.

The not-so-funny side of Delmore's impersonations was that he also did them when he wrote. In *Humboldt's Gift,* Bellow has Charlie Citrine say some harsh things about anthologists who, since Humboldt's death, have omitted his poems from their collections. I must admit that if I were making an anthology Schwartz's poems would not leap to mind. On this point it seems that Bellow wants to have it both ways. He chastises those who do not think highly of the poet; at the same time he has Charlie Citrine say, "As a poet or thinker his record wasn't all that impressive." Bellow seems to think that he alone has a right to pass critical judgment. Not that his judgment of Schwartz's poetry is that high, but he resents any sign of intellectual pretension in other people.

Schwartz was aware that he imitated. A section of the 1938 volume, *In Dreams Begin Responsibilities,* is titled "Poems of Experiment and Imitation." But awareness of one's faults does not excuse them—at least, not in the arts. Here we find Schwartz impersonating Yeats:

> The ape and great Achilles,
> Heavy with their fate,
> Batter doors down, strike
> Small children at the gate
> Driven by love to this,
> As knock-kneed Hegel said,
> To seek with a sword their peace,
> That the child may be taken away
> From the hurly-burly and fed . . .

"Knock-kneed Hegel" indeed! And here is Schwartz impersonating Auden:

> Pardon, O Father, unknowable Dear, this word,
> Only the cartoon is lucid,/only the curse is heard.

Schwartz's record as a poet, as the novel says, is not impressive. His long poem, "Coriolanus," is a crashing bore in blank verse.

When I expressed these opinions in a conversation with Alfred Kazin, he disagreed and advised me to have another look at Schwartz's lyric poems. Schwartz had a way of seeing things newly and a rare sense of form. The poems he wrote about art show a passionate enthusiasm. Kazin once quoted in Schwartz's presence the ending of Rilke's poem on a statue of Apollo: "You must transform your life." The effect on Schwartz was electrifying. In his passion for art Schwartz was naive, in the good sense of the term. It was the lover of poetry that people loved. Kazin wrote in an article after Schwartz's death that he had "a feeling for literary honor, for the highest standards, that one can only call noble."

Schwartz saw himself as one of the "drunken and fallen princes,"

> . . . the singers and sinners, fallen because they are, in the end, Drunken with pride, blinded by joy.

On paper, however, he was not as drunk as he wished to be. The prose of his stories is rather monotonous. He is a poet of brief lyric passages—anything longer tends to be just literary.

Many reasons are given when an artist destroys himself, but there is one we tend not to take into account: a failure of talent. We don't take art so seriously; we don't think that a man will go to pieces just because he can't write a story or finish a poem.

The psychiatrist points out that failure of talent is a symptom, not a cause. There is some psychological defect at the root of it. But the argument runs just as well in the opposite direction: artists become depressed when they have reached the limits of their powers. Some artists consume themselves in the process of creation—they have done their best, and there is nothing left to do. Then,

> . . . as it sometimes chanceth, from the might
> Of joy in minds that can no further go,
> As high as we have mounted in delight
> In our dejection do we sink as low.

I recall an evening in Berkeley when the poet addressed all his intelligence to the problem of ordering the next martini ("I concentrated my attention with careful sublety to this end"—T. S. Eliot). He had already had two martinis. The first didn't count. To order a second was O.K. But a third would be serious—he was giving a poetry reading that evening and his host might think he was going to have a drunk poet on his hands. So, when Delmore finished the second martini, he discovered that it had been all ice, not a real martini at all. He therefore ordered another, which by this method of counting was still number two. So it continued. The reading he gave that evening wasn't uninhibited, however—to the contrary, it was academic.

There was a small audience of people from the thirties who remembered his name. Delmore Schwartz stood for literary brillance and the *Partisan Review*. Though they didn't know it, they were about to become irrelevant, wiped out by Vietnam and the radical left. They would soon, with their memories of Spain, be as dated as Queen Victoria.

Bellow's poet is crazy, while Delmore Schwartz was so only at times and increasingly toward the end of his life. This brings us to the point of the novel, the message insofar as it can be separated out. Bellow sees the artist as a scapegoat. The ordinary sensual man looks at the life of the artist and says to himself, "If I were not such a corrupt, unfeeling bastard, creep, thief, and vulture, I couldn't get through this either. Look at these good and tender and soft men, the *best* of us. They succumbed, poor loonies."

The message is not new. Others have pointed out that the self-destructive life of a Dylan Thomas or Plath or Berryman serves to reassure the middle class of its values. Art strikes the middle class as an aberration, a kind of insanity. And some poets have hastened to conform, accepting the role assigned, and have drunk themselves into a stupor, slain themselves, played out a middle-class idea of the life of art.

"And poets like drunkards and misfits or psychopaths, like the wretched, poor or rich, sank into weakness—was that it? Having no machines, no transforming knowledge comparable to the knowledge of Boeing or Sperry Rand or IBM or RCA?"

Charlie Citrine, who says this, seems to be speaking for Bellow. In his view poets have to compete with Boeing and Sperry Rand, and if they don't survive it is because they are weak. So Bellow's view of poetry and the arts isn't fundamentally different from that held by the cynical people he has been explaining.

Bellow faults Humboldt for not finding "the next thing, the new thing, the necessary thing for poets to do." Humboldt's behavior—buying a pistol and going after the critic he thinks has seduced his wife—is hopelessly old-fashioned. At this point, Bellow confuses art with life—he takes Humboldt's behavior to mean that art too is out of date. It appears that poets will have to develop a new kind of intelligence. "There's the most extraordinary, unheard-of poetry buried in America, but none of the conventional means known to culture can ever begin to extract it." So poets will have to give up writing poems. Bellow is saying to the artist, "You poor sap, you'll never make it." He advises him to give up his art and find "the new thing, the necessary thing" that will enable him to compete with RCA and IBM.

What is "the new thing?" Bellow does not say. Charlie Citrine speculates about new kinds of consciousness and the immortality of the soul, but his thoughts are too vague to be comforting. All that we can be sure of is the destruction of the poet. And there is no difference between life and art—as the poet is doomed, so is poetry. Bellow has undertaken to show that art as we have known it is no longer possible in a world of machines. He seems determined to take it with him, leaving nothing for the rest of us.

But it is not necessary to accept this point of view. From what we know of Delmore Schwartz he did not accept it. In contrast to the cynicism of Charlie Citrine, disguised as philosophy, Schwartz had this to say about the future of poetry: "In the modern world, poetry is alienated; it will remain indestructible as long as the faith and love of each poet in his vocation survives." Schwartz's life, unhappy as it was, seems to stand for something more—a devotion. And there are others who continue to write poetry for the pleasure it gives them.

American Poetry Anthology

There are energetic and imaginative poets in Daniel Halpern's *American Poetry Anthology,* a gathering of American poets under forty. Michael Benedikt, Jim Harrison, Lucille Clifton, and a half dozen other poets are already well known among readers of poetry, and there are others such as Stanley Plumly and Louise Glück who are in the process of becoming so. The anthology also shows certain tendencies that are very much of the present time: freedom of form and disengagement from political or social involvement.

Freedom is a mixed blessing. I am not the first to point out that, in the present overwhelming vote for free form, verse tends to collapse in an inert mass.

> Below me was a railroad track,
> and a shelter surrounded by log palisades
> across from that. Along came an engine and
> a little car: foresters, and for a minute I wished
> I was with them, one of them. Someone
>   appeared . . . .

This review first appeared in the *New York Times Book Review,* January 4, 1976.

This is from a poem by Kenneth Rosen titled "Abstinence." There is no movement of verse; the words just go galumphing along anyhow.

The disengagement is a more recent symptom—only yesterday poets were writing against the war in Vietnam or as members of an oppressed minority. But these poets, like most people nowadays, seem to have retreated into their own private lives. There are poems about dead fathers and live babies and considerable writing about nature. Some of the poets are positively bogged down in their surroundings—it's a wonder they can extricate themselves far enough to use words at all. "No ideas but in things," said William Carlos Williams. The advice was badly needed at the time, to offset vacuous, sentimental writing. But for some poets this has become a prescription for describing one damned thing after another.

> Cousin to codfish, an eelpout's liver
> can't shrink goiters, but crossing moose
> are sometimes whales, and any random otter
> is a shark. Spawn floats the tinkling moon
> downhill to a glacier's melted thumb . . . .

David McElroy, who wrote these lines, will also tell you how to copulate with a fish. And Fred Levinson will tell you what it's like to kill a rat with a stick.

It's not just disengagement—it's disaffection. It's impossible to know what the poet feels about killing the rat or expects us to feel.

> he didn't die easily
> bit the shaft of the spear
> squealed mournfully . . . .

Are we supposed to feel sorry for the animal? For the poet? Or are we supposed to take pleasure in the mere description? I showed this poem to a woman because it struck me as typical of a certain kind of unemotional violence that is taking place these days, and she said it was machismo. She may have been right—I can think of no other reason for poems, novels, or movies in which a man does something filthy or violent and tells you about it in detail.

What separates poets from mere versifiers is a quality of feeling based in experience. This is why the poems of AI, for example, make the poems of most of her contemporaries seem like kid stuff. Here is her poem titled "Everything: Eloy, Arizona, 1956."

> Tin shack, where my baby sleeps on his back
> the way the hound taught him;
> highway, black zebra, with one white stripe;
> nickel in my pocket for chewing gum;
> you think you're all I've got.
> But when the 2-ton rolls to a stop
> and the driver gets out,
> I sit down in the shade and wave each finger,
> saving my whole hand till the last.
>
> He's keys, tires, a fire lit in his belly
> in the diner up the road.
> I'm red toenails, tight blue halter, black slip.
> He's mine tonight. I don't know him.
> He can only hurt me a piece at a time.

I confess to a bias—I think that the ability to say what you mean means that you have something to say. Obscurity is not necessarily a sign of intelligence—stagnant pools are the ones you can't see to the bottom of. It's a pleasure to have clear narrative writing such as James Tate's "The Distant Orgasm" and Gregory Orr's "Gathering the Bones Together." In the poem by Tate the reader seems to grasp the point before the man who is telling the story—a nice effect. Orr's poem has tragic feeling—a welcome contrast to the casual pose adopted by the majority.

Casualness, the throwaway, is the besetting mannerism of the age. Most of the poets don't want to be thought to be taking themselves too seriously. There is a danger, however, that the reader will take them at face value as poets of no importance. There are a handful of writers who break through the fashion of keeping a "low profile"—in every age, whatever the fashion may be, there are writers impelled by an inner necessity. Jim Harrison and Diane Wakoski are obviously poets of individual character; they have a great deal to say about themselves, and they write it out in full. The anthology also produces a fair number of surprises, poems of considerable brilliance that one has never seen before, such as Roger Weingarten's "These Obituaries of Rattlesnakes Being Eaten by the Hogs."

This is a useful collection of younger poets. It should be very useful, for with a few exceptions—Allen Ginsberg, of course, and perhaps Robert Bly—the poets of ten years ago are no longer leading the young. Not that the over-forty poets have ceased to write—far from it! But younger people must find new voices for their own experience. The voices are here in Daniel Halpern's anthology.

James Merrill's *Divine Comedies*

Auden would have liked this book—in fact, he is mentioned in it as one of the spirits who, from the next world, act as "patrons" of the living. A spirit named Ephraim tells the narrator, J. M., and his friend, D. J., that spirits must return to earth repeatedly, as to a school, until they have worked through their ignorance. Then they obtain "peace from representation," graduate to the lowest of "NINE STAGES/Among the curates and the minor mages" and become patrons themselves. Ephraim was once a Greek Jew living in Asia Minor; in another incarnation he was a favorite of the Emperor Tiberius.

> Died
> AD 36 on CAPRI throttled
> By the imperial guard for having LOVED
> THE MONSTERS NEPHEW (sic) CALIGULA

The system seems vaguely familiar, a mixture of Buddhism and Christianity. James Merrill is not too explicit: J. M. and his friend arrive at their ideas of

This review first appeared in the *New York Times Book Review,* March 21,1976.

the afterlife by using a Ouija board; a teacup moves from one letter of the alphabet to another as Ephraim speaks. In this manner the universe is assembled—rather like a crossword puzzle. The method allows for surprises; at one point J. M. goes so far as to think that Ephraim may be the unconscious. There is nothing naive about Merrill's view of his own creation. *Divine Comedies* reads like an extended conversation with the poet; there is hardly any conventional plot or drama; these supernatural carryings-on, however, afford a welcome quality of suspense.

J. M. is a much-traveled, erudite, somewhat ironic storyteller. He moves with no embarrassment among rich people and the owners of expensive automobiles. He has none of the American embarrassment about being well educated. He does not hesitate to use unusual words and dispense esoteric information. He likes to rhyme. Auden would have liked all this very much—he had small patience with simplicity, whether natural or assumed.

The "comedies" range from Asia Minor to Japan, with look-ins at different places in the States. It isn't a panorama; it is more like a kaleidoscope—a brightly colored pattern or scene twitching into another pattern. In the following passage J. M. is informed by his patron, Ephraim, that J. M.'s father, who died recently, has now been reborn in Kew.

> To Istanbul. Blue DJs, red JMs
> Or green or amber ones, we sweat among
> The steam room's colored panes
> I DECK MYSELF IN GLIMPSES AS IN GEMS
>
> YR FATHER JM he goes on (we're back
> At the hotel now) WAS BORN YESTERDAY

To a greengrocer: name, address in Kew
Spelt out.

"Oh good," J. M. exclaims, "then I can look him up/Do something for him?" Whereupon the spirit has something like a fit: "WILL U NEVER LEARN," and adjures him to "LOOK LOOK LOOK LOOK YR FILL/BUT DO DO DO DO NOTHING." The reason for the spirit's excitement is that on a previous occasion J. M. and D. J. did meddle in the process of reincarnation. When two spirits were about to be reincarnated, D. J. advised their patron that there was a vacancy open—a Virginia West, wife of a friend, happened to be in a sufficiently advanced state of pregnancy. As she was 'A skier and Phi Bete," the new life couldn't find a better home. But there was a mix-up—apparently there are inefficiencies in the divine postal service—and the spirit was born to a "VIRGINIA WEST IN STATE ASYLUM." As a result, their patron has been sternly reprimanded and put on probation.

Ingenious? Witty? Merrill's writing is all of that. But the reader who wants to be gripped by strong feelings or a plot will be disappointed. Merrill has staked out his claim very nicely, thank you; I have the impression that he would think the demands made upon poetry by a certain kind of reader—for example, the reader who is looking for strong feelings—irrelevant if not absurd. There are two kinds of poets. The first believe that poetry is a language-skill, that poems are constructed with words, not emotions. Auden was of this opinion and said so more than once. He said that if a young man wanted to write poetry in order to say something important, then there wasn't much likelihood of his being a poet. On the other hand, if he wanted to see what he could do with words, then there was a possibility. James Merrill and one or two other American poets—John Ashbery and W. S. Merwin come to mind—have taken Auden's way. For these writers, poetry is a word-game of a high order. It is a matter of style. It is not circumscribed by nature and, in the long run, it may adopt some form of religion. For Auden toward the end of his life, Pope was a great poet and romantic poets of any kind were anathema.

The other kind of poet believes that poetry is a product of feeling rather than wit. He believes that words are not chosen by the poet's rational mind but, to the contrary, may be forced upon him, and the best writing is done this way. Poets are not quite sane when they compose their verses, said Socrates, they are possessed by a god. There may be a god in the process, but rarely is there a clear form of religion. This kind of writing is romantic and more likely to be a tragicomedy than a divine comedy, especially for the poet himself—a Coleridge or Rimbaud or Sylvia Plath.

For getting through life with sense and charm, even with some sybaritic pleasure, as Merrill's narrator evidently does, the first kind of writing is the kind to choose. It can be worked at intelligently and it leads somewhere. It is likely to wind up with the prizes. Auden was a brilliant writer of verse, unfailingly articulate and witty. I suspect, however, that his way of writing will be of interest to fewer and fewer people as time goes by—especially in the United States where life is not witty and does not aim to be articulate.

James Merrill, too, is a brilliant writer, operating on a level of high style. A society of cultivated readers might give his *Divine Comedies* a high place. At its best, as in the poem titled "Chimes for Yahya," his writing is exotic and picturesque. The tone of easy, intimate conversation is a stylistic achievement. It is hardly the poet's fault that there are few readers of this kind of poetry. For that matter, there are few readers of poetry of any kind—people seem just as oblivious of the poetry that intends to render "feelings" or describe "real life." So Merrill may as well please himself and his friends, and be as capricious as he likes.

The Split Lives of W. H. Auden

Bringing together "all of the poems that W. H. Auden wished to preserve" is reason enough for a new *Collected Poems*. But readers who want all the poems, not just the ones Auden approved of at the end of his life, will have to wait. The editor promises that the excluded early poems will be published in a volume titled *The English Auden*. But poems will still be missing, and some of the approved versions will be different from the original. Auden was continually rewriting his poems and switching things around. He had an idea of his life as a construction into which the poems had to fit. If they didn't, out they went.

In the middle of Auden's life was a mystery, a secret he was trying to hide. It accounted for the splitting of his life in two—the first part in England, the second in America. In 1939 Auden left England and took up residence in the United States. He told Stephen Spender that he had done so because the future for writers lay in America; New York was the model of Cosmopolis, the city of the future. Auden's critics on the other hand were saying that he had

This review first appeared in *Ideas,* October 17, 1976.

fled England in her hour of need, on the eve of World War II, in order to be safe and to flourish in the lucrative pastures of the New World. Both his friends and critics were naive: they found intellectual reasons for everything he did, just as he wanted them to. The truth, however, was that as a homosexual Auden found life in England too confining. He was a public figure—he had even been awarded the George Medal—and when he thought of what would be expected of him in the years ahead, as a member of the literary establishment, it was a dreary prospect indeed. But in the States there would be plenty of room—no one paid much attention to writers. In the Village or on Fire Island he could be "cosy"— one of his favorite words. He could live with those he preferred, emerging only to teach, then again retiring into obscurity. Besides, he felt easier in his mind about being a homosexual in America. England was home, but what you did abroad didn't really count.

It is impossible to understand Auden's poetry, its style, the form it took, and the attitudes it expresses, without taking into account his homosexuality and his wish to conceal it. The wish is understandable; back in the 1940s people were not as tolerant of homosexuality as they are now. In order to conceal his feelings Auden wrote in pseudodramatic, "impersonal" forms. He wrote essays in verse, putting a distance between himself and the reader. He did not *present*—he was always careful to explain.

This was the later Auden. The young poet had been quite different, a poet of feelings—feelings that he himself could not explain. Influenced by Thomas Hardy, Edward Thomas, T. S. Eliot, and Icelandic sagas, the young Auden invented a compact, elliptical language that was strikingly original. He was obscure and prophetic. After leaving Oxford he went to Berlin; there he absorbed the ideas of Groddeck, Homer Lane, and Freud—as well as the homegrown theories of D. H. Lawrence, which he already knew. These men argued that people were sick because they willed to be, that nervous and physical disorders were symptoms of spiritual disease. When Auden returned to England he wrote poems that diagnosed English economic and cultural life from a Groddeckian point of view. He seemed gifted with double sight; the characters in his poems, lonely vicars, repressed spinsters, languishing esthetes, bluff and hearty types, each in his own way testified to the malaise of England as a whole. Auden's poems hinted at secret guilts and criminal wishes. As he saw it, the whole nation, in these years of economic depression, was suffering the effects of psychological repression. Readers felt that they were privy to the secret. *Poems* (1930) sold only a thousand copies in three years, but the copies were in the best hands at Oxford and Cambridge. When Auden's poems appeared in the anthologies *New Signatures* and *New Country* edited by Michael Roberts, they launched a movement. By the middle of the 1930s dozens of poets were trying to write like Auden.

He addressed himself to the public. He had always had a journalistic flair, a photographer's eye. His descriptions of modern landscapes were written with zest, though the view might be sinister:

> Smokeless chimneys, damaged bridges, rotting wharves
> and choked canals.
> Tramlines buckled, smashed trucks lying on their side
> across the rails . . .

He now wrote about history. It was widely assumed that he was a poet of the Left—in the thirties Marxism was fashionable among intellectuals. Auden did not deny it, though in fact he cared little for Marx and felt some contempt for the common man. He even made a brief journey to Spain. What he saw of the Civil War must have frightened him, and he was offended by the repression of the Church. He had been brought up in the Anglican faith; his mother was a stern Anglican; at any rate, the poet who had been urging his countrymen to some sort of revolution, overthrowing the Old Gang, after his return from Spain said no more on the subject of revolution.

In 1938 he traveled with Christopher Isherwood to China. On their way back they crossed the United States and met some congenial souls. This was why, as Auden told Cyril Connolly, he decided to live in the States. The decision had little to do with history and everything to do with his personal tastes.

It was a mistake as far as poetry was concerned. He had been at ease with England, he knew country and town like the back of his hand. His poems with their views of an industrial landscape anticipated the subject matter that would be explored by novelists after the war, the Angry Young Men. Auden knew the secrets of the English vicarage and public school. But in the States he hardly knew anything. Unlike the American expatriates in Europe—Eliot or Hemingway—Auden had a reputation when he made his crossing. He was immediately accepted into the American literary establishment, and in a little while he was advising editors and sitting on prize committees. He never had to scrounge for a living, he never had to learn about America in his bones, and so he knew nothing of the way Americans thought and felt.

Auden's long poem, *The Age of Anxiety,* presents as American speech passages such as the following:

> After a dreadful
> Row with father, I ran with burning
> Cheeks to the pasture and chopped wood, my
> Stomach like a stone. I strode that night
> Through wicked dreams: waking, I skipped to
> The shower and sang, ashamed to recall
> With whom or how . . .

This is camp. And writing camp was Auden's solution for not being able to write American. As time passed the mannerisms became more precious until, so Jonson said of Spenser, he wrote no language at all. The distancing from American scene and character made the language of the poems distant from any kind of reality. Auden's later poems were full of ideas, but none of them had any urgency. They were not rooted in life.

In his later poems Auden played games with words, shifting from one level of usage to another. One critic, Justin Replogle, argues that Auden is a comic poet; all his inconsistencies are consistent with this. The comedy is created by "jamming together words that are ordinarily used only in very special environments, with widely varying degrees of solemnity," and by using dozens of highly technical terms and phrases. He quotes from Auden's poem, "Mundus et Infans":

> Kicking his mother until she let go of his soul
> Has given him a healthy appetite; clearly, her role
> In the New Order must be
> To supply and deliver his raw materials free . . .

Replogle comments: "The basic incongruity here is between the infant subject and the adult language used to describe him." And he proceeds to show "smaller incongruities" that "flourish endlessly in the diction." Most of Auden's later poems shift about and giggle in this manner. It isn't comic, except to readers whose idea of life is tea at the Faculty Club.

In later years Auden was opposed to experiment. The voice in the later poems is that of a querulous, aging man who is attached to his creature comforts and who fears that any rebellion of youth may take them away.

The message did not appeal to young people. They preferred Dylan Thomas, the roaring Welshman who seemed to be living passionately. From the day that Dylan Thomas came to America, Auden was a back number.

Auden hated biographical criticism—he would have hated this essay. Writing about a writer's life, he used to say, casts no light on the work. But in Auden's case it is not possible to see why he wrote as he did, in strict forms and in a language so far removed from the language of common speech, if we do not see the personal reason that lay behind it. Auden came to the United States in order to be a member of the sexual underground. It was a matter of personal freedom. And in order to preserve this freedom, he made his art less free. His poems were masques, eclogues, essays . . . anything but expressions of the poet's character. His habitual concealment of his deepest life led him to write in a trivial manner until—at an age when Hardy and Yeats wrote their greatest poems—he was writing light verse.

Lowell's Indissoluble Bride

Robert Lowell once wrote a poem that began, "Writing,/my indissoluble bride for forty years. . . ." Whenever he has written about writing he has written his best. He can describe the night sweats, the many ideas that come to one, and the uselessness of them all as far as writing a poem is concerned. And the stupidities one commits in between poems.

He has written with sympathy about other writers, both living and dead: Ford Madox Ford, Robert Frost, Propertius. But the writer Lowell has known best is himself, and this is his constant theme. It is not to be taken as "confession." Those who think that he has been writing about himself in order to purge his soul have mistaken the shadow for the substance. He has not been writing about his personal life, but about his life as a poet. He has written about his life in order to write poems.

Not that Lowell himself has been aware of this. For a while he was trying to speak to and for America. He published many sonnets under the title *Notebook* (1969) and then rearranged them under the title *His-*

This review first appeared in *Saturday Review* 5, no. 1 (October 1, 1977).

tory (1973), whereupon his friends and critics—it has been Lowell's misfortune that the two are usually the same—mistook the book to be what it said it was and discussed it as an epic work on history. These were New Critics—that is to say, no critics at all—trained to assume what the writer assumes and then to explain how the parts fit together. They don't ask radical questions: for example, whether there was a connecting idea between the sonnets on Sir Thomas More and moon landings and the "Pacification of Columbia."

The sonnets in between that came from Lowell's life were not windows on the world. If one were to turn the life of a president into verse it could possibly be an epic (in Pound's definition, a "poem containing history"), but Lowell's life has been much too sheltered. He has kept the best company, he has made his political protests under the best possible conditions. Besides, he can have very little understanding of the kind of people who make up the mass—the poor and unlucky and obscure.

In his new book, *Day by Day*, Robert Lowell has given up his pretensions as an epic poet and he has stopped writing unrhymed sonnets. We are back with the fascinating, superbly gifted poet of *Life Studies* (1959) and *For the Union Dead* (1964) who is capable of riveting down the "flux of experience" with details, scenery, gestures, and words. He has returned to the life of the poet, and as no one knows more about this than Lowell, the book rings absolutely true. The subject may seem limited, but the poet's urgent need has taken him to many places, no good as history, but perfectly adequate as settings for his angst. He has turned back once more to confront his parents. He has gone back to "St. Mark's,

1933," to Louisiana State University, to England, and, in a sequence written with a humor that must be all his own, he has revisited a mental hospital. It is all consistent, for the poems are about a sensibility, and this is rendered by the writer's voice with no apparent holding back. The book reads like a talk with a friend—especially if you both happen to be writers.

The other good thing about *Day by Day* is the recovery of form. Lowell said years ago that he was divided between his love of a narrative, as in Tolstoi ("his work is imagistic, it deals with all experience, and there seems to be no conflict of the form and content"), and "another side of poetry: compression, something highly rhythmical and perhaps wrenched into a small space." The first love gave us *Life Studies;* the second gave us *Near the Ocean* (1967), hailed by the reviewers who had been offended by *Life Studies* and who couldn't wait for Lowell to be his old, compressed, Lord Weary self again.

Then came *Notebook*, which fell between two stools, being neither imagistic and free in form nor compressed. Some of these unrhymed sonnets were good. I remember one that was written to a woman. It ended with the happy remark that since they were now both fifty, they were free "to be old, do nothing, type and think." But in general the lines were loose, and there was no sense that the poems were shaped by the excitement of writing. His new book shows that the fit of trying to out-Wordsworth Wordsworth is over: the lines have the rhythm of living speech.

Ever since *Life Studies*, Lowell has turned away from writing imaginary narrative. His last attempt to do so, *The Mills of the Kavanaughs* (1951), was a failure. Moreover, the age demanded confessions. In *Life*

Studies he gave the age something better than it asked for—not confessions, but the life of a poet. That age is past, however, and even Lowell's version of sincerity will no longer serve. He seems to be of the same mind, for at the end of *Day by Day* he says: "Those blessed structures, plot and rhyme—/why are they no help to me now/I want to make/something imagined, not recalled?" This is troublesome, however; I am afraid he is on the verge of a mistake. He seems to think that imaginative writing in verse calls for plot and rhyme.

Plot, in the old sense, and rhyme were exactly what was wrong with *The Mills of the Kavanaughs*. Lowell doesn't need plot and rhyme; he needs Chekhov. He ought to try getting inside the skin of a few people who aren't like himself. And he should continue to use the living speech and forms of his new book. If he can do this he may write narrative poems that will astonish us all.

Not Made for the World of Moloch

At the age of twenty-six Allen Ginsberg already could look back on a life of intellectual excitement. It had almost been catastrophic. At fourteen he had wanted to be a leader of the political left and President of the United States. At nineteen, as he describes it, he was a practicing homosexual, an anarchist, and a hipster, and he wanted to be a great poet. Then he became a mystic whose ambition was to become a saint. And at twenty-three he was "a criminal, a despairing sinner, a dope fiend." His aim was "to get to reality."

When he says that he was a criminal, Ginsberg is referring to his arrest as an accomplice of his friend Herberg Huncke, who stole things in order to support his drug habit. But Ginsberg was innocent—he had merely let Huncke and his partners in crime stash their loot in his apartment. He himself was thinking of poetry and not paying attention to the entrances of Huncke and his friends, bearing radios, phonographs, and chests of silver.

Ginsberg may also be referring to an earlier epi-

This review first appeared in the *New York Times Book Review,* October 23, 1977.

sode, when his friend Lucien Carr killed a man named David Kammerer with a knife. Carr pushed the body into the Hudson River and Kerouac helped him hide the knife. Kerouac and Ginsberg were already social rebels, and the Carr incident pushed them over the line. From now on they would sympathize with the outcast and criminal. This was the side of virtue. On the other side were the hypocrites, so-called respectable people who sent people to jail while they themselves prepared to make war.

As a result of the episode with Huncke, Ginsberg was sent to a mental hospital. When he came out he resolved to make order out of his life; he had been living too much in fantasy. In 1952, when these *Journals* begin, he is making an earnest attempt to fit in. He describes himself as "shy" and says that he is going out with girls; he is freelancing as a literary agent and is a registered Democrat. "I want to find a job," he writes, "who cares?"

By this time his wish to be a great poet has produced enough verse to fill two books. One is of rhymed poems written in imitation of traditional English poets he has studied at Columbia, the other consists of unrhymed poems in imitation of William Carlos Williams. He has recently come to know Williams; listening to Williams read his poems aloud has wrought a great change in Ginsberg's notions of prosody. Williams writes just as he talks—this is the stupendous secret.* Poetry isn't a foreign language: This realization started Ginsberg on the painstaking road to "Howl" and "Kaddish."

Journals: Early Fifties Early Sixties is a record of his

---

*Ginsberg is in error, however. Williams never wrote just as he talked [Author].

actual travels and his mental journeys. In the next few years he discovered that there were people, millions of them, who lived in ways completely different from the money- and war-oriented life of people in North America, whose culture he would describe in "Howl" as devoted to Moloch. Ginsberg could never really have made it in the world of Moloch: he was perfectly capable of writing advertising copy and paying his analyst, but the voice of William Blake kept breaking in. On the other hand, he didn't want to be crazy. This was a dilemma. His travels, however, showed him that Moloch and insanity were not the only alternatives. If Mexican Indians and men who knocked about in seaports could make a life for themselves, so could Allen Ginsberg. The solution he found was one that has been discovered by others: the life of art. There was a competing attraction: religion. Ginsberg has never quite decided whether he wants to be an artist or a saint.

At the end of 1953 he set off for Mexico and lived for six months there. The *Journals* skim over the years 1955–56, when he lived in Berkeley and made his big push as a poet. His reading of "Howl" at the Six Gallery in San Francisco in 1955 was the event from which some literary critics date a renascence of poetry in the United States.

He went back to New York for two years. He traveled in the Mediterranean, and at the end of the *Journals* we see him setting off for India to complete his education and become the guru we have all seen—the Ginsberg who puts the palms of his hands together and says "Om."

It has been a spectacular career, and some of the thinking that went into making it is recorded in these *Journals*—but not enough. With all the traveling he did in these years, and the thinking he must have done to change the "shy" imitator of Williams into the astonishing poet of "Howl" and "Kaddish," Ginsberg's *Journals* do not yield episodes that reveal his development as a poet. There are trivial details and, at the other extreme, some mystic musings, but Ginsberg's strength as a writer is in neither of these: it lies in his ability to deal with the whole visible world, drawing sounds and images from it, so that we see things in a new way. Here and there in the *Journals* we come across a passage that has this quality, as in the description of roosters crowing in a village: "challenging in various cockly hoarse tones as if they existed in a world of pure intuitive sound communicating to anonymous hidden familiar chickensouls from hill to hill." But there is too little of this. Instead we have his dreams, acres of them—perhaps because he had been treated by psychiatrists and was undergoing psychoanalysis. But dreams do not make good reading—no wonder psychiatrists are paid large fees for listening to them! The reader of the *Journals* will have to wade through this kind of stuff:

> "He-she walks in—a feminine boyish face, real curious, round eyes & 1939's Brecht hair—I'm impressed—I remember him as the one I noticed in childhood—There he is in clown costume from the Freak show of the Circus, coming in under the awning of the breakfast tent for morning communication with the gang & audience—a round face like young Naomi, I gaze at him knowing my own amazement he's reincarnated in a movie-dream. Is he made up? I can't tell if it's a girl or boy or girlboy monster. He looks sweet—"

As a record of Ginsberg's formative years during which he produced many good poems, the *Journals* have some factual value and must be of interest to serious readers of poetry. Ginsberg has been one of the most influential poets in America in our time.

Robert Bly once said that people disliked Ginsberg's poetry because it expressed feeling. This strikes me as wrong: it wasn't the feeling they disliked but the attitudes. Ginsberg had his own brand of morality, which consisted of views directly opposed to those held by the middle class, by businessmen, and politicians. And he was given to promoting his views—for example, he often spoke about the beneficial results that could follow from the use of hallucinogens. I wish that his wide reading had included the part in the New Testament that speaks of misleading children, and how it is better to have a millstone tied around one's neck and be cast into the sea.

Yet, though Ginsberg may take himself to be a prophet, in other moods he is warm and sympathetic, at times even humorous. His "America" is one of the few truly humorous poems in the language. And there are some entertaining "political ravings" in these *Journals,* including insults to some people at Columbia who did not pay sufficient attention to his poems when they first came out. As I was one of those people, I am happy to have this opportunity to say that I was wrong—not merely wrong, obtuse. I still don't care for "Howl"—Lucien Carr and Neal Cassady were not my idea of "the best minds in America"—but other poems in the volume are superb, and "Kaddish" is a masterpiece. Anything the author of these poems wrote deserves to be read, including his *Journals.*

III

Life and Work

What's in It for Me

I write poems but teach for a living. Some writers and teachers are only half-writers and half-teachers, but I think a man can be both a full-time writer and full-time teacher. It all depends on what you want to write. If you wish to make writing pay, then of course you must give all your time to it, like any business. But if you write only when you have something to say, then you will have a lot of time left over. During that time I teach. I certainly would not recommend teaching to everyone. In the first place you must enjoy it.

W. H. Auden once said that poets should not marry. But not every poet is able to resist the temptation. Certainly there are drawbacks to being a married writer, as there are to being a married anything. There's the house, the car, the kids shouting, "Gimme!" But the unmarried writer is in no better pickle. For one thing, he will always be fretting that he is not sufficiently loved. The unmarried writer travels more, but he knows less about the ordinary lives of men and women. However, when you get

This essay first appeared in *Harper's* 231, no. 1385 (October 1965).

down to cases, being married or unmarried does not determine the quality of a man's work. Keats and Flaubert were not married, but Blake and Tolstoi were. What matters is the writer's intelligence.

If writers may be put in two categories, those who live in artistic circles and those who have ordinary lives, I belong in the second category. This does not mean that I agree with middle-class ideas; it is simply that I find it less distracting to live as others do than to spend my energy trying not to.

Also, in my experience, people who build their lives around art become ill-informed, arrogant, and stupid. On the other hand, if you move among ordinary people—and not as a stranger, but subject to the things they feel—you can learn much. Indeed, unless you do this your thoughts will have no importance. But you must also be able to detach yourself. It is necessary to have a little of the cunning that Joyce recommended, if you wish to "forge the uncreated consciousness of the race."

There is material in everyday life for a poetry that will be neither esoteric nor banal. Except in Whitman and Hart Crane we have had very little of this poetry in America. We do not find in writing images that correspond to the lives we really have. Most poetry is mere fantasy; most prose is merely reporting the surface of things. We are still waiting for the poetry of feeling, words as common as a loaf of bread, which yet give off vibrations.

Advice to the English

When people worry about the state of poetry in Britain, especially in comparison with the States, I think that what they are worried about is not poetry as much as it is literary movement and excitement. Good poets are nice to have, but movements are more fun, and these days the Americans seem to be having all the excitement.

Isn't this what is felt to be lacking—a British group to put up against the Black Mountain poets the next time they come over? Or against the San Francisco or the New York poets? There is the Mersey Sound:

> Love is the presents in Christmas shops
> Love is when you're feeling Top of the Pops
> Love is what happens when the music stops
> Love is

But this seems like kid stuff in comparison with the Ur-texts of Charles Olson:

> Off-shore, by islands hidden in the blood
> jewels & miracles, I, Maximus
> a metal hot from boiling water, tell you

This article first appeared as "Opinion," in *Review*, no. 25 (Spring 1971).

Though wanting a movement has its funny side, it is not as ridiculous as it seems, for a movement means some discussion of technique. Without an involvement in <u>technique</u>, the practice of any art must degenerate into a desperate exertion of mere personality. Now, Graves and MacDiarmid were wise in their generation, but what about the present? What is a young poet to do? What ideas are there to sustain him?

This concern will strike some people as unnecessary. Who cares what ideas poets have? Poets shouldn't think, they should just turn out the stuff, and in Britain they've always managed to. Blathering about *le mot juste* is all very well for Frenchmen, and Americans of course are obsessed with technology, but an Englishman should be able to write poetry without kicking up a fuss.

Am I exaggerating the point of view? I have just been reading a bit of advice given by an English poet to other English poets. He says that they should "worry about *what* they are saying first, only *how* they are saying it as an afterthought." I have also been looking through forty-six books of verse published this past year in Britain, and the above attitude explains much of the writing—it was an afterthought. The main difference between contemporary American and English verse is that, as a rule, Americans are much concerned with technique, the English are not. The English poet tends to tread the old worn paths. These, for example, are new lines by an English poet:

Let the Secular City thrive, the dream-projections
Thrown on the All Night Cinema's circular screen . . .

But this manner was exhausted thirty years ago. Nor will making it topical make it any livelier:

basin of the Mekong Delta watched over by the wings of
helicopters. Out-generalled
by the Granddaughters of The Revolution, they die for
the inalienable right
to six feet of Republican ground. At Forest Lawns

Remarks, as Gertrude Stein said, are not literature.

Essay writing, I have come to think, is the English vice. English writers too often fall into a jog trot of remarks. This vice began in the public schools, where they learned to write in a chatty way about everything. But poetry isn't a conversation, it's a "made thing." It's an experience in itself, as the Englishman (Ford) told the American Pound some sixty years ago.

I suppose that by this time several readers will have misunderstood what I mean by technique—they will think that I mean a mechanical process. But I mean the exact opposite—writing with the living breath. The life within the poet is his subject and his individual breathing determines the line and shape of the poem—not a concern with love, or God, or asparagus. If these matters come first, why doesn't he write prose?

I don't like all that W. C. Williams wrote, not by a long shot. But he did point toward a way of writing that has unlimited possibilities—finding the language and form for the particular experience. In Britain, D. H. Lawrence said much the same thing, but no one paid him much attention at the time.

From Williams a poet, especially an English poet, could learn how to write of his perceptions rather than his opinions. There are still many things to be described, as Williams said, in their "natural colors and shapes." And there is no end yet in sight to the possibilities of Pound's ideogrammic method, "the examination and juxtaposition of particular specimens."

Also from Pound and Williams the poet could learn how to write living speech. As I've said, the English writer too often falls into the style of an essay. Too often he loses the sense of poetry as drama, with downs as well as ups. But a poem may include bad grammar and clichés—if the dramatic situation needs them. University-educated poets for the most part don't write as people actually think and speak, for fear of writing incorrectly.

And, of course, the poet could learn how to write in free forms. I shall not argue here on behalf of free verse, for surely the quarrel has been fought out long ago. The antifree verse people—there are still some around—think that to write free verse is to attack the traditional forms they prefer. But no one would object to a poet's writing in the old meters and rhymes, if he wrote with energy. Tony Harrison does, for example:

> I'll bet you're bloody jealous, you codgers in U.K.,
> Waiting for your hearses while I'm having it away
> With girls like black Bathshebas who sell their milky
>   curds
> At kerbside markets out of done-up fancy gourds . . .

I don't at all mind remembering that the last time I heard this sort of thing was "Mandalay": "I've a neater, sweeter maiden in a cleaner, greener land!" These ideas, derived from Pound and Williams, have been the basis of the "modern" in American poetry, and I think that English poets, too, could improve by using them. Oh yes, and Eliot—out of fashion these days with the Poundians, for they seem to be afraid that if Eliot is a great poet, then Pound cannot be. At this point, however, it is necessary to say that some Americans don't hold with Pound or Williams or Eliot. Take Robert Bly, for example, who said recently ("Poètes Americains d'Aujourd-hui," *Les Lettres Nouvelles* 41 [December–January 1971])—speaking of Robert Creeley and myself:

> Their poetry tends to be restricted to certain limited areas of the psyche. The reason for this is that this fourth generation, instead of going to the sources of "free verse" in Europe, is founded on models such as Eliot, Pound and Williams. You won't find "convulsive association" in the work of Eliot, Pound or Williams.

Then, having produced "convulsive association" out of his hat (where on earth did he find it? He never ceases to surprise me), Bly goes on to compare Eliot, Pound, and Williams, to their disadvantage, with those poets (European writers of "free verse" such as Blake and Trakl) who operate "by secret paths of the imagination." In his *Cantos* Pound only puts one text next to another, and one anecdote next to another, and goes from one to the next. This is the typewriter trying to do the work of the imagination.

> In American poetry we have not yet reconquered the rapid movement through the psyche, from the conscious to the unconscious, from a table made of fir to repressed, wild desires, such as the ancient poets were possessed by, as Lorca and others have rediscovered for Spanish

poetry. And why? Every time we start going we get lost in technique.

I have quoted this criticism at length, and shall try to reply to it, in order to show English readers what some American poets, of whom they may not have heard, are talking about. I hesitate to call this talk "criticism." When you discuss the connections of the "psyche" and poetry, you find that conventional literary terms won't serve at all. How can you describe and evaluate the subtle, instant, some would say invisible, movements "from the conscious to the unconscious?"

Against the charge made by Bly that I don't go beyond a limited consciousness (I won't undertake to defend Creeley—he can take care of himself) I shall begin by remembering Jung's observation on some attempts to bring over, suddenly to transplant, the ways of another culture into your own. Jung said that for a Westerner to adopt Oriental modes of thought, for example, resulted in emptiness. If this is true of psychoanalysis or philosophy, how much truer must it be of art, for if the artist is not familiar with the *texture* of his materials, he cannot be at all convincing. In writing a poem you must write with your thinking processes, in your own time, in your own place. You may have learned something about concentration, perhaps, from reading haiku, and something else from Lorca—but you must come back to writing out the poem in the terms of your own culture, not theirs. I would say of some of the poets who think as Bly does that too often they sound merely pseudo-Oriental or pseudo-European. They sound like dilettantes. A poetic image of the refrigerator they use every day would be more convincing—and ultimately also closer to the Japanese and the Spanish—than attempts to be deep by putting "Oh" at the start of the poem and an exclamation mark at the end of it, and saying that suddenly there is within them a sea afloat with butterflies. The word "policeman" simply doesn't have the same connotations in America that it has in Spain, and a horse in Japan does not look or behave like a horse in Newark, New Jersey, supposing that you could find one. You can't transplant things so easily from one country to another—you have to go through the Customs.

Bly might say that he wasn't speaking of images—he was speaking of a "movement" from the unconscious to the conscious. But I have dwelt on the question of images because, it strikes me, any discussion of the transformation of the unconscious into the conscious must be a discussion of images—the kind of images you use, and how you use them. I don't know how consciousness is to be extended other than by means of an image (remember that sound, too, is an image). Pound's definition of imagism—an image, Pound said, is that which transforms something outward and objective into an inward, subjective feeling—isn't it this, after all, that Bly is talking about?

Still replying to Bly, I would like to underline the point I have made above in parentheses—that *sound is an image*.

About this, it strikes me, Bly is unaware. He pays little attention to the rhythm of verse. Frequently he doesn't seem to hear the sound of poetry. This doesn't harm his own writing—he seems to hear his own poems all right—but it goes far to invalidate his criticisms—enabling him to praise some poets who have no essential poetic ability—i.e., rhythm—

and to ignore others who have a great deal. This is a serious fault in a critic who insists on "secret pathways" by which the poem must move. Of all the ways in a poem, rhythm and sound come first. Visual images put together without a rhythmic flow are not poetry—they are prose. Rhythmic flow is what makes the parts of a poem cohere, and only through rhythm and its utterance do we indeed feel the psychic energy of the poet.

Some pages back I took issue with an English poet for his advice to other English poets. But with another piece of his advice I find myself in agreement. In speaking of the current criticism of English poets as lacking in energy, etc., in comparison with their transatlantic colleagues, he says "Beware of self-conscious transatlantic borrowing." I can hardly quarrel with his attitude, as I have just been expressing a similar attitude in regard to American borrowings from abroad. I agree that, yes, you have to forget about mere comparisons of English and American poetry. But it is necessary for poets to pay some attention to ideas about poetry, and stimulating ideas have been coming from America for some time.

I do not belong to a school of American writing, but I do have certain ideas about poetry that, I believe, other American poets would sympathize with. Speaking for myself, yet with the hope that what I have to say will be to some extent representative, I shall try to explain these ideas.

The symbol of the symbolists was an object taken from nature that evoked mysterious associations. Then came the image of the imagists (1910). This, also based on nature, was a symbol without associations. The next step was the invention of the surrealist image. This differed from both the symbol of the symbolists and the image of the imagists in that the surrealist image did not represent nature—it was a dream. To quote, yet once more, Ezra Pound's little poem about faces seen on a train: "Petals on a wet, black bough"—the connection between faces and petals is perfectly understandable according to the laws by which similes are made. Both faces and blossoms are yellow, white, or pink. They are both soft. They are both organic. Therefore, according to the habit of metaphor by which the human mind brings together things that have an element in common, faces and blossoms merge to create an image. But there is no connection we can find in nature to justify bringing together the following objects: "Funnels smoking with hyacinths and propelled by blue serpents." The image is purely invented. André Breton, who wrote this line, says in another place, "I am the plaything of no sensory power." Sense perception and a natural relationship between one thing and another are no longer the basis of the image. The surrealists were living in a dream:

> A farm was prospering in the heart of Paris
> And its windows looked out on the Milky Way

The surrealist movement was very much the property of André Breton. A French writer, Sarane Alexandrian, has said, "To be a surrealist, one had first to be granted the title by Breton; no one ever raised a murmur of protest against this obligation, so self-evident did it seem." A view of literature such as this could exist only in France, where, more strongly than the image of liberty, there is impressed on the mind of the artist the image of the concierge, the person who lets you into the building. In the history of French surrealism one has very much the impression of a political enterprise limited by the tastes of André Breton. The same writer, Alexandrian, says that surrealism was not merely fantastic art of any kind; true surrealist art had to come out of "inner need," but it is clear that the need could not be "inner" as long as the artist had to apply for approval to André Breton.

Breton's concept of surrealism was automatic writing, in the course of which he invented images and destroyed the conventional structures of the sentence. It never seems to have occurred to him, however, in his attack on syntax and punctuation, that it might be necessary to change words themselves. As Eugène Jolas pointed out, in order to hold to a program of purely irrational poetry one would have to invent new words. If the surrealists were sincere, their poetry would make no sense at all. But the surrealists still wished to be considered as artists, and their poems were to some extent intelligible. Therefore, they were as much a product of the rational mind as anything else. Indeed, they seem more rational, for as long as surrealism makes a program of being spontaneous, it must seem less spontaneous than other kinds of art. Systematic surrealism does not permit moments of true unselfconsciousness to occur. The effect of systematic surrealism is the opposite of what André Breton said it would be. Instead of emphasizing the irrational, it seems to emphasize the calculating mind. Systematic surrealism makes us think of store window decorating—calculated shocks.

This is the kind of thing I mean, by an American poet writing today:

218

You are one for colonial lizards
and over bathhouses of your ear
skulls shall whisper
of a love for a crab's rude whip
and the rimless island of refusal shall seat itself
beside the corpse of a dog
that always beats a hurricane
in the mad run for Apollo's boxing glove.

Surrealism such as this rapidly grows monotonous. The construction is predictable: "bathhouses of your ear," "island of refusal." This is only a series of forced juxtapositions. Two things forced together by conscious effort do not make an image. In the writing of the better surrealists, however, there are images that move us because they strike a chord in the unconscious. The true surrealist image rises out of the unconscious. The elements of the image, however disparate they may be, have been brought together and fused in the depths, so that when the image comes to the surface we cannot perceive the separate elements or the manner of their joining. But in the pseudosurrealism I have just quoted the unconscious is aware of itself—that is, it is not the unconscious at all.

French surrealism failed for the reason that many fashionable movements fail. It substitutes a part for the whole. Literary movements begin with a discovery; then the discovery is claimed to be the one possible technique; then the movement becomes academic. But underneath a literary movement there may still be a movement of literature that remains valuable: in the case of surrealism it was the invention of images. As one surrealist said, new images are new realities. This is what has remained in the poetry of the present, in the poems of writers who do not claim to be surrealists but whose work draws on images that represent the unconscious rather than what they have observed in nature. These have been called "deep images." The writings of Sylvia Plath contain such images. Here are five stanzas of her poem, "Berck-Plage":

> This black boot has no mercy for anybody.
> Why should it, it is the hearse of a dead foot,
>
> The high, dead, toeless foot of this priest
> Who plumbs the well of his book,
>
> The bent print bulging before him like scenery.
> Obscene bikinis hide in the dunes,
>
> Breasts and hips a confectioner's sugar
> Of little crystals, titillating the light,
>
> While a green pool opens its eye,
> Sick with what it has swallowed—

Here are other "deep images" in contemporary American poetry:

> The lamplight falls on all fours in the grass.
> [Robert Bly]

> Suddenly I realized
> That if I stepped out of my body I would break
> Into blossom.
>
> [James Wright]

And one of my own:

> And the angel in the gate, the flowering plum,
> Dances like Italy, imagining red.

Breton and the automatic surrealists went wrong in their insistence on writing purely irrational poems. What is this but rationalism run mad—stiff and repetitious as the gestures of a man in an insane asylum? There is nothing spontaneous about the gestures of the insane—to the contrary, they are limited to repeating some little technical trick that they have mastered. Total poetry, like the total human being, must include so-called rational as well as irrational states—the poem must be logical as well as unpredictable. Images that move us do so because they are connected to logical thought processes which we all share. They are connected to the psyche of the author and an understandable feeling, or idea if you prefer, underlying the poem. Poetry in which there are no dream states is trivial, but dream images may be trivial, also, when they are produced by automatic writing, without a necessary direction by the psyche of the poet. The answer, therefore, seems to be that the poet dreams and produces the images of his dream, but that only by meditation and selection can he discover poetic images—those which move other people. Poetic images are not picked up in the street or from a common stock of clichés such as can be obtained from a textbook of psychoanalysis. The poet must discover the logic of the dream.

"Deep image" writing has not been much practiced in America or in England. The tendency of writers in English is to be merely reasonable. The later writing of W. H. Auden is an example of this. In recent years Auden has taken to praising Alexander Pope, and he has said that the object of poetry is to remove all traces of magic. From attitudes such as these we might expect, and we do get, light verse.

> . . . When they look in their bedroom mirrors,
> Fifty-plus may be bored, but Seventeen is faced by
>   a frowning failure, with no money, no mistress,
> no manner of his own, who never got to Italy
>   nor met a great one: to say a few words at banquets
> to attend a cocktail party in honour of Nor M
>   can be severe, but Junior has daily to cope
> with ghastly family meals, with dear Papa and Mamma
>   being odd in the wrong way.

The poetry of Auden has become as shallow as the verse of John Betjeman and Ogden Nash, whom he admires.

English and American poets come from a civilization so powerfully dedicated to triumphs of the conscious will that it requires an extraordinary effort to dream. I do not think that this can be entirely changed, and any attempt to transplant modes of thinking from one culture to another is bound to seem awkward and unconvincing. We could not turn overnight into Tibetan monks or Navajo Indians or Spanish surrealist poets, even if we wished to. But we can bear in mind our tendency to make remarks instead of creating poems, and be on guard against a drying up of the imagination.

Capturing the World As It Is

An Interview with Wayne Dodd and Stanley Plumly

Athens, Ohio
February 9, 1973

I gathered from a remark you made last night, that you are now engaged, sort of officially for yourself, in writing a new book of poems.

That's right.

And so I was wondering to what extent now you write poems for a book?

Well, when I say I'm writing a new book of poems, what it really means is this: I am getting a new vantage point from which to write. That is, I have to figure out again who I am and what kind of a stance to take toward the new material. You can always write random poems and even publish them in magazines, but you don't start to do anything that excites you until you have a new sense of yourself. Now what happens with me—I think—is that every

---

This interview first appeared in *Ohio Review* 14, no. 3 (Spring 1973).

book of poems I've published has represented a really new stage of development, and what I'm talking about is that right now I'm asking myself what my stage of development is.

And writing poems out of that stage?

The poems have to mean something new to me, and therefore I put aside a lot of stuff that doesn't have that feeling for me of depth or onward movement. I now have a few poems I've written in the last two years which do have that sense of onward movement: that is, they are making a real book; they will lead towards something real; whereas I have about ten other poems which I've written in the last few years—some of which I've published—which I see now were, from this point of view, aimless. They don't go anywhere. They are isolated. In fact, a couple of them have already been taken for anthologies, but they don't mean much to me. Actually if I have a real book, I mean if I have a book with a development in it, these little poems, these random poems might fit in somewhere. But I never feel that I have a real book until I have some important poems that are moving beyond me, beyond myself. Now I have, I would say, at this point about seven new poems which are moving that way, which seem to me to be quite important.

Then I guess the logical next question is where are these poems taking you? If I may make an observation: it seems to me that they are taking you towards a greater sense of fiction in your poetry.

That's true.

I mean that in terms of the persona as well as in terms of the technique and nature of the poems.

That's true. And also, you see, there is this question: a lot of poets in the last few years have been very much writing about circumstances, about society, about politics, about their lives. Now I am not going to write about that. I'm not concerned with that really. Not that these things wouldn't come into a poem, but for me, a real poem is not about these things. These things are just incidentals to what has to be, after all, a development of a sort of symbolic life in the poems.

You would call that other kind "confessional"?

Yes, a lot of it is confessional. A lot of it is just referential. Confession implies some emotional outpouring, but in many poems today there is only conversation. The man sits down and writes a poem that says, "You know, there's a war, I feel terrible, other people feel terrible, I'm calling up my friend and we're going to meet and have a little conversation." That's not a confessional poem; it's just a poem about daily, ordinary life, what he does every day. To me, this is kind of a pointless poetry. There's been a lot of it and it's not getting anywhere. I think what I'm talking about is the thing I just mentioned: the symbolic life. I think a poet ultimately has to shape his life in some way beyond the surface, so that he gets down to what it means really in some depth. I have a very funny sense of myself in the poem—I'm not talking about me, I'm talking about how the poems make a self for me. When I finished my last book of poems, *Adventures of the Letter I*, I was really resolving certain questions for myself, and then I was through with those questions. Not that the new poems won't relate to the last book; they obviously will. But it will have to be a new development, a different thing—coming out of that. Until I can make a development I really don't think I have a book at all. I don't think it's interesting.

As a part of this, I gather the use of narrative in poetry is important to you. Now I was wondering, what do you yourself see as the difference between the kind of narrative you employ in your new poems now and the kind of narrative you employed early in your career in poems like, say, "The Bird."

Well, there I was relying on traditional forms and a traditional voice. After all, I couldn't really have written "The Bird" unless I had read Heine, for example. I could rely on the audience to be carried along with me by certain literary associations. Not that I think "The Bird" depended on those entirely, no. But I was working within a tradition. The new narratives I'm writing now I don't think there's any tradition for. For one thing, the forms are very free. Each poem determines its own form and exactly how it's going to turn out—it is not traditional. I've just finished a new one about a wedding in Russia. And the question for me was, why was I telling this poem at all? It wasn't a real poem until I resolved this question in the last few lines. The point of the poem is that in fairy tales people get married and live happily ever after, but in real life they don't live happily ever after. The actual conclusion of the real-life story is that you're related to the people. When you are a child and someone tells you a story taken from real life, the ending is not "then they lived happily ever after," but "this person was your cousin." This is a much better ending, if you think about it. Now until I had grasped this idea I didn't know I really had a poem. I needed an original idea and I finally got it. It wasn't just an event I was describing, it was a perception into the nature of fiction and the nature of reality. I had to get that depth. I had to ask myself "Why are you telling this? You're not just interested in Russia, you are interested in reality and make-believe. Why you're concerned with these happenings is the question you have to solve." So narrative poems lead into very deep waters for me. I think some of the stories in *The Adventures of the Letter I* also go beyond just the interest of happenings.

These lead into further discoveries for you of what it means to you, what the material really means as you're playing, as you're fooling with it?

Yes. The happening, or the mere field of events, is very little. Of course we all know that. The real problem of fiction is, what is the significance of these events? Now this is very true of poetry. People say there is not much narrative poetry being written nowadays. Well, that is true largely because, I think, writers don't realize what can be involved in narrative poetry, what a real narrative is in a poem; it's not just surface events.

Let me ask at this point, then, what is the advantage or strategy that you see in terms of the narrative structure in one of your poems?

Why should it be in a poem, you mean, rather than prose?

Yes, what is its advantage?

I think that you get tremendous compression. Let me put it this way: you get a depth, you get an element in a poem that you can't get in prose because there is compression. You see, things happen when you compress that cannot happen when it's extended in prose—much greater echoes and resonances and interplays occur in a poem. If we can get a narrative to work in a poem, the compaction makes for depths and resonance that you'd never get in prose, except in a very rare bit of writing. But then there are the other usual elements of poetry, of course; there's the rhythm of it and so on, which you don't have in prose, the movement of the poem—the line.

Do you think of any particular or peculiar limitations to the use of narrative in a poem aside from the danger of falling into a prosy flatness or something?

Well, the danger would be particularity, a lack of general interest, that you would be telling a story and someone else would say, "Well, I don't care about trout fishing," if it happened to be about trout fishing, or "I don't care about this man weeding this patch of yard; this is not part of my life." When you tell a narrative in poetry you must get beyond the particular into some general human element. This is what the whole thing is about, and this is why until I've done that, it's not a poem. And it's very difficult to get at it. But when it does work I feel terrific, because I've done this thing which is based in life, which I think my poetry must be. My own poetry has to be based very much in life, that is, in the recognizable world. But, at the same time, it carries the recognizable world into the infinite or into something magical or mysterious. That to me is exactly what I want to do in a poem.

That's a very creative world in your work, though, that symbolic life. What's the relationship of the surreal and a lyrical kind of intensity and passion, then, to this kind of narrative?

Well, I think there should be as much of that in the narrative as you can possibly get in. Anything, after all, that will make the narrative move and have vitality is desirable. For example, in this poem I'm talking about, the one about the Russian wedding, there is a man named Brodsky who comes from Kiev with a team of horses. In fact, every time I heard this story—which is true, incidentally—this is the way the man was described. They remembered the name Brodsky, and Kiev, and, obviously, they were impressed with the horses. These things had some magical importance—I've tried to convey the importance as the people themselves felt it, by telling the story in a simple, narrative manner, without being ironic. I have tried to keep their sense of wonder.

I'm just wanting to make sure I understood all the things you said a moment ago. I think you said that one of the major attractions to you, or advantages of the narrative to you, is that it enables you to get more of the density of the actual world into the poem. Is that right? Something of that sort?

Yes. Well, I mean more than if I were doing it in prose. You see, when you put things very close together, which you do in a poem—sometimes two things in the same line, or two perceptions or three in the same line—you get a fourth dimension: something else happens, which hardly ever happens in prose. It is like surrealism, where the sudden juxtaposition of objects creates the surrealist image, a thing that we have not seen before. In a narrative if you can move things fast enough or jump from one place to another fast enough, the very juxtaposition, as in moviemaking, gives you a surrealist feeling.

In a recent interview we did with Galway Kinnell, Kinnell expressed at one point very clearly the desire to start depending less on narrative, which of course has been always so important to his poetry, and said that he thought it had been too much of a crutch and he wanted to reach for the poem that didn't require narrative. So what I wonder is what exactly you see as the advantage to you of narrative as distinct from nonnarrative poetry.

In American poetry today a lot of poets are making a mistake: they are preaching, they are sermonizing. They are telling you directly what they feel, and this is preaching, ultimately. Now the point of narrative, or narrative elements, or dramatic elements, in a poem is that you don't preach at somebody. You give them an experience. Art doesn't say "you must do this or you must feel that." Art says "come with me and let us go through this experience together." Now I think Galway is making a mistake. No, I shouldn't say that. One can never say of another artist he's making a mistake; besides I don't really know what Galway has in mind. But what I do know is that many of my contemporaries write poems that only say "I feel this." Some of them say "I feel this and you *should* feel it," and this is very boring. Actually what poetry must do is say "See this," and "I'm going to show you something. I'm going to take you by the hand through an experience," and then you are persuaded that way. Or maybe you're not persuaded at all, but you live with greater enjoyment.

There's a deadly solemnity in American poetry today. Many poets seem to have the feeling they must be serious men. That's fine, but they think that this means they must be solemn men, and must at every moment be terribly in earnest. Now, seriousness is quite different from solemnity. Solemnity is deadly, and some of my contemporaries have gone after it—they would call it sincerity. For the last fifteen years maybe, we've had this great sincerity in poetry now, an outpouring of sincere feelings. Ultimately this may be a failure of imagination and a failure therefore of love, because expressing your sincere feelings may be oblivious to the feelings of the people you're talking to. And it may not do them a bit of good. Whereas, a narrative or a drama, something of that nature, something created out there, enables you to communicate with them. That is love. But just pouring out your sincere feelings is a solipsistic, self-indulgent thing which doesn't communicate with anyone. That's not love at all. At the best it's therapy of some sort, for yourself. They're making a terrible mistake, some of my contemporaries. They're boring themselves and other people to death. I don't want to say who they are, but I pick up books of contemporary poetry, and I read them, and I can see that the man is serious and earnest, and he's read the newspapers. He's sincere. We know he's good, and he's well-intentioned and he's not a phony. But he's terribly boring, because he's not creating anything for the imagination at all. He's telling me about the life that we see around us every day, but he's not creating anything. He's sincere—so what? Now if he would tell me something exciting, or if not exciting, *true,* which I never knew before . . . I'm not asking for a cult of beauty or a religion, but I am asking for something beyond what we know already. Not just mere sincerity and earnestness.

The cult of sincerity is the present-day equivalent of the moralizing in nineteenth-century American poems. Baudelaire attacked it when he was writing about Poe; he thought it was almost impossible for Americans to have poetry because they demanded a moral purpose. We haven't advanced much since that time, though of course we don't see our own moralizing for what it is. Perhaps American poetry will always fall into moralizing, for the country is held together only by idealism of one sort and another; it is certainly not held together by love of the soil, or religion, or the love of art. So the poets dedicate themselves to one cause or another; they feel obliged to show that they are sensitive and "relevant"—good citizens, in fact. At the present time in poetry, just as with the old Puritans, there is widespread suspicion of drama and fiction. The poem must be a "naked" statement of the poet's thoughts about some serious subject, or a justification of his life. To read a new book of poems by an American— or worse, an article on poetry by an American—is more often than not to find yourself back at school in the civics class, or back in church in 1850.

I think part of what you're saying is that some poets have abrogated or disowned the possibility of translating that life into the symbolic life you spoke about earlier. The symbolic life is the life that we can read into and share.

Yes.

Is there some connection, in your mind, between your fond-
ness for the narrative and what I perceive in your poetry as
a persistent concern all the way through from early to now:
a very strong sense of, what shall I say, moral history or a
morally historical vision?

Yes, I think there is. I do think so. I've become
aware of it myself. I never cold-bloodedly went
about this, but I've become more and more aware of
it lately. I suppose with the struggle to write some
new poems in the last year, and start again from the
beginning, I'm beginning to realize I have certain
values, certain historical values. For example, in the
last book, *The Adventures of the Letter I,* I was using
Chekhov as a sort of a guide. After all, Chekhov was
a man who had very strong ideas, which he got
partly from himself and partly from Tolstoy, about
what life should be like. Chekhov is a very great
entertainer but he always has something to say about
human beings and what the value system is. I now
realize that I have a very strong historical sense and
also that I have strong ideas about human values.
The poems that I write now must say something to
that effect or else I don't consider them poems. If
they just say something about my own discontent,
for example, I don't consider that at all important.
It's so easy not to think. A lot of writers for
example . . . as I say, they read the newspapers and
they jump at the clichés, and they strike conventional
attitudes. There are writers who adopt the conven-
tions of the Right and writers who adopt the conven-
tions of the Left. But the poem or story demands that
you see for yourself, think what a thing really is, not

what it should be according to some group. I have been developing, I think—in the last few years more consciously, although I always had it somehow in flashes unconsciously—a viewpoint about what life is. And it's a very simple viewpoint. I mean it gets simpler as time goes by. It really is . . . I suppose I put a terrific value on imagination. I think human beings need it and are imaginative creatures primarily. I want art that will extend that. And the other thing is that I do believe that human beings are socially responsible and that there are vicious ideas. There really are vicious ideas. And those things, I think, are what my poems are about. But not by preaching.

When you say imagination I have a sense that you're talking about something else from what Bly means by imagination.

Something very different. Robert and I have a big difference which has become clearer to me over the last few years. We have never been able to thrash it out because—well, I don't know why. We have not had time to meet each other and discuss it. I think the difference shows in our ways of writing. I think that, for example, images, to have any depth at all or real meaning, must be related very tightly to the environment. Now I think Robert's idea is quite different from mine. Robert, I think, believes that images can be taken out of some—I don't know what: I suppose what Yeats might have called the *anima mundi* or Jung would have called the collective unconscious. It can be grabbed anywhere and put into a poem. That's the way some of Robert's images seem to me sometimes. Now, when he does that I don't get a feeling of resonance or relationship at all. Now he might say of my images: well, that writing doesn't give me anything at all, that's just a flat description. This is a big difference between us. When I write a poem the images can be very unusual or even have a surrealist feeling about them, but they must be related to the world around me. That way I think they get to someone else's unconscious or whatever you want to call it. They relate to someone else. I don't think you can just go wildly jumping around putting everything together and expect anything to happen. That's just very peculiar. And I mean peculiar in the strict sense of the term: it's peculiar to you.

You're certainly talking—and I mean this not in any pejorative sense at all of course—about a much more intellectual imagination, imagination much more in control of itself with respect to the environment of the poem as well as the surrounding matter of the poem, than Bly employs.

Well, I suppose so. Now I think another thing is that Robert wants to extend . . . Robert doesn't have the picture of the reader that I have. I have a vision, which is probably perfectly idiotic, really I have a sort of Wordsworthian vision: a picture of a very ordinary human being who is also highly intelligent and likes to read poetry; he is the one I write for. This man knows what a garage looks like, this man knows what a milk bottle sounds like on the back porch in the morning.

He's your roof-repairer.

Yes, the man who repairs the roof. In a sense, I want

to write a poem for that man. I want to write a poem that—in fact I think my poems are poems that can be read by anybody without any . . . I hope most of my poems are perfectly readable by most people. Now I think Robert has a more exotic picture of a reader than I do, at least I think he really would think that he is writing to expand the mind into some new realm of consciousness. And I think the disagreement there is very basic. It is between people who like the world as it is and those who want to change it—and I know that remark can be attacked as that of a very smug person, but I don't mean that at all. I mean I like the terms of existence as I understand them. I like the terms of perception as I understand them well enough, whereas I think there is another kind of man who wants to change the terms of perception and the terms of existence.

Would you even perhaps extend that to say that the one has greater affection for the phenomenal *world than the other?*

I don't know. I won't go that far. But let me put it this way: that my poems nowadays are very much a struggle to talk about ordinary situations and to find in them something that would make life not just tolerable but imaginative for people. Like a Chekhov play or a Chekhov short story where you have an ordinary situation and you walk out of the theater and say, "My God, there's no break between the inside of that theater and the sidewalk outside." I can walk out of that imaginative experience into my ordinary life and my ordinary life *now* seems more interesting. My feeling about other poets is that they run away from their ordinary lives in their poetry. They want to create either an alternative life or a better world in which they will live, and where they will take their readers. I don't want any part of that other world. I like this world. I want art to perceive what's fascinating in this ordinary life around us and present it with a lot of the confusion removed so that you see what's really essentially interesting about it. Therefore, to me, uninhibited surrealism is nonsense, for it doesn't make life more interesting—to the contrary, it makes it seem like a letdown. Whereas the absolute perception of what is there, really there, on the surface as well as underneath, is to me enriching life for everyone. That's why I said in the poem in my last book called "The Foggy Lane" that I wanted to keep my eye on the uneven muddy surface and to see what is really there. I don't want to make up a fantastic world for people to live in, which they can't stay in anyhow. So this kind of preoccupation determines largely how you write a poem and the kind of images you use. Very often, writing a poem nowadays, I find, over and over again, that I'm striking out what I call exaggerations. When I was starting to write, when I was twenty-one or so, the more exaggerated, the more farfetched, the more surprising something I wrote was, the better I thought it was. I was consciously trying, or not so consciously, but I was trying, to be exaggerated.

"Elevated" might be another word?

Maybe elevated. Now I eliminate that. I want the whole poem to be poetic, goodness knows, and imaginative. But I don't want it to lie. I don't want to distort, for the habit of distorting makes it impossible for poetry to relate to someone else. I remove exaggerations. This is very hard, and my contemporaries, most of them, don't do this. For one thing I think that some of them are infantile, you know. They are going around categorizing people, for example, and situations so that they . . . look, let me give you an example. In that poem I just mentioned, "The Foggy Lane," I mention an insurance man who tells me that I need more protection. Now another kind of poet could have made fun of this man. I didn't. I just said what he said. Another poet could have made this man ridiculous, foolish, less clever than the poet, etc., etc. You know what I mean? This is a very limited thing, that kind of a satire or that kind of superiority of the poet to the world around him. It is a very, very limited operation.

And very unattractive.

Yes. I try not to make statements I can't stand behind in some way, not to make statements for mere effect. Some of my contemporaries are completely untrustworthy in their poems. I wouldn't believe a thing James Dickey, for example, said in a poem. Not because a poet doesn't have the right to make up things. But Dickey just regurgitates words. There's very little thought in all his words. Dickey is an example of what Yeats talked about: will trying to do the work of the imagination.

Is this why you stopped rhyming and left the formal patterns? Everyone did this of course, for different reasons I'm sure in each case.

I think that mine was partly the feeling of the times. I think a lot of poets were just moving out into new forms and I was one of them. I don't think that this is particularly related to what I'm speaking of. In an attempt to write a poem that would be perfectly natural . . . I can't imagine how I would do it in rhyme now. I can't imagine how I would go about it now.

Throughout these last few minutes one line of yours has just leapt to the front of my mind as an epitomizer of what you've been saying about your whole strategy and approach and conception of poetry, and that was the line "despair." Period. Blank space. Then "an intelligent household."

I was able to make that leap from the word "despair" to "an intelligent household" by knowing Chekhov, whose characters are always full of despair and are always terribly full of words and ideas.

And despair is always just below the surface or on the surface. "An intelligent household." I found it very telling. Why do you write about Russia so much?

Well, I don't actually write that much about it. There's the new one we've been talking about—the poem called "The Intellectual," about the Russian wedding. But I wrote this not so much in order to talk about Russia as to make a point about the nature of fiction. I'm not going to write about Russia any more, I don't think—maybe one or two poems, that's all. It was just a—it was one of those preoccupations in which one works. Actually what I am tackling now is the poetry that is characterized by poems such as "Vandergast and the Girl" and "Simplicity": poems about contemporary life, set in contemporary scenes, particularly where I'm living. I want to get some good poems written about the new world we are entering—a lot of people are entering—which is neither the city nor the country: these spreading interconnected villages. Millions of people are living like this now. I wonder if any poetry can be written about these places and. . . . This would be the area of scenery I'd be writing about. But I tend to be interested in many different kinds of things. For instance, I have a poem about the first moon launch, which I've not published yet. It was accepted for publication but I withdrew it in order to rework the ending. I was down there when the first men left for the moon, you know; I was invited to go and watch. The same thing that Mailer wrote that huge book about. And so I wrote a poem about it. I get dispersed in different directions and this gives me a problem, because *then* when I start to think in terms of an ongoing body of work, *how* do I pull it together? Now you see, there are two ways to go about this: a man can say to himself, "I am going to write on one subject. I'm going to write about (let's say, for example) life in the middle of Mississippi. I'm going to start with the Mississippi River." And then he writes a lot of poems that are obviously connected. This seems to me to be a deadening kind of poetry. It tends to run down into a series of tasks. You set yourself the farm, and you have to do the barn, and then you're going to do a poem about the cow, and then one about the woman giving birth in the house, and so on. You know, all these poems are terribly predictable. Actually what I have to do is two different things: I have to write about things as they strike my fancy and then hope to God that after a few years I'll start to see the development of a major direction, underneath the randomness, coming forth. What I mean is, one shouldn't be too programmatic about what one is going to do in poems. I think with a book of prose it's quite different.

We've already talked about this, but I want to go back to it and make sure we've said enough. I'm not clear in my own mind about the relationship between you, the I, Louis Simpson, and the I who is the adventurer, for example, in this book, or in any of the poems before this book.

Well, you see, the title *Adventures of the Letter I* came to me in Stratford-on-Avon. I went up there to the Shakespeare Festival, three years ago, and leaped out of bed one morning with the title *Adventures of the Letter I,* and the minute I said it to myself, I knew it was right for this book. Obviously the title has several different mysterious even confusing meanings. "What does he mean by *Adventures of the Letter I?*" For one thing I wanted to put a distance between himself and the "I" character who appears in the poems, who is not me. He's someone I think I understand very well, but he's not me. For example, I am not the character who goes up the stairs in "Simplicity." I never did such a thing. I knew the woman, but we never had the conversation in the poem. So these are, well, these are make-believe *myselves.* "What would I do in this situation if I were there? Or what would a man like myself do or think in this situation if he were there?" In writing narrative poems it is important whether you use the first-person voice of someone who is taking part in the action, or you tell everything from outside, using the third person. For example, "Vandergast and the Girl" is in the third person, and I am able to move around Vandergast and his problems in a knowing, expansive, somewhat ironic manner. Now the "I" in the poem "Simplicity" is a much more involved character, and it's a much crazier poem, and it's a much more intense poem in that it comes out of his own voice. The dramatic monologue there is much more intense than the descriptions in "Vandergast." "Vandergast" is more scenic, more panoramic, moving over distances of time. Whether you use "I" or write about characters in the third person can determine the whole feel of the poem—perhaps even what happens. I use the "I" as someone who is—let me put it this way: someone I understand but who is not me. In some ways he's had the same experiences I have had.

You mean the way Eliot uses Prufrock?

Yes.

What about the generation of poets coming up? What do you see happening? You can look back on the sixties, now that we've moved into the seventies, and describe the experience. But what do you anticipate?

Well, I'm very encouraged. I've just very recently been reading people like yourself and Bill Matthews and Simic and a few others. And what I find most encouraging is the fact that you are not only writing poems, but you are also publishing magazines and discussing poetry. Now I think that some of us in the sixties served a function of keeping certain lines open to the seventies. We did. I can think of some men of my own age who didn't keep lines open, you know, who went off either into seclusion or else into some sort of commercial success. Now people like myself, those of us who were writing poems and were never very popular—I was never a popular poet, I can't claim to have a little *bit* of the audience that a man like Snyder or a man like Ginsberg has; those were the great successes of the 1960s but those of us who were not popular poets kept lines open to the next generation, perhaps *because* we were not popular poets. And we were not . . . well let me put it this way: we were not so . . . we were not creating such an absolutely public mask of ourselves. So we had to be devoted to poetry for its own sake. I think a man like James Wright, for example, should mean something to the next generation; he is the figure of a man who is devoted, just simply devoted, to poetry.

Yes.

I think this is true of Robert Bly too. And besides, both of those men have shown tremendous generosity towards younger people. When I was a young poet, which would have been in the late 1940s, just beginning to write, when I looked above me there was no one. There was literally no one I could have thought of learning anything from. There were the great figures of the twenties, but they weren't around in person. No one I knew had ever seen Eliot, or Stevens, or Pound. I had no sense of a living connection with those men. And the generation directly above me—the Lowell generation. Lowell was rapt in the pursuit of his own fame. He would have had nothing to do with a man like myself. Now that has not been true of my generation. We have been open to the young. And while some of our generation became famous, those who were not accomplished a great deal. If I were a young man now and I looked above me I would see several figures that I could feel very strongly, very good about. *They* would have been there before me. Bly, Kinnell, Merwin, Ignatow . . . and there are others, several others who have given possibilities to young people. They can look and say, "I like what he does," or they can say, "I like some of his work." There are many alternatives. There are bodies of work done. I once said this. I had a vision of this long ago in a poem. I said, "Grave by grave we civilize the ground." And it has happened. In 1948 a young poet looked above him and who were the poets? Karl Shapiro and Delmore Schwartz were the well-known younger poets of that time. And that was all.

Yes.

Nowadays the younger poet can look above him and see—above him in the sense that they've lived before—and see how many? Maybe twenty, thirty people whose work is worthy of reading and thought. And different life styles, if that interests him. Different possibilities. There are all these possibilities. There's a lot to read! If I were a young woman poet today I would see lots of women. I could say to myself, "Well look at all that good poetry to read. Look at Diane Wakoski. Look at all these women who have written poetry. Look at Lucille Clifton, look at. . . ." You know, there are wonderful women poets. Each in her own way. There's something there before you.

America's had a lot of business traditions, we've had a lot of war traditions, we've had all that, but our literary figures have been lonely and disconnected. There's Hawthorne. He's a great writer. And there are Mark Twain and Whitman. But these are solitary monsters. American writers of the past have been solitary figures. With nothing around them. Now, however, in this generation you could look out and see a lot of people.

That's right.

And there's a lot to be thought about. I mean, I could imagine a young man or young woman saying, I want to study the works of Gary Snyder, or I want to study the work of Robert Bly. There's quite a lot there to read and to think about. And this is rich, it's very rich. American poetry of the last twenty years is tremendously rich. There are so many good poets in America now . . . I don't want to sound sappy about it, but there are so many good poets that we don't have time to get around to them.

Unfortunately, that's true.

For example, Robert Francis may not be the greatest American poet—and who is the greatest, anyway?—but his work is worthy of serious attention. Or take a man like Robert Duncan. There is a great deal there to be read. Some lucky young guys thirty years from now or forty years from now are going to have lots of American poetry to read. When I started reading American poetry there wasn't that much to choose from. I have heard it said that in every generation there seems to be a lot of poetry. I don't think so. If you look at the anthologies of 1918—American poetry of 1918—it is not just because I'm living in 1972 that I can say this, but I can say it objectively: an anthology of 1918 was nine-tenths nonsense. It was ladies' verse, society verse, obviously. Now an anthology today will have a lot of junk too, but there's a much larger proportion of serious and very good work. I think that in general the quality has gone up tremendously.

Do you think we're forever beyond the time when there will be major figures that will loom so large or tower so high above everybody else that they stand out as the great luminaries of the time? We certainly are not in such a time now.

We don't know. We never know this. You see, when I came to the United States in 1940, William Carlos Williams had done, well, I would say about three quarters of his work, and a great deal of his best work. He was almost unknown. It is hard to believe that in 1940 with his best work behind him, nearly all his best work behind him, this man should be unread. But he was read by very few people. Wallace Stevens was, you know, less known than Williams. Wallace Stevens I would say was almost completely unknown in 1940 and he had done most of his best work. Now in our time right now you hear this cry about there being no major figures, a lot of good poets but no major figures. I'm not at all sure about that. I think that Ginsberg . . . I won't contradict anyone who wants to tell me that there's a lot of bad writing by Allen Ginsberg. There certainly is. But I could make a selected volume of Allen Ginsberg which would, I think, put up a pretty good argument for his being a major poet. And I'm not using the word "major" lightly, the way the publishers do on their dustjackets. I could argue that Gary Snyder is as interesting a poet as William Carlos Williams when he was the age of Snyder. I think that I could do this with a handful of other poets, prove that they are as important at this stage as some people of the last generation. But it seems we can never see this until the man is dead. We never see this until—twenty years from now they'll look back at 1970 and say, "Well the work he did then, in that year was fantastic. It was a great year! It was a great year of poetry for this writer!" But when we are living alongside a writer we don't see so clear. Especially if the man is busy writing and not talking in *Time* magazine.

You mean promoting himself?

Time magazine is the *death* of poetry. But I'm very optimistic, and it's not because I want to be foolishly sentimental about it. I do think that there's a lot of good poetry being written. For example you take a man like Michael Benedict—there's a very special kind of humor. It is very good, of its kind. There's William Harmon, with his big poem. I find it very interesting. And I know a couple of younger poets who aren't published yet, that I'm working with— well, that I'm a friend of—and I have a great hope for them. There's a man named Jimmy Nolan with a wonderful manuscript. And all the little magazines, the *little* magazines that exist are making this possible.

Do you have any opinions or theories about why there are so many good *poets writing in America today?*

Yes, I do have. I think the teaching of poetry in colleges has had a lot to do with it. This would not be a popular remark in certain quarters. For example I can imagine it would give a man like Kenneth Rexroth fits. But it is a fact that people have been taught in universities how to read poetry. And as a matter of fact, some of the people who have fits when they think about universities, like Rexroth, seem to spend an awful lot of their time around them.

Well, we've sort of coursed through a kind of contemporary sensibility—a sense of the present in poetry. And you said that when you were younger and starting out as a poet there wasn't anyone above you really to lead you—I don't know if that's a fair word. But surely there were influences.

The influence when I was young, the presiding influence was, now that I look back on it, a very bad one. That was W. H. Auden. I think he did a great deal of harm. I don't think he ever understood American sensibility. And his recent works have been appalling, his attitudes are appalling. Fortunately, however, that kind of thing is seen through. Very few American younger poets care about Auden at all. But he was the influence when I was young. He was the tone that everyone was imitating. Even a good poet like Delmore Schwartz, certainly a poet like Karl Shapiro, if you look through their early work, half of it is an imitation of Auden. Now I educated myself, largely. I read poets, I discovered poets for myself, and they were all sorts of poets.

International poets or strictly American?

Unfortunately in those days we didn't have all the translations that are being made now, and the pipelines weren't open. People didn't come from abroad to give poetry readings, so that unfortunately we were rather limited to English and American poetry. I was very affected by Eliot, obviously, and I knew Yeats's poems when I was young very well. Those two men. But they were rather remote figures. I didn't know—

I didn't read Williams and I didn't read Stevens. It wasn't until I was in my thirties that I read those men. When I began reading poetry I was pretty much on my own. When I was learning how to write a poem of my own I would study very carefully a man like . . . oh I did study Hart Crane very carefully, and Whitman when I was young. But these are the people you'd expect everyone to know. Nowadays a young poet will be introduced by very bright teachers to, for example, Yannis Ritsos. He may hear Voznesensky on a platform reading his poems. Very exotic foreign poets. He may hear a South American poet like Nicanor Parra, or Tomas Tranströmer from Sweden. And he'll have all sorts of exotic ideas of poetry to choose from. Now we didn't have these opportunities. Poetry readings were very rare when I came to America. I never heard of any, except down at the Museum of Modern Art, where a few famous foreign poets were promoted. You might go to hear Edith Sitwell or Dylan Thomas. Some big name. But there was nobody else around giving readings, so you were never exposed to different ways of writing, and your teachers didn't know much about contemporary poets. Even the very good teachers would be teaching Yeats and Eliot and so on. They wouldn't introduce you to surrealist poetry, for example. But now, my goodness! One of the problems of the young—I was looking in the bookstore this morning—one of the problems of the young must be just sheer confusion. I mean a lack of direction. Too many choices.

I think that is true: too many choices.

In view of this I would think that a man like Frost, even a man with Frost's attitudes today . . . actually maybe what we need now is a moratorium on choices. A man fixed in his place like Frost might be a welcome change. I think Frost never read a foreign poet—outside of a few Englishmen—in his life. At least, he gives that impression. He wouldn't have anything to do with them. We could use a little concentration now to stabilize the minds of the young, who must be reeling with all the infinite possibilities there are. Shall they be like—who knows—should they be like a South American surrealist, or should they be like, oh goodness knows what? There must be an infinite succession of choices, if they are going about it in a literary manner and not out of the inner necessity that determines what you do.

Would you like to say anything more about the differences between your writing and Bly's? You said you were disagreeing about images.

There's something I would like to discuss with him. We started writing each other letters about it, you know, and he gave me hell in a letter recently. He said, "Ridiculous!" You see, I wrote to Robert and said, "I'm tired of this business about the inner life and the outer life. There is no such division in nature." He wrote back and said, "Ridiculous! You know there was a fall of man and you know from your own experience how you feel, that there is a fall of man and a split between the inner life and the outer life." I shall have to write back and say: "When you say there was a fall of man you're talking revealed religion, and there is no more discussing it. If you're talking about my personal experience, that sometimes I feel bad and therefore I know that there is a split in my psyche, that there is an inner world which is good and an outer world which is bad, or something like that . . . if you're going to bring that up, it's only a split because I think it is. If I didn't think that I have feelings of guilt and sin then I wouldn't have such a split."

This is an important question, because the split between the inner life and the outer life that Robert is supposing, has a bearing on how we go about writing poetry. I want to write the poem that looks, as I said before, directly at the outer world, and through the outer world at some deeper meaning. Now Robert seems to be saying that the outer world is not as important as the inner world you make up surrealistically. Now there, that's the real basic difference between the ways we actually go about writing a poem. So I think this is an interesting and important argument. Writers have all sorts of ideas, but what counts is the created work. I believe that my attachment to the surface of things will create in the reader a greater affection for life. In American writing we have had a number of weird creations: a woman who wears a scarlet letter, a white whale, a hero who cannot make love, and so on. But it seems to me that we are short of people who love their lives. Do you know the saying by Goethe? "Prophets to the right, prophets to the left . . . the child of the world in the middle." Well, I'm a child of the world. I want to write poetry for people who want to live in the world.

Therefore, as I said earlier, I am writing poems based in experience and the images are related to the environment. When one of these poems works there is no split between an inner and an outer world. There is only one life, and we are here to enjoy it.

To Make Words Disappear

Emotional intensity—this, as far as I can tell, is what poetry consists of. A poem will move from one moment of intensity to another, and there will be a connection. This, I suppose, is where I part company with surrealism and with some of my contemporaries—they don't care about the connection, don't feel a need to get a narrative line into their work. They seem to think that it is enough to say that they are having a feeling—but they do not try to convey it in an image or a narrative line. I'd rather not read such poetry—I don't care about writing that merely tells me that the writer is having a feeling. I want to be able to experience the feeling—I want lyric or narrative poetry.

As for poetry that preaches, I can do without it entirely. I don't want to listen to a poet berating people for their shortcomings—for example, for not being as "politically aware" as he is. It would be better to give them some pleasure rather than make them feel inferior. The most pleasurable poetry I know is lyric or narrative, and sometimes it's a

This essay first appeared in *American Poetry Review* 3, no. 1 (1974).

poetry of ideas, but the ideas are transformed into emotion, as images, so that the reader can experience them.

None of this is new, but it seems to have been forgotten in recent years. There is a lot of hard breathing going on—you see the poet straining to say something important, and you may feel sympathetic, but it doesn't do a thing for your life. It would be better if he were less self-absorbed and told you something that was interesting. To be interesting is an act of love—it may be the best thing we can do for each other.

I would like to write poems that made people laugh or made them want to cry, without their thinking that they were reading poetry. The poem would be an experience—not just talking about life, but life itself.

I think that the object of writing is to make words disappear.

The Poetry of Searching

An Interview with Lawrence R. Smith

Eastern Michigan University
Ypsilanti, Michigan
October 16, 1974

In North of Jamaica *you include a poem called "Before the Poetry Reading," which satirizes some of the aspects of that university institution. Do your comments extend to the status of poetry in the university in general, that is, to the relationship of the poet to his public, as well as to the poetry reading itself?*

I think that poem is aimed directly at the institution of traveling from one place to another and being bewildered by your reception. And the sort of wonder one has sometimes about what is expected. And the funny things that happen to you; there are very funny things that happen on poetry readings, half of which I didn't put in that poem. (You can't make a poem out of everything.) But I think that the situation of poetry in the universities is a different scene from what I was talking about. The poet in the

This interview first appeared as "A Conversation with Louis Simpson," *Chicago Review* 27, no. 1 (Summer 1975).

university is a lot better off than he was twenty or thirty years ago. He has a recognized place now, which never used to be true. And I am not one of the poets who say that the university is antipoetic, you know. I've met my colleagues who dislike poetry, met many of them, but you can avoid them. And I think the poet can have, nowadays, a pretty good life in the university, and get out of it when he wants to, too. Universities have not been bad for poets. I mean, they've been better than anyone else. Who else has been supporting poets in the last ten or twenty years?

What about the poet and his public in general? Say that a university audience, small or large, would be a sample of the public. Do you feel that there is a problem in relating to the public through the spoken word?

Well, the university audience—that's a definite disadvantage—the university audience is not representative of the public. It's only representative of a certain segment. It represents a small, rather specially educated part of the public. And you should be aware of that if you teach in a university, or write, or are a poet in a university. You must not take the people in front of you as a complete picture of humanity. Fortunately, I arrange my life so that I don't live in a university. I live outside it. My life is set up to relate more to the external world than to the university itself. I go teach my classes, hold my office hours. I don't skimp on that, but on the other hand, when I'm not teaching and I'm not holding office hours, I'm away from that university. I don't consider myself bound by the campus. After all, you're talking about students who have a very special view of American life and politics and all that—they tend to be much more liberal, for example, than most Americans.

After your celebrated change from fairly formalistic poetry to the more colloquial free verse of At the End of the Open Road, *I assume that a lot of people have more or less concluded that you have forsaken an interest in rhetoric and meter and so forth. Is that true? Or are you still interested, say, in quantitative metrics?*

I write with a very strongly marked rhythm in my work. Even though it is not a traditional line, it usually has a pretty strongly marked beat, which I think comes out very clearly when I read. It may be very irregular at times, but my poems for me aren't real unless they have a rhythmic unity. Now I just simply got away from the old fixed patterns because I couldn't speak in them freely, and I couldn't move around in them freely enough. But I didn't lose my interest in rhythm. As far as interest in the old formal poem, of the sonnet or the quatrain or the fixed stanza—I have no real interest in that. In fact, I am like a lot of people turned off by it. The reason being that I feel too much is being sacrificed in terms of a subtler music by that kind of form. The argument seems to me a bit academic at this point. I mean, so many writers in the twentieth century, and before the twentieth century, have written what could loosely be described as "free verse," that surely by now it's recognized as a very old form. I write poems that depend very much on a rhythmic line, which is determined somewhat by the rhythm of my body, the motions. And also by a syntactical sense of speech—what at that moment do I need to say to sound natural and convincing? And therefore, if the line has to be suddenly longer, it will suddenly become longer; if it has to be shorter, it will suddenly be shorter. There is no line, regular repetition of meter, foot, stanza, that is going to do the work for me. I have to do it in terms of speech, and the rhythms of speech.

You mention free verse as an old form, and Walt Whitman is one of your great thematic concerns. Are you interested, or were you ever interested in Walt Whitman in terms of the mechanics of his free verse?

I never made a formal study of Whitman's line, but I probably know as much about it as anybody does. I've studied the device of parallelism he uses; he gets his effect of holding a poem together by the repetition of sentence structure. And then I was interested in the sense of how much he could get into one line, or the sense of movement in his line. And I think he's an extremely good teacher from that point of view, like Pound; they can both teach—so can William Carlos Williams, so can Eliot—teach you how to move around in a line that is ostensibly free, but actually is rather tightly controlled by a concept or by speech patterns.

At the end of Lolita, *Nabokov says in his afterword "It had taken me some forty years to invent Russia and Western Europe, and now I was faced by the task of inventing America." That sounds similar to what you have done with both Russia and America. What do you think are the advantages and disadvantages of being a nonnative commentator on a country?*

Curious you should mention this. I think the first review of *Lolita* in this country—not that it matters—was mine. I gave it a rave review. And also, a curious thing happened; I compared Nabokov to Gogol, although I had not known that he had written a book on Gogol. I thought I saw a tremendous resemblance between *Lolita* and *Dead Souls*. And there is. You see, in both books, in the Russian *Dead Souls* and in *Lolita,* you get the sense that for the first time a man is looking at these scenes and characters. There's a delight you feel in *Dead Souls* as he describes all these strange characters that live in the Russian countryside—some of them half mad, all eccentric, very strange—and he's having such delight in describing them. Now to get back to your question, I think now that you mention it . . . I had not thought of myself in comparison to Nabokov, for obvious reasons; we work in very different media and in very different ways. I think that I have been inventing a United States, because I came to it from the outside. And I think this is true of Nabokov, too. Now that has certain advantages. It means that I will look at a character and think "How strange," when nobody else would look at him twice. Or I would look at a scene in a street or something and think "How odd" and . . . "These Americans!", you know? And think in those terms when they themselves don't see it. Now those are the advantages. The disadvantages, of course, are enormous. Things which an American knows instinctively, I don't know. For example—when I came to this country I was seventeen—I'll never be able to understand a large part of the American character, because I didn't go to an American high school. If you've been to an American high school, you know a lot about America. You can never find that out again. On the other hand, I did when I was nineteen go into the Army, the American Army. If I had not done that, I don't think I would be an American writer at all in any real sense. Three intense years in the Army taught me an awful lot about being an American. But I regret that I don't understand the high school view. So there are a lot of instinctive relations between people that I don't understand. I see a lot of things from outside. And I don't understand them quite. So I feel a little uneasy from that point of view. On the other hand, as far as probing it from outside goes, and looking into America from outside, and traveling around in it, I've done more than most Americans. I mean, I've been all over America; I've spent nights in strange small towns, I've dug holes in fields, I've seen a lot of America. But there are certain instinctive things that you spend your youthful years doing that you'll never get again. And that I regret.

Like Nabokov, you traveled around more than most Americans to get your experience. New York and California seem to be almost polar symbols in your poetry, yet there are similarities in your references to them: a kind of mechanical life, capitalism, realtors, business, and so forth. And the same images come up with respect to both New York and California. How do you think those two places function in your poetry?

Well, California is, as far as I see it, a place that is living almost entirely in the present and talking about the future. It has decided that's where life is. And New York is a place—I don't care who you are—where you are in a kind of pressure cooker, where a lot of people are still connected somehow with the past—their past, their family's past—they're still European in a sense. The West Coast is not connected to Europe, and it is turning, if anything, toward the East. However, I felt a sense of dissipation out there. I felt like there was a certain energy, American energy, that was going off into a vacuum. And another problem is this: I come from the Caribbean. Now to many Americans going to California is just wonderful, wonderful—freedom, you know, exotic flowers, tropics. I came from the real tropics, and I know what it has to offer and I know what I didn't like about it. And I left Jamaica by choice. I left because I wanted a more intense intellectual life. And a place where people really cared about things. I found in California that people cared too much about their barbeque pits. You see, I'd much rather live in Michigan than I would in California, because I love the land mass, I love the sense of enclosure, I love the idea that you are somehow turned in upon yourself, and have to make your life inside your mind. Whereas in California I always had the sense—and it's not just my illusion—that their object was to escape. My object was not to escape. I think that my strongest criticism of California is that it's basically hedonistic, as in the H. G. Wells story *The Time Machine*. There's a race of people who live underground and do all the dirty work, and they eat— they're horrible cannibals—and they eat the people up top.

The Morlocks.

Yes. And then the people up top are these mindless people who sit by the river while somebody is drowning, and they just watch. And I always thought that Wells must have been to California, because these are the people there. They just sit there and they watch someone drowning and they say "Oh, how nice. He's doing his thing." That's their attitude.

Are the New Yorkers the Morlocks?

In a sense, they are. Life in New York can be brutal and dark and unlovely, but I understand it. See, I went to college in New York and I spent many years there and I understand that life. And it's very unsatisfactory in ways, but also a lot of the people I've known have been connected there. I don't live in New York City now, though, you must understand that. I live outside it. I live in a small fishing village which I love. It's very nice, and I have trees around me and so on. But I don't think that my statement that a lot of Californians are looking for escape is untrue. They say a lot of things about my attitude towards California. It's getting to be a joke, I think, in some quarters. "Here's another Simpson poem about California." "You know what to expect from Simpson on the subject of California," I saw in a review recently. All right. But I still say that if your object is to escape, California is the place for you. If it's not, I think you could get a little tired of it.

In one poem, "Love, My Machine," you call San Francisco "the darkest of all cities." What in particular did you have in mind there?

Oh, that was just an insult. And sheer self-defense. I went out there and these people in Berkeley, particularly, some of the people in the English Department kept telling me that this was the greatest place in the world. Nowhere else in the world was equal to San Francisco. And after all, I'd been around a bit. I'd lived in France, I'd lived in Italy. I thought this was ridiculous! I met a man who had moved once across the Bay, and then decided there was no point in moving, and moved back to San Francisco. I mean, he'd seen the whole world. So, in front of this attitude, I just decided to call San Francisco "the darkest of cities."

In North of Jamaica *you mentioned being thrown in, during the Vietnam antiwar readings, with San Francisco poets, with all kinds of poets with whom you didn't necessarily agree. Did that result in any kind of mutual understanding? Or modification in your own style?*

No modification in my own style. But I understood those others. For the time we were doing those readings, we got along fine. I mean, we had a common objective. I remember an early reading; I went up to Reed College and read up there, alongside Ferlinghetti and others, you know. And actually the Vietnam War readings cut across a lot of lines; a lot of poets who ordinarily wouldn't have been on the same platform were. And I thought it was fine. I liked that fine.

Another thing that has interested me particularly is your recurrent use of references to ancient civilizations, and especially decayed, ruined ancient civilizations. Especially Rome, as a matter of fact. In the first place, is that based on your own experience of Europe, and in the second place, how does that particularly apply to the ruined civilization of America?

Well, I think when I talk about ruins—it's not just a nostalgic thing, goodness knows—I'm really seeing America as a ruin. I frightened my students the other day by saying to them: "Let's understand one another; in this room we're all dead, and have been dead for a hundred years. So don't give me any of this crap about your generation and my generation, or that you can't read John Donne, or that you prefer something that you really grew up on. Let's start from scratch. We're all contemporaries of everybody." The point is, when I look at America, I think: "Oh, this is all well and good, but in about five hundred years we're going to be as dead as Rome." So I look at it to try to see what's alive. Thinking of ruins enables me to feel what is really worthwhile in living. These people with their big monuments. I look down Park Avenue and I can just see it so clearly. I can just see Park Avenue five hundred years from now, just a bunch of pyramids. And so I say to myself: "What is life really about?" These buildings are not going to be around long, or they're going to be in very bad shape. So I suppose I think about ruins because I'm really thinking about death. And thinking about what is the "antiruin." Maybe I should publish a poem called "Antiruins." That's a nice thought. I hadn't thought of that. I'll write a poem called "Antiruins" about living moments of real life. I suppose that's very wily of you. I never thought of this before. No one has ever asked me this question of why I write about ruins. But now I realize why I do it, because it's sort of the antilife . . . ruins are antilife, and I'm going to write a poem called "Antiruins," I think.

Going back to H. G. Wells—you were talking about H. G. Wells—his famous remark upon first seeing New York

City: "What a magnificent ruin this will make!" Another outside view of America. I was also interested in a remark you made in North of Jamaica *about Indian poems. You were talking about being up at Robert Bly's place in Minnesota with James Wright. And you mentioned as an aside that everybody seemed to be writing Indian poems. I think you also mentioned William Stafford. After mentioning that, you said: "The Indian, I have no doubt, was as foolish as the white man, and the people who settled Kentucky would have wondered at our sympathy for howling savages." Weren't you saying essentially that this was the old "noble savage" bit again, and really wasn't getting any deeper than previously?*

There is an Indian poet who is very angry with me for that, who, in fact, wrote me a letter saying: "This is a terrible remark to make about Indians in your book, that they're all savages." "My God," I said to him, "Can't you read? I didn't say that. I said 'To the Kentucky settlers, they were howling savages.' And they certainly were." What I was actually saying in my book about this Indian question is that, yes, the new poems that we were writing in the early sixties were a literary construction. We were trying to use the Indian as a means of expressing our feeling about the repressed side of America that should be released. However, if I or anyone were to continue to try to write Indian poems, we should know more about Indians than we did, than I did. I was writing with sympathy and a historical sense of feeling, but to write about Indians you really should in a sense become an Indian. You have to know how they think and feel. And *that* I know I could never do, so I wouldn't even bother trying. I have enough to do to write about what I do know.

*Take for example William Stafford's "Returned to Say,"
where it seems to me he is more than sympathizing with the
repression or the oppression of Indians. He is talking about
a whole new world, which may indeed be a poetic construct.
He talks about a new, an alien philosophy that may be the
real America that is as yet undiscovered, the antimaterialis-
tic America. Do you think that that's possibly a different
kind of direction than the noble savage business?*

I don't know exactly what Stafford is driving at
there. I don't know the poem. I think that there are
many kinds of Indian poems. There would be the
poem which you wrote like an Indian, where you
understood how he thought, his magic, his life, his
values. Then there's the white man's Indian poem,
in which after all the Indian is not just the Indian, he
is a concept, like the "noble savage" which the white
man has had in his head for a long time. Now that
you mention it, is that invalid? I have been saying it's
invalid, but I may be completely wrong. Why
shouldn't you have an idea of the Indian which is
really the white man's Indian, whom the Indian
might not care about, but who is very important to
the white man? Like D. H. Lawrence's concepts of
the Indian. Lawrence, for example, was always talk-
ing about "blood knowledge." Now, I'm not sure In-
dians thought that way. But Lawrence thought they
did; and thinking they did served a purpose for
Lawrence. And I think a lot of the so-called Indian
poems that I read now are very much "noble savage"
poems. They present the Indian as a man who has
mystical experiences with animals. You know, we're
back to "Hiawatha," I'm telling you. But the point is
that a lot of Indians I'm sure were not different
from me. Maybe they had their equivalent of televi-

sion. There must have been an Indian equivalent for just wasting time. There was an Indian equivalent, I'm sure, for having too many drinks. There was an Indian equivalent for even sitting down and talking seriously about poetry. But, you see, when you construct a symbolic Indian, you don't let him do any of those human things; you just have him being very mysterious and silent and in touch with mystic deep things all the time. No race of man that has ever lived has been as solemn as some of the Indians that these white poets are creating. Or as boring, may I say.

A theme or concern that seems to me to be linked to this Indian poem business is orientalism, especially in the sixties and seventies. In North of Jamaica, *you make several sly cuts at orientalism on the West Coast, especially the popularity of Zen Buddhism. It seems to me that in one of your poems, "Pacific Ideas—A Letter to Walt Whitman," your final image recalls Li Po embracing the moon, a kind of conscious orientalism.*

That was actually a girl I was thinking about. She was not Oriental, either. I really had great designs on that girl, but they didn't work out. But that was really on my mind at the end of that poem. Now the question of Buddhism: you must understand that I like it a lot. I have done a lot of meditation. The point, however, is this: I am making those cuts at what I call "bargain basement Buddhism." There is an awful lot of cheapening and stupidity in California. Their attention span—not just California, let me get off California—the attention span of some people is about ten seconds. Now Buddhism is a very intense meditation. It can be instant perception, as in

Zen Buddhism, but it also can take years and years of training. And what irritated me was the way some people talked about Japan; they had these wonderful sweeping generalizations. I would have students who would talk about "nonselfness," you know, that sort of thing. And I would say to them: "Isn't that in Christianity too?" As if they'd never heard about Christianity, never read Jesus. But they were sure that there was something new in the world that was purely oriental. They were so ignorant! They had this vision of Japan as a place where everyone went around meditating. I used to say to them: "Where do you think all those automobiles are coming from, or those radios?" I'm not knocking the real thing, when it happens, but it's not instant soup.

A poem like "The Morning Light" seems to be almost consciously oriental in its tightness. Do you believe that's true?

Yes, in my poetry there are elements which are very close to real oriental meditational feeling. I think there's an intensity in some poems, with which I look at things or try to just present the bare thing without any similes or metaphors—just the thing in itself. A lot of my more recent poems, which are apparently "flat," are really very carefully selected to direct attention to just the object, which, after all, is a meditation process: to get away from abstraction and to realize that you're here and now with every fiber of your intellect. The curious thing about it is that the more you realize where you are, with the material universe immediately impinging on you, the more removed you become, the more you get into real deep space. It's a curious thing, but that's the one process I learned. I don't know about other peoples' processes. I think some of my poems are very close to that feeling.

It's interesting that you mention people are thinking of some of your recent things as "flat." In your poem in At the End of the Open Road *called "American Poetry," you talk about the shark that is "uttering cries that are almost human." In your latest poetry, you seem to have moved toward conversation a great deal, and away from a concentration on concrete objects. Do you think the reference in this poem a kind of prophecy of the movement you were going to make?*

No. I think at that time that line was meant to suggest an inhuman life which poetry has, a shark life. A lot of American poetry is too domestic. My new poem about the search for the ox is moving back in that shark direction. It's talking about things which aren't domestic, aren't recognizable. I'd like to do both kinds of poems; I don't want to be limited to one. But in the last few years it's certainly true that a lot of the poems that I've been working on have been about people, speech, and so on. I'd like to do both things, because I think both directions are good for me.

I have the feeling, in listening to "Searching for the Ox," that when the "tube of darkness" rises from the water and comes into the beam of the lighthouse, it is almost like the proverbial "deep image" coming back.

Yeah, I think it's almost my definition of the "deep image." Incidentally, that passage has taken me years to write. I've written it over and over for years. I put it aside. I knew it belonged somewhere, I wasn't sure where. But I think this poem is where it belongs. And that's a real image. It's been haunting me for years, that thing coming up to the surface.

Let's go back to orientalism. From your very first poems, it is almost a unifying theme that you are in a constant search for a spiritual guide. For instance, in "There Is," you talk about "the word" and "the light," in "The Redwoods," you talk about a giant poet whom the redwoods are waiting for; in other poems you talk about the Torah, and in "Good News of Death," it's Christ. And, of course, Buddhism and Zen Buddhism can also be included. But it always seems to be a dissatisfied search.

Chekhov and Whitman. It *is* a dissatisfied search. I was talking to my wife about this—she's really tremendously useful to me as a critic and a helper, in poetry—and she said: "You know, you don't have a country." And she said, "In a way, it's very sad, but you must realize that." I was talking about Robert Bly, saying how wonderful it was that Robert had this center in Minnesota. I've discussed this with Robert many times over the years. I never had anything like that in America. You can never be at home unless you are in the place where you were born. You may do many things: you may be a great musician or a writer, or you may be a wonderful citizen or something, but you never have that absolute mother-child relationship with another country which you have with your own. Now I broke completely with my own birthplace. And that means that in a funny sense the rest of my life, as my wife pointed out to me, I am going to write the poem of searching and looking for guides. Whereas somebody who was born in a place, and so on, might speak with more authority out of one body of knowledge. In a way I have got to keep thinking and looking for spiritual guides. And another reason I do that is because I believe, with Yeats, that you choose your opposite and work toward it, and that keeps you really alive: the antiself. Now I'm not a terribly spiritual person. I'm not a mystic. In fact, I have some very cynical moods. Therefore, what is good for me is to read people who are slightly mystical and religious and deep in that way, and to use some of the control for myself. It prevents me from becoming stupid, you see. I'm sure that I'm completely different from Whitman in my likes and dislikes as a man. But I love Whitman, because he explores those areas which I know I should be conscious of.* See?

You deny being a mystic, yet so many of your poems from the "deep image" middle period were read as just that, as mystical, as being of another realm. Is it possible you're a split personality?

I think so, I think that I have a definite split, and I have a tendency to go off into days, weeks, even a year of a kind of superficial thinking and writing. It's a physical rhythm I have. About three or four years ago I was at a rather superficial level. I go through phases of intense work and getting deeper and deeper, and then creating a new . . . oh, to me a "new" set of ideas. It exhausts me. And then I become very superficial for quite a while. And then I have to get back into a new complex of ideas. I think

---

*Reading this six years later I cannot understand why I thought Whitman either mystical or religious. He is a naturalist throughout [Author].

right now I'm entering very deeply into a new set of ideas. In other words, I'm saying that I'm going to have a book in a couple of years, a real book. Because for me, a book is a very real thing; it's a living organism and it's produced from a new set of ideas. There's a physical rhythm. I have to go through a certain seven-year span of gathering ideas for a new phase and coming into it again. And I think I'll do this all my life. Undoubtedly, when I say I'm not mystical, I'm exaggerating. I've had moments, and tried to represent them. But I love this world. I don't like asceticism. I don't eat much, because I'm just too vain to get very, very plump. It's sheer vanity, that's all. There's nothing mystical about it. And I think I go through these rhythms. Somebody should study something like this. You see, critics never talk about things like this, but I wish they would. These are fascinating questions, about a man's creative rhythm, and the letdowns in between. Literary critics should get together, for example, with psychiatrists more than they do. And they should get together with religious leaders more, and bring back into literary criticism some real ideas. Robert Bly has been very important—he can also be infuriating to me, but he's very important—because he's been willing to cross these borders and to bring into literary criticism a lot of deep ideas. Now I don't agree with Robert on certain ideas. He's a Jungian. I don't like that. But still, he does it. I do it too, in my own way. This fascinates me. Poems do not come out of just talking about meter. That's the smallest thing. Poems come out of a lot of preoccupations.

You were talking about your cycles, the "ages of man" cycles of your books. Donald Hall was remarking that he thinks that your new poems, like "Searching for the Ox," are a synthesis of the best of all the past—that is, of the newer conversational style as well as the "deep image" style. Is that true?

I don't know. He might be right, but I'll tell you one thing, I sure ain't going to think about it much. If I think in those terms, I'll get too self-conscious about it. I really only have the problem of writing the poems. And that's what I've got to do.

No critical thinking while writing. Is that right?

Not that kind of critical thinking.

Everyone Knows But the Poet
(What Poetry Is)
An Interview with Kraft Rompf

Do you still hold to your definition of poetry as thought set to rhythm?

It would not be just any thought. You see, the problem with anything you might say about poetry is that it's not comprehensive. And quite often it is a matter of degree that makes something poetry, rather than kind. Now, you can set many thoughts to rhythm and they wouldn't be poetry at all. It would be a certain thought expressed with a certain kind of intensity; it is very much a matter of emotion that makes something poetic or not.

There has been a movement in your poetry away from rhyme and meter. Why?

There was a period from about 1949, between *The Arrivistes* and the 1959 book, *A Dream of Governors*, when I worked very intensely on formal poems with stanzas and rhyme. I think part of it was because the critics beat up on me so much for *The Arrivistes*, for being too free. Also the spirit of the time was such

---

This interview first appeared in *Falcon* 7, no. 12 (Spring 1976).

that there was a great emphasis on form. And it was a challenge.

Did you find any problems in reconciling meter with the American landscape?

No. It doesn't have to do with the subject whether you use rhyme or not. It has to do with your feelings. Some of the most rugged landscape in the world has the most formal poetry. There is no correlation between the thing you're writing about and the freedom with which you write about it. That depends entirely on you and the methods available. You can hardly imagine a more rugged landscape than that the Welsh or Scottish bards had to deal with, and yet their poetry was extremely formal. Americans think they have a big primitive country, and therefore art for them must be naive. This is a complete fallacy. Primitive societies did not have simple art, they had very sophisticated forms of art.

Do you think the artist might be a throwback to a kind of primitive man who insists on defining the world in his own terms?

No, because the primitive artist did not redefine the world. That was exactly what he did not do. The primitive artist grew up in a society where things were known, values were known, and his relationships to other persons were predetermined. He was not experimental in our terms. He came from a very stable culture, too stable in fact. There were certain known things he could do; anything else was not acceptable.

In your poem "The Peat-Bog Man" you give an image of the primitive artist:

> *Yet, there is delicacy in the features*
> *and a peaceful expression . . .*
>
> *that in Spring the flower comes forth*
> *with a music of pipes and dancing.*

He had a definite function; he was a consort of the mother goddess figure, the moon. He was a magician and a poet, and at the end of his time he was executed ritually by garroting. However, he was fulfilling a seasonal function; it wasn't up to him to decide if things would grow again in spring. He would perform the magic which would enable it to happen, but he found the magic and he left it behind him when he went. He didn't make it up.

To get back to rhyme and meter for a moment, do you feel people no longer need it to help them through longer poems the way they did during an oral tradition?

Yes. We have printing now, which makes things permanent. But you know there is a form of rhyme that people still seem to demand today. You find it turning up in popular songs—just rhyming for its own sake. We have a childlike need for that.

Could rhyme make a poem more accessible?

To the general person, yes, the person who does not read poetry but can remember a song. To some people anything that rhymes is a poem.

You mentioned earlier your fear of getting prosy in your new poems. Do you think the old poets avoided that problem through rhyme?

They had the problem and didn't know it. When people attack modern poetry as being unreadable they don't remember how much of that old stuff was terrible. A poet could go along for pages and pages rhyming away, writing prose with a jingle at the end. Many of the books written in the eighteenth and nineteenth centuries were written in impeccable rhyme and were really flat unreadable junk.

Did the novel in any way purify poetry?

Certainly the narrative started moving out of poetry into prose by the eighteenth century.

Do you find that the poet needs the narrative or a strong rhythmical device to help him sustain a longer poem?

I think so. If you're not working in a regular form which moves by itself you have to move the poem from point to point by some sort of dramatic or narrative art. It may be a very subtle kind of drama or narrative, but it has to be there. It may even be a drama of ideas, but it has to move.

How do you deal with those lines in your longer poems, those words which set up lyrical passages?

This is a very hard thing to describe, but it is the voice, the sense of a presence still there. It may not be doing a great deal, but that sense of presence must be felt.

The difficult thing for me in a poem is not the individual phrases or images; it is the structure of the poem. I must have an overall structure which enables me to get everything I want to say across as a whole. Once that is settled the poem is no problem for me. I usually have the details long before I have the structure. Now as to these passages, once I have the overall structure I just let things come together, and they do link up pretty well.

In your poem "Doubting" you separate the poem into clusters. Is this a way of sidestepping the issue?

Yes, there are certain clusters which look like little poems but not one of them says completely what you want to say; just put by itself it would be misleading.

I know when I am writing well because I start to trust the reader. When you start to have a sense of the reader, a strong sense that you can trust this person, this mind listening to you, then you can move in all directions. I find when I do not have a sense of the listener I try to explain everything and the poem goes dead.

In North of Jamaica *you state if the poet wants to write better poems he should lead a better life. Would this in any way tie into your concept of movement?*

Oh, yes. You're not the only one who's remarked on that. One critic remarked that my attitude there was rather unusual. It seems to me obvious that poems are written by poets. It's an unfortunate fact that you just have to be a poet to write poetry. What does this mean? It means you have to be in a poetic mood to write a poem. However, this can be misunderstood, and often is, by writers. They think this means they have to be in a exalted mood or out of their mind. This is a mistake. This is not a poetic mood; it's OK for a party but has nothing to do with writing a poem. The kind of poetic mood I'm talking about is that state where you can make connections. In your own life you may be quite depressed but you may be in a good mood to write or finish a poem. In fact, Eliot when he finished *The Waste Land* was in just such a mood. In fact he was ill. Somehow in his case that illness removed certain prohibitions, which enabled him to write. It may very well be that your feeling of good health and well being and functioning is a very unpoetic mood and very antithetical to poetry because the will may not let the something real come through.

Something may obsess you, and when you are obsessed with a poem you may be quite unable to finish it because you are trying to will it finished. But if you're distracted something real may creep to the surface and take over. You have to learn how to try and how not to try. The will, sometimes, must be suspended and something more deep and perhaps more casual must be allowed to come through.

A reader must sense that the man writing the poem really knows what he's doing. If the man writing the poem wants too hard to write a good poem it's like watching someone dancing who can't dance, stumbling all over himself with the effort. The strain, the effort, must never show. The wish to be a poet must never show in poetry. That is why so many would-be poets are bad; you can see they want to be known as poets. They use the conventions of poetry, the conventions of their time. They assume the postures of an avant-garde. The bad poet today knows that he shouldn't sound like Yeats or Eliot or Pound or Williams. What he does not know is that he is merely conventional in a new way. There are poets writing today who sound like Bly or Merwin or Kinnell. It is hard to spot the conventions of your own time, but in another generation these people will be seen as mere imitators.

When the poet does not write from his own real life does he alienate himself from his society or tribe?

There is a great divorce between poet and community in our society. That's why you see some poets going into Indian poetry, for example. I don't mean Indian poets, I mean poets who twenty years ago would have been trying to write like Eliot, now writing like a Sioux Indian. It won't work; you have to really live into something before it works.

And it's silly; there are communities all around them, but they don't write about that. They don't know how to. They *do* belong to a tribe, a tribe that uses automobiles. But they don't recognize it and don't know how to handle it.

Every generation has its own forms of imitation but can't recognize them. It'll take about thirty years. Now the most fashionable one is a belief in some sort of magic; the poem which is reduced to a minimal statement about stones, or earth, or a tree branch. This is ridiculous among people who live in the most varied manner, who use machines. But they don't talk about that; American poets want to be pure, and then they impoverish themselves.

Has poetry become too pure, too pristine?

Sometimes poets feel they can't make contact with the general public and therefore retire into some kind of a limited operation. This is a mistake in two ways. First, poets should recognize that they will never make contact with the general public, at least not in this civilization, and number two, this shouldn't bother them at all. A poet will never be happy until he realizes he will not be accepted by the general public. But that doesn't mean he has to write about twigs or rabbits for the rest of his life; he can still write about the general life he has. You cannot write well unless you write about your own time and age. You cannot talk about eternity until you can talk about the present moment.

You have just finished a book on Pound; do you consider it a weakness that his imagery and language were so strongly influenced by the past?

I'm glad you brought that up; we should get it out in the open. When I speak of writing about your own age it may seem that I mean that modern subjects are better. I don't mean subjects. I'm not talking about writing about automobiles and dishwashers rather than writing about the marriage at Cana of Galilee. When I say a man must write for his own age I mean he must know the spirit of his own time. In 1975 a man may be writing about something that happened 700 years ago, but the spirit in which he writes must speak for the people of today. I'm talking about the spirit. Pound was very modern when he wrote about China and Provençe; he was extremely modern in his attitude, in his spirit. That was what made him a great modern poet—not the subject. It's the mood and feeling that you have, the sense of what is important to people of your own time. The subject doesn't matter. You can write the most modern poem in the world right now about the crucifixion of Christ; it could be an absolutely modern poem. And yet you could write the most old-fashioned poetry about the workings of an automobile factory. The Russian novel between 1930 and 1940 under Stalin was the most old-fashioned novel possible. They were writing about factories and tractors, but they were writing without any feeling of the twentieth century. A man like Proust, however, writing in 1914 about a society prevalent in 1880, with new psychological insights, was an innovative and modern writer. The subject is never the question. The question is ideas and feeling; those are the important things; they are what make a man modern.

And in respect to language, Pound was trying to break up a dead kind of speech. What he was trying to do was smash up a Victorian or neo-Romantic literary language that had become standardized in English, that you found in London in 1910. In order to do that he established new rhythms and possibilities for using words. He used archaic words when he thought it would shock or break up the old ideas of what language was. He reached for everything he could think of. And his sense of the line was extraordinarily new. He talked about free verse better than anyone I've ever heard describe it. He talked about an inner sense of the line, that this was what really made the greatest poets.

To work back to your poetry for a moment. "A Story About Chicken Soup" took you ten years to write. Why?

I didn't work on it for ten years, except inside my-self. There are certain things you have a vague idea you can do, but you're not right for them yet, you're not old enough, you're not . . . you haven't settled certain attitudes inside yourself: how do you really feel? It happens differently to people. In the case of Rimbaud, within one year he discovered how he felt towards almost everything. For the rest of us it takes years to work things out. For that little poem I had to determine how I felt about World War II, my part in it, what had actually happened to me at certain points; I had to think about my grandmother, and I had to come to terms with how I felt about my Jew-ish background.

Does this then tie in with your concept of the proper mood?

You have to live and write. It's no use working out ideas when your tools aren't there when you need them.

In Death In Venice *we find Ashenbach working three hours in the morning every day. Would you say this is necessary?*

No. First of all Ashenbach was a writer of prose. I would say for a prose writer this is pretty true. I know that when I write prose I have to do that. Last year I wrote a book, and every day in the morning I spent four hours at the typewriter at least. With po-etry it's different. The work of poetry goes on when you're walking around, you know, when you're talk-ing to people. It goes on all the time. The work of poetry is thinking of yourself as a poet. This is why I've had a lifelong quarrel with writing schools. This is something they never mention, because actually it's a little bit frightening. It's asking a lot of young people, but it's the one thing that should be asked. It's the one important thing, and, incidentally, it wouldn't frighten young people. The only people it frightens are instructors in the universities. Let's say you do have a poetry writing workshop. You have to ask them, do you know what being a poet means? It doesn't mean getting a certain number of poems published in a magazine. You must say to them this is a very important thing you're considering, it's just as important as if you decided to be a heart specialist or a saint. It means you have to think of yourself as a poet. Now this doesn't mean you have to walk around with a solemn look on your face, telling everyone you are a poet like so many of my contemporaries do, but that you have a reason for living, a special way of looking at things and that you have a duty to say these things. It is expected of you; the public may not expect it of you, but somewhere it is expected of you that you do this. It is a mission.

What are your writing habits?

Well, you just saw them. I come in here in the morning right after breakfast, about 8:30, and I sit down and work for a couple of hours on poetry.

Do you do this every day?

I do it three or four days a week. There may be a year when I don't do it at all. Last year I worked on a book of prose, but this year I'm back to normal. I come in here and work a couple of hours and stop when I get bored. I don't stop exactly when I hit a difficulty, but if I see that for a half an hour I've just been sitting around, I stop. I just stop. I write to the point where I enjoy it and then I stop. If it starts to get too damned difficult or cantankerous I cut it out before I drift into prose.

Did the opposite ever happen?

It can become obsessive. The results aren't very good. As you see, I fill up whole boxes of poems that don't work out. But then I stop battering my head against the wall. I'll pick the poem up three years later and work on it. That often works out.

Does taking time off from poetry help you with your poetry?

It helps me a great deal. It doesn't help other people though, so they tell me. I know people who are terrified by the idea that if they don't say they're a poet, or try to be a poet all the time, they'll stop being a poet. I think that's kind of laughable myself.

Last year when I was working on sections of this long poem, "Searching for the Ox," I was battering away and couldn't finish. Then I went away for a year and came back and wrote it without any problem; things just fell into place.

You once remarked that the poetry written today is the most difficult to write because the poet must always start from scratch. Would you still say that's true?

Yes I think that's true. Each of us has to develop his own style, his own interest, whereas in the old days society gave you things to do and certain ways in which to do them. Now each poet is on his own.

There is an emphasis on originality. In the art world paintings have to be original in order to sell. Marxist critics make this point: Christopher Cauldwell—and I don't agree with him—attacked surrealism for being a capitalist enterprise. He said it was what happened when there was a complete alienation between the writer and his community. The writer would go in for experiments, anything to attract attention. I don't think this is the case in South American or European communities where surrealism is understood.

However, we do seem to stress originality. Or do we now? I'm saying something that isn't quite true. There is a kind of poetry written in the last fifteen years, in which one poet sounds exactly like another. What is the difference between poems by Michael McClure and Philip Whalen? Sometimes it's impossible to tell. They write in a style that is accepted among friends as a way of talking.

But for most poets in the twentieth century the object is to seem original. Now this is an odd, anti-communal activity, wanting to seem unlike everyone else. The idea that art should be completely original is very antisocial. Actually it is a form of capitalism: you're going to build up your own particular way of making something which no one can duplicate, and then you're going to be rich and famous. That's the mentality behind it.

Could this stress on originality be a reason for so much obscurity in contemporary poetry?

It is the explanation, and it is an explanation why so many young poets are unhappy with poetry. It's not giving them much satisfaction, and the reason is this damned notion that they must solve all of life, be completely original. Now I'm not arguing for mediocrity, I'm arguing against the belief that novelty is all-important. This is putting emphasis on the wrong thing. Instead of thinking so much about seeming original, poets should give themselves more to the subject, to the feeling, and say to themselves, "I want to express something."

Erica Jong, in an article about Anne Sexton, said that we are all writing one continuous poem, all the poets in America. Now that's a nice sentimental remark, but I would hate to think I was writing the same poem some people I know are writing, an extension of it. I would feel that I had failed as a poet unless I had done something of my own. I believe you should be original. At the same time it's a depressing and antisocial idea if it's over emphasized.

Is it a question of degrees?

It's a matter of where you put the stress. If they would think more of looking and feeling and getting the thing down on the page, then we could look at it and see it and hear it and touch it and worry less about what the hell the style was or the current was or what was passing for original these days. As I said, I'm writing these poems about New York, and I'm sure they are not like anyone else's, but that's not what I'm doing it for. I'm doing it because I've had certain experiences that I've never read about, a sense of the atmosphere of New York over a period of about fifteen years that I want to get down.

The concept of locale plays heavily in your books of poetry; there is a wide range, landscapes of war, of modern America, and lately of Russia.

A book is an organism, a separate entity. Every time I put together a book I go through a new complex of ideas. It's not enough when making a new book just to put together a bunch of good poems. The book has to be rooted in time and place.

Concerning Buch der Lieder, *Heine said the arrangement was as important as the poems themselves.*

Definitely. Wallace Stevens said much the same thing. The book I'm writing now, it's only within the last six months that I've seen it coming together as a book. The poems are starting to relate to each other. Sometimes between two poems there is a missing link—there should be another poem in there somewhere. It's exciting but it takes me years to get to that point. It takes four or five years of writing poetry and then about two more in which they begin to come together. I eliminate certain things and I add certain things. It takes me about six years to write a new book of poems, which I know is an appalling thought to some people.

In many of your poems the surface image is uncertain; the words pull into different levels of thought. For example the last five lines of "On The Lawn At The Villa":

> *We were all sitting there paralyzed*
> *In the hot Tuscan afternoon,*
> *And the bodies of the machine-gun crew were draped over the*
>   *balcony.*
> *So we sat there all afternoon.*

I think I'm a natural surrealist. I don't think I learned it. The parts of my poetry that have a surrealist effect did not come from reading the surrealists; actually I hadn't read them with the exception of Apollinaire, who isn't really a surrealist. His connections are too logical for real surrealism.

Is surrealism a quality of the surface or the spirit?

It should be a quality of the spirit if it's any good at all. It has been used as a surface mechanisim by the French surrealists, but it is a quality within, a movement away from rational connection to a realm of connection equally valid. If you were a disciple of Freud or Jung you could call this realm the unconscious or the preconscious or the subconscious. But it certainly is an instinctive sense of connections which we find hard to explain and should not try to explain. They do work in poetry if they are real. The person listening feels they are real; they can feel there is a flow in the poetry from one thing to another. Bad surrealist poetry is mechanically constructed; there is no flow, no real connection.

Is this one of the problems of the New York poets?

They operate, deliberately, in a very narrow range. They do not want to seem to be taking themselves seriously. Facetiousness is the quality they achieve. I agree with C. S. Lewis; talking about what he called flippancy, he said it excites little affection among those who practice it. I agree with that.

Would you agree that humor is one of your concerns? I'm thinking of your poem "The Redwoods":

> *O if there is a poet*
>
> *let him come now! We stand at the Pacific*
> *like great unmarried girls,*

turning in our heads the stars and clouds,
considering whom to please.

Humor for me is a rich and deep and nourishing thing. I do write humorous poetry. What does that mean? It doesn't mean it's not serious. It means I'm trying to get the quality into poetry that Chekhov gets in prose, a range of life that admits humor. Now one of my quarrels with some contemporaries who are going into what I call cult writing, like the imitation Indian poem, is that you can't write that way and have any humor at all. You are trying to be very solemn and wise and magical and therefore cannot at all admit real life, and you cannot admit humor. They strike me as deadly dull.

Roethke said the poet should work all facets of the language, from the joke to the epic. Would you agree?

I think so. But when you set yourself up solemnly, when you're faking an attitude you don't really possess, humor is the one thing you cannot allow to enter. So you get back to purity, the so-called pure poem, which is rather dull and thin. There is no substance or life in it. You're trying to be too significant, too important. You should try to forget this and write something that really connects with human feelings. The complexity of human feeling is what you should try to get into poetry.

When you're writing you discover things. I'm writing a poem right now about having an interview with an author. I just invented this idea while you were sitting there. The author tells me—I'm the editor—that literary agents have been stealing his ideas, that's why he no longer has them. This line was a pure find. I just found it in the writing.

Accidents have played a good part in many poems. Can you think of other examples from your work?

In the poem "On the Lawn of the Villa" there is this line: "Perhaps, after all, this is not the right subject for a poem." I was writing the poem, and I said to myself it's not working out, this is not the right subject for a poem. But instead of just saying it to myself, I typed it into the poem. And it's perfect in its place. It works absolutely in its place. That was accident, if you like. The accident was that a thought I didn't think should go into the poem went into it all the same. A lot of people when they are writing are having thoughts which they're censoring out all the time. I know one American having a boom right now; when I listen to him reading his poems I am conscious that the man reading the poems is no more than half the man I meet afterwards at the party. He has eliminated from his poems a great deal of himself. I think it's a pity; he's kept the solemn, pure self in the poetry, but the man I see standing around talking to people is not in the poetry, and I find the man in the poems impoverished for that reason.

Does this in any way tie in with your concept of the poet pushing too hard?

Audiences love someone who takes himself solemnly, adopts a pose. They like it as a performance, but when I say you must think of yourself as a poet all the time, I'm not saying you must become a solemn, self-conscious man. I mean you must be really thinking.

Seriousness is not an indication of quality.

Awareness is what makes it, not seriousness.

Most of your awareness always seems to be rooted in the physical world; the last stanza of "Port Jefferson," for example:

> *This is the place, Camerado,*
> *that hides the sea-bird's nest.*
> *Listening to the distant voices*
> *in summer, a murmur of the sea,*
> *I seem to remember everything.*

When I write I try to keep to visible images or things we could actually experience. But at the same time I like to give a level of life behind the visible. And this must be what poetry does. Obviously poetry could not just be description; there would be no need for it. It must be trying to reveal something behind appearances. I do not like poetry which does not present the visible world because there is no key. If you omit the visible world there is no sense of reality. If you try to leap directly into the mysterious, without dealing with the things we see and touch, then you cannot arrive at anything universal. The universal must include the particular, the local. On the other hand, if you just write about the trivial without giving the sense of mystery, why bother?

If you try to go directly to the universal, the meaningful, leaving out the particulars, when you get there you have a big hole. Poetry is a way of connecting. Poets are very different from religious people. Religious people don't need the here and now. Their object is to get away from it and to get beyond it into mystery directly. The artist is not a religious man. He may believe in religion; he may be motivated by it largely, but in the practice of his art he cannot operate the way a saint operates. The artist must cherish this world; this is what art is made of. Now I'm not saying an artist is a better man, just a different kind of mind. The artist is attached to this world.

A lot of the young people in the sixties who were involved with mysticism and today are involved with mysticism are profoundly antiartistic. To them, art with its involvement with technique, its involvement in making, is an interruption. They want to be happy. But the artist is not so concerned with making people happy; he is concerned with making.

Therefore, he must stay in touch with the senses. I know in my own writing I try to develop images, and that must be done by looking around me for a long time. I try to make the reader concentrate on the image itself. Now there is something very Buddhist about this technique. The Buddhist sees eternity here and now. I try to create images which speak now and for a long time. Someone who comes to them in a hurry will not be struck by my poems, but if he went back to them he'd see they're not that simple. There's something going on under the surface, and if you look at it it will start to unroll, all these layers of feeling and thought that I put into it.

How do you define the poet?

He has to be a certain kind of man or woman who believes he has a mission to make sense out of things.

The world is always incoherent. He is someone whose job it is to pull it together and make a whole of it that has meaning for other people.

Is there a difference between pulling together and explaining?

It's not the poet's job to say why things are the way they are. I think it's his job to show how things are beneath the surface of appearances. What is really happening.

Does this ever happen in spite of himself?

Yes. Every writer has the experience of writing something, intending one thing, and finding himself compelled during the process of writing to turn it another way. This is the real excitement of poetry, that you may sit down with one idea and wind up with a completely different thing.

At what point do you stop rewriting a poem?

I think one thing a poet should do is stop messing with his own poems. Once I've written a poem and it's printed in a book, I'm through with it. That's not true when I've printed in a magazine; I've rewritten or discarded many poems that have been printed in a magazine. If I've printed a poem in a book I might change a word or two when I do it again for some other book, but that's rare. I leave them alone. Let's say you're twenty-one or twenty-eight when you write a poem; you have certain awkwardnesses but they are part of your age; they ring true. You go back and smooth that out and what you wind up with is something that is neither that which you wrote at twenty-one or what you would write at forty-one. Also the impulse towards constant revision is a very bad one. What are you trying to do? Present a static image of yourself to the world? You were never perfect, finished, or shouldn't have been. So why try to make yourself seem so?

How about the poet of lilacs and the bleeding throat to whom you refer so often in your own work? Didn't he spend most of his life rewriting Leaves of Grass?

He added to the *Leaves;* I don't think you could say he rewrote it as much as you could say that he added to it. Using the original volume as a seed, he wrapped around it layer upon layer. You know some of his old-age poems are just magnificent. There's one I've never seen in any anthology and which I'm very sorry I never put into *An Introduction to Poetry.* It's about eight lines and he's an old man. I have constipation, he says, and I'm terribly sad to think now that I'm growing old I'll give way to whimpering like an old man. But I hope this will not happen to me, he goes on, that I will be able to continue singing my songs. It could have been written in 1975 by some frank, intimate writer. And written in the most natural language.

On his death bed Renoir reportedly said he didn't even know what a drawing was anymore, which seems a terribly honest statement.

That might well hold true for a poet also; everybody else knows and keeps telling him what a poem is. Critics know, professors know. But the poet writes the poem and then doesn't know anymore, until the next time. He never knows what it is; he has to work it out every time. A poet keeps writing because he doesn't know what a poem is.

The deeper you get into something and the more complicated it becomes, the harder it is to accept anything that is said about it. When you're a kid they tell you that this is what a painting is, or what a poem is, and you believe them. Then if you really get involved with these things, and you see different kinds of poetry—Chinese poems, Yugoslavian poems—you see that all sorts of things can be poetry. So a definition of what poetry *is* becomes more and more difficult to make. Ultimately people think you a kind of fool. And then almost anyone can come along and tell you anything.

I have a definition of an intelligent person and a fool which I apply frequently. A man who says to you, "Have you read Marx or the New Testament?" is a fool. I always assume on the part of the other person that he knows more than I do. A fool always assumes he's read a book no one else has. He's read a book by Dickens and sits down and lectures you on Dickens: "You should read Dickens some time." This is a fool.

Do you find at the academy things escalate from Dickens to Rilke?

Oh yes. I've been lectured over and over by people to read Rilke or Jung. These people assume you've read nothing.

The irony perhaps being that both Rilke and Jung make no claims on what art or poetry is.

The fool knows very early what the answer is to everything. How do people get so vain? The artist never knows; that is why when some of my contemporaries become assertive on a platform, or when they start to get a little group around them, I immediately see an apple start to go rotten. I begin to suspect they've passed into this realm of folly. I can teach but I can never band together with followers. I would start to hear myself and feel ridiculous. I would rather listen. I want to continue learning, not defend a position. There are real leaders, of course; but when a man starts laying down the truth he had better be the real thing, because if he isn't the very, very real thing, then he is a fool and misleads others. How does he know if he's the real thing or not? That's the chance he takes. I have never taken that chance. Maybe I don't know enough. Maybe I don't think I know enough. On the other hand, maybe it's a great vanity. Maybe I think, well if they come to it, fine; if they don't, I don't give a damn.

In your poetry you do reach out to the reader. In the poem "After Midnight," in the last two stanzas, we run into an image that reaches far beyond itself:

> *Who lives in these dark houses?*
> *I am suddenly aware*
> *I might live here myself.*
>
> *The garage man returns*
> *And puts the change in my hand,*
> *Counting the singles carefully.*

Yes, that poem and that ending seem to me to be absolutely valid. You know there are certain poems you write which you feel are so true that you could give them to somebody else. You don't care that you wrote them. And that's one I feel like that about. The poem is completely valid, and the ending is exactly what I want from an image, which is that it be, perfectly, something anyone could recognize. Any modern man would recognize a garage attendant counting back dollar bills into your hand after you've paid for your gas. At the same time it has a depth of feeling behind it. Now I haven't defined what that feeling is; I've left it hanging there because it should hang there at midnight outside the garage. This is what poetry is supposed to do for me; it reveals the life behind appearances. Certain things are upsetting to you, or exhilarating to you, that you don't quite understand as the writer. At that moment you are finding out as much as the reader. The image of the dollar bills has at least three kinds of meaning that I don't want to explain. But I know they are there.

Do you feel that if you explained them the reader would no longer be able to realize the poem for himself?

That's right. I think you should not explain too much because, as you well know, the things you write are quite often a choice among several alternatives, and even when you have made that one choice the alternatives are still hanging around and you should leave them there. I try to make my poems absolutely clear with these images, and to concentrate the attention upon those images the way a Buddhist in meditation concentrates. Of course the quick readers, those who want a lot of words—there are too many words in American poetry—will slide over my poems.

Do you feel one of the poet's concerns is to create a link between the past and present?

I have a great belief in tradition. I know it's not fashionable to say this, but I can't imagine anyone living in the present with any intensity who does not have a sense of the past. The poet must also show the link to the future. The future as far as we know is just a gas with no reality. But we live in the present with all the excitement of the life that's come to us from the past.

What about T. S. Eliot's technique of tying the past into the present by taking the lines of other poets and putting them into his own work?

That's fine. That was done by Chinese and Japanese poets for hundreds of years. Nothing wrong with that. He never intended to deceive. Eliot's position is an interesting one; he was a poet for the community. Eliot was using lines by other poets because he felt they were all working in one continuous process. He was using the poetry of the past as communal property. Now if you believe poetry is your own private possession and that you're going to make a killing out of it—you know, big capitalist or rock star—then of course you don't want to use anyone else's lines, and you don't want them to use yours. You charge like hell. Eliot felt as anybody would who has a sense of tradition. Tradition is the same as community. It means doing things together with other people, not against them.

In North of Jamaica *you mention how the Celtic bards*

learned to compose: someone placed a stone on their chests and they would then have to sing praises.

A *real* poetry workshop would be a great thing. If I ran a writing workshop or if I taught writing, which I don't, the first year would be given to not writing at all. It would be given to requiring the students to read key works and discuss them for a year. They would have to have read the Bible. They would have to have read the Buddhist writings. They would have to have done certain meditation exercises. They would have to have taken long walks with a friend. Maybe I would even demand they take care of an animal. I would do all sorts of things like that before I asked them to write poetry. They could have alternatives—learn to ride a horse, learn to sail, perhaps build furniture. I would give them definite tasks. But I don't teach writing because no university takes it seriously. Their idea of writing is so stupid. If I came to a department meeting with these ideas, they would think I was out of my mind. But anyone who knows something about life and poetry knows this is the only way you make poets, if you can make poets at all. If I ran a writing school I would make them do emotional exercises, physical exercises. Young people still have an antiuniversity attitude, and they are right in respect to the arts, because universities like the prestige and money of running art schools, but God knows they don't want any serious involvement.

In the poem "The Foggy Lane" you state in the first two lines,

> *The houses seem to be floating*
> *in the fog, like lights at sea.*

and then you conclude,

> *Walking in the foggy lane*
> *I try to keep my attention fixed*
> *on the uneven, muddy surface . . .*
> *the pools made by the rain,*
> *and wheel-ruts, and wet leaves,*
> *and the rustling of small animals.*

Could this be interpreted as your way of looking at life and art?

I recently quoted that as a statement of my poetic belief. By the uneven surface I mean life; it's uneven and it's muddy, and I keep my attention fixed on it rather than on a dream.

If I can state a problem truly in a poem I feel I've written the poem. I try to state the answer but I never arrive at it. What I really think I'm doing in poems is presenting a situation or a problem as clearly as possible or giving the reader a sense that different things are coming together at this point. Many of my poems end with a statement, but it's a dramatic statement. I write very much in the dramatically narrative form. My poems are human beings in a certain situation, so if I do make a statement it is understood that it is in relation to this time, this place, this action—not my personal final solution. God I hate that phrase—remember, Hitler had the final solution to the Jewish question. It is characteristic of the Judaic tradition that you do not come up with final solutions. You leave that up to God. In that respect I am a Jewish writer. A lot of my poems end with a shrug that says I don't know. On the one hand, yes; on the other hand, yes, and I don't know which way to choose. And damn it, that's how we live. I don't know any people who go through life with a view of life. I know people who go through life with a lot of ideas. I have general ideas myself which sound sappy actually; I know they're right, but they don't help people—love, forgiveness, things like that.

But you know the poem has a reality which is not that of life; it creates its own world. The symbolists were right to a large extent; when you enter a work of art you enter something which creates its own reality. Discussion of philosophy and religion is very nice, but any writer knows damn well that when he sits down to deal with a poem he is dealing with a particular work which has certain limits and certain breadths which he has to understand. You are as much at the mercy of the work of art as a man working on a car. You have to deal with the material. That's why writing is such a back-breaking task. You can have the best attitudes and the most comprehensive soul, but if you can't write, forget it.

What do you do to help you with your writing?

I read. I read good writers. I'm filled with envy all the time. But they are such great friends. I'm conscious of their presence. I never envied Tolstoy. He was a magnificent, formidable human being, but I never felt his presence, any sympathy, although I love his writing. Well, I don't love it, I admire it. On the other hand there are some writers who I feel sometimes when I am writing would have understood the shade of emotion I'm after: Chekhov,

Conrad, Keats. Apollinaire? I don't know. He was too busy to pay attention to anyone else but himself.

I love paintings. I know very little about music, but painting I feel I'm an instinctive expert on. I'm probably wrong. But I've looked at a lot of paintings. I've often thought of writing a poem the way one thinks of a painting: landscape, people sitting in a room. I'm much more tolerant of painters than I am of poets. They don't make me feel that I have to work. Looking at the work of a writer in your own time you always feel that you have to go out and do some work, not because you're competing, but maybe he knows something you should know.

On the other hand music is very exciting. It gives you the feeling you must write big poems. I listen to Shostakovich and I say, my God where is that huge poem I should be writing? How can this man pour out such stuff? I have the same feelings, why can't I pour out ten pages?

What poetry are you working on now?

Whatever it is I'm probably going to be told that it's just like the rest of my poetry, although I work on each poem as hard as I can to make it new. I'm working on individual poems. There are certain groupings. I'm working on a manuscript; it's broken into four sections. My problem right now is to work on poems about things I've known for about twenty years. I'm trying to write about being in New York in the late 1950s, what it felt like coming off the news-paper shift in the morning. Very heavily narrative. What it was like being a young man seeing all this. It's very exciting to me, like a novel. The second part is the questionable part so far: a lot of poems somehow related to being a poet. And also about American suburban life. The third part is different; it consists of one fairly long poem called "Searching for the Ox," which is about searching for a way of life. And then the fourth part I don't want to talk about because it's not written yet. If I can pull the fourth part off it will be the hat trick.

For the last few days we've been sitting here doing this and you've seen me fuss. It's the same poem I've been working on. I have all the material for it, all the lines, but not in the right way. There are too many lines. I want to eliminate all the flat, unnecessary details. The prose is what I'm working to get out right now. Also I don't want my poems to be satirical. It's very easy to satirize life in the suburbs, for example, or middle-class people. It's very easy to satirize anybody you don't like. This is the easiest possible thing to do. But it isn't even the beginning of the serious work of poetry, which is to show how ridiculous people are and how important they are at the same time. This is what I mean by humor. You can see in a character by Chekhov that the man makes all sorts of foolish gestures and has foolish characteristics. But in a very short time you realize that his life is extremely serious and a tragedy not just for himself but for others also.

There is a poetry of ordinary life we haven't even started to write in America—with exceptions. Williams knew what had to be done and he did it. In the fourth section of the new book I'd like to demonstrate how poetry can be written about the way we actually live, but a poetry that can move to Mt. Sinai in the desert if I want it to.

What advice would you give a young poet?

First of all I'd tell him not to worry about becoming part of the literary world. Definitely not to worry about that. People who spend their time doing that, that's what they spend their time doing. It takes a certain talent. What you ought to worry about is simply the writing. I believe if you write well and you work at it, if you work on your psyche, you'll be published when the time is right. Young people come to me and ask how do you get a book published. I say I don't know; they think I'm being snotty. They say you have to know somebody. I say that's nonsense. It's possible that a poet will get published because he knows somebody, but, believe me, he won't get published the second time. You should be concerned with the writing. Rilke says that you have to get into another dimension and forget about getting published. My poetry goes weak when I start to worry what other people are doing. The minute I start to write I don't care what anybody else does. I don't care if I ever publish, I don't give a damn. And a good thing to learn is not to respond to slander. You realize soon enough that some people are not interested in straightening out a few points. Hecklers, slanderers have their own axes to grind. You can't talk to them; they're not interested in shades of meaning.

Would you recommend seeking out other poets?

Write to your friends. I'm a lousy correspondent but I should do it. And go and see them now and then. You know we're crazy the way we plan our lives. I know writers who would spend a hundred dollars to buy a lens for a camera but wouldn't spend the money to visit another writer, a friend whose work they respected. Take some money if need be and visit a friend. And get something going locally. Find people who like to write and talk to these people.

If you are at a university avoid the English department types. I mean there are good people, but my God an awful lot of them are clods, just unimaginative people who—and there's nothing paranoid about this—hate literature. And they detest the idea that you write. They think you're judging them—with the contempt they would have if they were in your place.

And as you get older avoid becoming that American writer who gets sentimental and foolish and stops trying to be a writer. Can you imagine a man like Cezanne giving up the struggle with technique? Of course not. Or Picasso? Of course not. But the American often falls back on good intentions and the big warm heart of democracy, some damned notion that we are really nice people.

Would you recommend travel?

One of the reasons I like to give a poetry reading now and again is that you get to see a new landscape. It's fine, especially if someone else is driving.

Preface to *Searching for the Ox*

Most of the time I lived at school. There was plenty
to say and do—a hundred and thirty young males
penned within walls on the top of a mountain.

But during vacations, especially the long summers,
days would go by when I hardly spoke to anyone. I
had an older brother. Our parents were divorced.
Our mother had gone back to America and we lived
with our father and stepmother. After a while no
one was invited to the house. Our father was a
lawyer; he was accustomed to dealing with cases; I
suppose that he did not want his own life examined
in the same way. So we were isolated. I spent most of
the days by myself, communing with sea, sky, and
my thoughts. The opening poem in this book, "Ve-
nus in the Tropics," tells of this period.

We lived on Kingston harbor. Stretches of the
shore were unfenced and apparently belonged to no
one. You could walk along the beach without en-
countering another human soul. There were sea
birds and beasts; many of them would be washed up
on shore sooner or later. It wasn't unusual, on look-

This preface first appeared in *Searching for the Ox* by Louis Simp-
son (New York: William Morrow, 1976).

ing up, to see a line of porpoises or the fin of a shark cutting the surface.

I still have dreams in which I am walking on a beach of white sand. There was such a place. To reach it you had to drive out of Kingston on a road that passed through a tunnel. Beyond lay a beach where waves of the outer sea came rolling in. The sand was fine and there were shells of all shapes and colors. There were pieces of flint, and yellow seeds as hard and smooth as stones, and flat brown seeds called "horse eyes." In the dream I am picking them up as fast as I can, for I shall soon have to leave.

Isolation turned me to reading stories and poems. It was stories I was after in either case; I didn't want fine emotions as much as I wanted something to happen to break the silence of the island. I read Conrad's "Youth" and *Typhoon* against a backdrop of palm trees and waves as exotic as any in his tales. But there was a difference: in Conrad there was passion and adventure. I saw none in the life around me.

Therefore I set about creating adventures of my own and setting them down on paper. This may be why I believe that we make our lives by ourselves, their meaning and excitement. It is generally thought that writers have a point of view and write in order to put it across. I am inclined to think the opposite: they write and so create a point of view.

When I first read Camus I was struck by the similarity between his early years in Algeria and mine in Jamaica. In the tropics where nature is everything and man is nothing, a man may decide that he alone is responsible for his life. When I left Jamaica and went to New York I felt a difference between my sense of the world and that held by friends who had grown up in the towns of New

York and New Jersey. They thought in social terms and were aiming to get ahead in the world. Later, when I was in the army and they were in medical school or one of the other professions, I felt the distance increased immeasurably.

Searching for the Ox is in four parts. The first two parts describe the life of a young man coming from a background similar to my own. Poems in the third part are more meditative; they are about a way of life. And the concluding section is made up of poems rising out of my interests as a writer.

Many of the poems are narrative or contain elements of narrative, for I wish to represent life even when there is an idea to be expressed. The idea should be felt, seeming to rise out of an event rather than being imposed.

But though these poems have their origin in things I have seen or heard, they are not, as Gatsby says, "just personal." Poetry has frequently been based on personal experience, but the incident that moves us has been transformed in the telling from the merely personal into a work of art. The poet dares to imagine and to explore the unknown.

Beside the narrative element in these poems, I am struck by how much they attempt to capture the atmosphere of a time, the concrete specificity of a place. I might have put Conrad's words in front of this book: "My task which I am trying to achieve is, by the power of the written word to make you hear, to make you feel—it is, before all, to make you see."

I have moved from place to place. After the war I lived for a while in France—the poem titled "Lorenzo" speaks of this. I worked in a publishing house in Manhattan. In years that followed I lived in Italy, in California, and England. Now from my window I gaze out on the north shore of Long Island.

Walking along the shore I am aware that nothing much has changed. The tide comes in here, across mud flats covered with weeds. The sides of the channel are carpeted with stalks of dead weeds, thick and springy underfoot. There are some boards nailed together, half buried in sand; I sit on them and contemplate the backs of houses on the far side of the channel. A few feet away there's an upheaval in the sand, an inch-high eruption. A living creature slides up and halfway out. A saffron-colored packet. It's the flash of its withdrawal, however, that really makes you know it's alive.

Then I notice there are holes in the sand all around. A dozen tunnels with alternative exits. Down there it must be like the photographs you used to see of the Maginot Line underground: long tunnels with pale Frenchmen playing cards, looking up at the photographer. *"Drôle de guerre!"*

Sea and shore are the same. If I followed them around I would come to the shore where I used to walk as a boy. But I have changed; I am different from the boy and the man I used to be, the one I call Peter.

These changes cry out for a life that does not change. The less we are at home in the world, the more we bear witness to that other life.

Rolling Up

For some time American poets have been writing almost exclusively about their personal lives. We have become accustomed to poets' telling us what they are doing and thinking at the moment. The present moment is everything—there is no sense of the past. Nor is there any sense of a community. If poetry is the language of a tribe, it seems there is no longer a tribe, only a number of individuals who are writing a personal diary or trying to "expand their consciousness." But the stress on the individual does not seem to stimulate imagination; we have almost forgotten what it is like to read lyric or narrative poems.

It seems, however, that we are coming to an end of a period. After the life studies, the case histories. . . . We are tired of looking in mirrors. Every year there is a new style in personalities. Everyone exhibits himself, we try to draw attention to ourselves . . . and soon, what does it matter? No one is listening.

In order to feel anything at all, we exaggerate.

This essay first appeared in *American Poets in 1976,* ed. William Heyen (Indianapolis: Bobbs-Merrill, 1976).

And then we don't take pleasure in anything, because we don't believe it.

In order to break out of the prison of the self, poets have tried meditating. Some poets have used drugs. Others have studied the ways of the Indian. It is clear that meditating can make a difference. Fifty years ago in Paris the surrealists used the technique of free association. This released images from the unconscious, or wherever images come from, and enabled them to write more freely. Meditation can have a similar effect. I suspect, however, that poets who rely on drugs for inspiration will exhaust their ability to write. Images may be released, but the desire to arrange them will be weakened. As for images and sounds without an arrangement . . . there is nothing more monotonous than the material produced by chance, if thought and feeling are not brought to bear upon it.

There is much to admire in the life and poetry of the American Indian. But it is not easy for an American of the white middle class to think like an Indian. I would go so far as to say that you can write convincingly only about things that you have been compelled to feel. It is easy to put on the costume of a nation other than your own . . . to share the emotional life of that nation is another thing entirely. Americans like to dress up and play at being what they are not. This has a good side—the social mobility of Americans, which is envied throughout the world, stems from the same impulse. But in poetry the results are not convincing. A hundred years ago Longfellow wrote about the Indian. In some ways "Hiawatha" is an impressive performance, but it remains a performance. Under the feathers and paint there is an American tourist. Ugh.

To read some American poets you would think they lived far away from roads and supermarkets, that they never had the thoughts of the people you meet, that they looked with the eyes of the crow and listened with the ears of the beaver. That their habitation was darkness and their house made of earth and stones. That they were pure in thought and deed.

But the Indian must have lived as a man. I would not be surprised if the Indian had an equivalent for television. He could not always have been thinking about animals and gods and having significant dreams.

Why is it that magical events are always happening in faraway places where we cannot see them?

The reader may think, What harm does it do? If an American poet wishes to think he is a shaman, or imagine he is a moose, what's wrong with it? Shouldn't we welcome the chance to expand our consciousness? Besides, what do we really know about the mind? Why try to set limits to it?

To the contrary, I believe that a great deal is known about the mind and that there is no shortage of consciousness. We have more consciousness than we know how to use. There is, however, a shortage of wisdom. We seem unable to live together without maiming one another. And we are running out of space; we have to learn to live with one another. This goes for people everywhere, not just in the United States. What we need is not to expand consciousness but to increase understanding. And there is no mystery about it—the tools are at hand if we wish to use them. But this would require work, while going on a trip does not. Americans like to go on trips. To the Virgin Islands, the moon, or an Indian reservation, it is all the same—an attempt to escape from necessity, the need to live an intelligent, useful life.

My objection to the pursuit of esoteric knowledge, shamanism and so on, is that it neglects the life right under your nose. While you are playing children's games you cannot think like a man. While the American poet is imitating the language of a tribe to which he does not belong, he is not learning to speak for the tribe to which he does belong. And this, like it or not, is the tribe that uses supermarkets and roads.

Here I must make a confession—but it has a point, it isn't just the expression of a personal grievance. I don't like the tribe that uses supermarkets and roads. These days I find that when I am in the company of Americans, the people down the street, I feel as if I were living in Germany after the gas ovens. With this difference—the Americans got away with it.

I am referring to the recent war. We still haven't paid that bill. The refusal or inability of Americans to atone for their war crimes has brutalized American society. If we can't admit our guilt, what can we admit? It is necessary not to think seriously about anything at all. Consequently, Americans have become callous, violent, and inwardly disgraced. This is not a society that inspires you to write; these are not people who understand poetry.

I seem to have painted myself into a corner: it is necessary for the American poet to write about his tribe, the nation of roads and supermarkets. At the same time, I don't want to.

Here Confucius comes to my aid. Speaking of the philosopher, he says, "When the government is rotten, he rolls up and keeps the true process inside him."

I've been rolling up. But this isn't, as some may think, a refusal to face life. To the contrary, it is the real work that has to be done if poetry, or any feeling life, is to survive. If the nation is to survive we have to recreate a sense of the spiritual, imaginative life that we have lost. My disagreement with the cultists is that what they are talking about has no connection with the life of the nation. There is not the slightest chance that Americans will become Indians. There is not the slightest chance that Americans will cease using household appliances and, instead, attempt to sustain themselves by magic. Therefore poetry written out of these ideas has no reality.

But poets are needed to recreate the image man has of himself and in this way reconstitute the nation. There have been precedents for this. Wordsworth, for example. . . . He was for the French Revolution. Then he was frightened by the bloodshed and went back to England. Subsequently, England declared war on France, on the revolutionary ideals that Wordsworth still cherished. This was a profound shock. He tells us how, during church services when everyone was praying for the success of British arms, he hoped for their disappointment. He felt like a traitor; at any rate, he was cut off in his affections from the people around him. It is hard to imagine a more desolate situation for a poet, and it is the situation American poets have found themselves in for some time. It would be bad enough if poets alone felt so, but what poets feel many other people are feeling too. The United States contains a large number of people who no longer like it.

Wordsworth removed himself from the centers of English culture and went to live in the mountains. In effect, he left England. Then, among the mountains and lakes, he set about creating imaginary men, a race of people in his mind. He imagined men and women who were full of feeling, who communed silently with nature and loved one another. He gave them heartfelt words and high sentences. These people are not found in nature but in the imagination of a poet. Wordsworth's aim was to hold up models for human behavior. He created the nation that he could not find.

In his broodings on human character he perceived new states of feeling. He became a psychologist in poetry and enlarged our sympathies. The political revolution failed—therefore he attempted to replace it with a revolution of feeling. He wished to reveal the deep springs that join one man to another and constitute a real nation. Indeed, if this nation does not exist, there is no other.

Blake was a poet for the sixties—I mean, in America. He was for people who wished to blow their minds. Wordsworth is the poet of life—he shows the way to the future, a community built on human feeling and sympathy.

There was never as great a need for the poetry of feeling as there is in the United States at the present time. By this I mean poetry that addresses itself to the human condition, a poetry of truth, not dreams. The poetry I am speaking about depicts human actions and the way we live. I do not mean poetry that merely talks about the obvious, automobiles and washing machines. Poetry must express the reality behind appearances. The poetry I mean can be subtle and mysterious, but it is related to the way we live. There is as much poetry in a suburb as by a lake, if we have a mind to see it.

As it deals with life, this poetry will frequently be in the form of a narrative. Not a mere relation of external events, but a narrative of significant actions. The poet will aim to convey states of feeling. In our time poets have stayed away from narrative because it has often been merely descriptive—there has been too much dead tissue. But this can be avoided if the poet reveals a situation with no more than a few words, and concentrates on the feeling.

In my attempts to write narrative poetry I have used the rhythms of speech. I bear in mind what it would be like to say the poem aloud to someone else. This helps me to form the lines. At the same time it eliminates confusion—I have to make my ideas clear. I eliminate words out of books, affected language, jargon of any kind.

I have tried to bring into poetry the sense of life, the gestures that Chekhov got in prose. And I have tried to bring in humor. I do not believe that this is common; there is plenty of satire, but this is not what I mean by humor. I have mixed humorous and sad thoughts in my poems, because this is the way life is. People want the sights and sounds of life; they ask for life in poetry. They ask for bread, but instead they have been given stones.

The poem "The Foggy Lane," states my ideas about poetry and its relation to life. By "the uneven, muddy surface" I mean human life. There is no end to the material—the question is what to make of it.

This kind of poetry requires a sacrifice of the individual, his peculiar fantasies. On the other hand, it is an on-going process.

The Foggy Lane

The houses seem to be floating
in the fog, like lights at sea.

Last summer I came here with a man
who spoke of the ancient Scottish poets—
how they would lie blindfolded
with a stone placed on the belly,
and so compose their panegyrics . . .
while we, being comfortable, find nothing to praise.

Then I came here with a radical
who said that everything is corrupt;
he wanted to live in a pure world.

And a man from an insurance company
who said that I needed "more protection."

Walking in the foggy lane
I try to keep my attention fixed
on the uneven, muddy surface . . .
the pools made by the rain,
and wheel-ruts, and wet leaves,
and the rustling of small animals.

The Hour of Feeling

> Love, now a universal birth,
> From heart to heart is stealing,
> From earth to man, from man to earth:
> —It is the hour of feeling.
>
>   Wordsworth, "To My Sister"

A woman speaks:
"I hear you were in San Francisco.
What did they tell you about me?"

She begins to tremble. I can hear the sound
her elbow made, rapping on wood.
It was something to see and to hear—
not like the words that pass for life,
things you read about in the papers.

People who read a deeper significance
into everything, every whisper . . .
who believe that a knife crossed with a fork

This essay first appeared in *Fifty Contemporary Poets: The Creative Process,* ed. Alberta T. Turner (New York: David McKay, 1977). It was written in answer to a questionnaire. Authors were asked, "How many drafts did the poem go through?", "What rhythmical principle did you use?", et cetera.

is a signal . . . by the sheer intensity
of their feeling leave an impression.

And with her, tangled in her hair,
came the atmosphere, four walls,
the avenues of the city
at twilight, the lights going on.

When I left I started to walk.
Once I stopped to look at a window
displaying ice skates and skis.
At another with Florsheim shoes . . .

Thanks to the emotion with which she spoke
I can see half of Manhattan,
the canyons and the avenues.

There are signs high in the air
above Times Square and the vicinity:
a sign for Schenley's Whiskey,
for Admiral Television,
and a sign saying Milltag, whatever that means.

I can see over to Brooklyn and Jersey,
and beyond there are meadows,
and mountains and plains.

The poem began with an experience: living in
New York and working as an editor in a publishing
house. One day a woman came in to pick up a manu-
script that had been rejected. It was a peculiar piece
of writing. She had invented a machine for choosing
a mate. It looked like the electric chair. You put your
prospective partner in it and the pointer swung to a
number. Then you made some calculations. After
that you were supposed to consult astrological
charts. Finally you would consider whether you were
compatible. The whole thing was ridiculous. The
woman, however, did not look like the kind of eccen-

tric you might have expected. She was about thirty, red haired, slender—in fact, quite attractive.

I explained to her why we couldn't publish the manuscript. Then she started to tremble—her elbow rapped on the desk as it does in the poem. I saw that the situation was getting out of hand and tried to calm her down. Then she said, "I hear you were in San Francisco. What did they tell you about me?" I had just come back from a short vacation in San Francisco; she had been told I was there when she called to find out the fate of the manuscript. I saw that I had to deal with a person who was not sane. I wasn't the only one to see it. There was a woman sharing my office; she saw what was up and stayed at her desk during our interview, so as to be a witness if one were needed. At the end the woman with the mating machine took her manuscript and left. I was glad to see her go.

As I say in the poem, such people "by the sheer intensity of their feeling leave an impression." The impression was indelibly etched on my consciousness. A few years ago I began trying to write poetry about this period of my life. In these poems I set out to record images of Manhattan and the atmosphere of the city. I tried to work in this episode in my descriptions. The trouble was, I couldn't see what made this episode and one or two others hang together. It isn't enough to describe, you have to know why. Finally I saw what linked this character and the others: it was a feeling in myself, a sympathy I had for them. The insane view held by this woman was, in its way, an act of poetic imagination. She wished to make events in the real world conform to her vision of things. The doctors' name for her condition was paranoia.

The actual writing of the poem, as with some of my poems, took years. I had no idea how it would work out; I had some images and clusters of lines that I would push around. Sometimes I would think I had a poem in view, then it would disintegrate. I would be ashamed to have people see just how hard it is for me to finish what I consider a real poem. Some of my contemporaries don't have this problem: they write down whatever they feel like writing, hardly revise, if indeed they revise at all, and publish it right away. Some of them are able to publish a book every year or two. It takes me five or six years to finish a book of poems.

I saw the woman in the poem in the early 1950s. The images of New York were accumulated over a span of years. Here is a page from a notebook I kept. You will see the bearing this has on material in the poem.

13 Nov. 1962. Monday

```
B'way & 42nd St. looking North (at my back, Crossroads
Cafe).
Distance: Canadian Club
          Admiral Television Appliances

N. E. corner: Florsheim (on corner)
              Books/Souvenirs
              Trans Continental Airlines Agency
        Globe: Exclusive New York Showing: No Morals/
        Midnight Frolics—strictly adults only
—above, Times Square Bowling Lanes

To West (7th Ave)
        Rialto: First New York showing: West End Jungle,
        the film that London banned—adults only—with
        Naked Terror

          Cameras   Kodak Films
          Records   Columbia Records
```

These notes were a source not only of "The Hour of Feeling" but of two other poems as well, "The Rejected" and "The Springs at Gadara." It sometimes happens that many things are conceived at once.

I don't usually make notes—only when I travel and come upon a scene the details of which strike me as important. As a rule, drafts of unfinished poems—of which I have boxes full—are my notes for future poems.

Here is another entry from the notebook, two pages further on. Again, you will see the connection with "The Hour of Feeling."

```
42nd bet B'way & Ave. of the Americas

Sweetville   candy   U. S. A.   nuts
Ice skates golf hunting ski equipment
American Irving Savings Time
   time          temperature
   12 27             46
   flashes off   flashes on
```

These notes proved useful—notes aren't always useful, they can be a waste of time. But what was much more important in writing about New York was to relive the period imaginatively. This required "immersion." I would imagine myself there, immerse myself in the atmosphere of the time and place, try to see what was significant, concentrate on certain images and eliminate others, and arrive finally at my true feeling about the experience. This is the way I write poetry. I hope also that something will be given to me in the course of writing—something more than I can arrive at by the immersion I have tried to describe. If you recall, Wordsworth said that poetry "takes its origin from emotion recollected in tranquillity." Most people think he said that poetry is emotion recollected in tranquillity. But for Wordsworth, remembering an emotion was only the beginning. Something new would happen in the course of writing—more than could be accounted for in the original experience. Poetry was a discovery, a making, not merely a recollection. I agree with his view of the process. Though I may have done everything I can to get at the truth of an experience, I don't consider that I have a poem unless it begins to excite me by telling me something I haven't consciously known.

Here is a draft of a poem that was never published. It stands halfway between the notes I have given above and the poem "The Hour of Feeling." You can see how I am groping in this draft. In fact, the last line says that I am groping.

SIGNS

```
Standing with his back to the Crossroads Café
this is what he observed:

Signs advertising Canadian Club
and Admiral Television Appliances.
On the North-East corner, Florsheim Shoes.
Books   Souvenirs
Trans Continental Airlines Agency

He observed that the Globe was playing
No Morals and Midnight Frolics Adults Only
Continuing to walk East
past Sweetville Candy U. S. A.,
glancing at his reflection
in a window exhibiting ice skates
golf  hunting  ski  equipment . . . .
               at the American Dwing Savings Bank
He saw that the time was 7:27,
the temperature 46,

and he asked, What does it prove?
```

The corrections above are exactly as they are in the original draft.

Obviously something was lacking in "Signs." What, indeed, did it prove? Years later—just this past year—I began another version of the episode of the woman with the mating machine. I made some changes—the incident took place in a restaurant instead of a publishers' office, and I cut out the business about the manuscript. The mating machine seemed ridiculous, and I didn't want to be satiric—I was after bigger game. In the new poem, after I left the woman and started to walk, I began to notice the signs. The advertisements in the sky, the objects in windows, the avenues, the whole city was charged with her emotion. Not only the city . . . "and beyond there are meadows,/and mountains and plains." It was human feeling that made these things memorable.

The epigraph, from Wordsworth's poem "To My Sister," had been in my mind for years. The mind is the best notebook. When I had written the poem, my mind handed me the quotation and the title, "The Hour of Feeling."

"How many drafts did the poem go through?" Maybe fifteen, though that is only a guess. "What intervals of time elapsed between the drafts?" Thirteen years from the notebook entries to the finished poem. "Did the poem shrink or expand? At times it expanded—then, rapidly, it would shrink. As for changes in the lines: sometimes these were changes of rhythm, sometimes of imagery, sometimes of sound.

I "lineate" my poems according to my patterns of thought and speech. I don't follow a literary convention—i.e., meter.

I make verse paragraphs so that a group of lines will be read together. They usually make a unit of thought. Sometimes, however, I will break a long passage into paragraphs because a pause seems indicated, as in speech, for the sake of a little silence. I sometimes make a verse paragraph so that the poem will look better on the page—a shaped form rather than a spate of words.

"What rhythmical principle did you use?" I write according to speech cadence and the cadence of idea groups, to use your terms. I try always to write "with the cadence of a particular emotion, the cadence of a bodily rhythm." Incidentally, I am interested to see you using these terms. I started using them myself some years ago. I don't think they were in general use—they would certainly not have been approved by New Critics and their followers.

I don't have any principles for the use of sound repetition, assonance, alliteration, consonance, onomatopoeia, et cetera. I play these things by ear. As for "exact rhyme," I hardly ever make rhymes. Rhymes occur in some of my recent poems but they are unobtrusive and irregular.

The poem could be read either silently or aloud. I have no preference. To read it to a musical accompaniment would be absurd.

In answer to the question about "metaphorical process"—I don't set out to make metaphors. Similes strike me as awkward. On the other hand, I do write so that my presentation of literal details will have a metaphorical, symbolic, or surrealist effect. I hope that my concentration on details, the thought that has gone into selecting them, the imagination that has gone into moving from one detail to another, will give my descriptions a meaning beyond the literal.

I avoid using abstract language, "poetic" diction, or any other kind of mannerism, unless I am being satiric—which I sometimes am.

I shall not answer all the other questions, so as not to weary myself or the reader. I shall answer those that strike me as more interesting.

I make allusions only when they seem necessary and then I try to explain the allusion within the poem itself. I don't think that anyone who reads my poems has to go to a library to look up allusions. This brings us to the question, "Whom do you visualize as your reader?" It's a touchy question. I certainly don't write for people who read Rod McKuen. Nor for people who want political poetry. In fact, as far as I can see, I have very few readers. On the other hand, my poems have been translated into some nine foreign languages and have been taught in schools in Africa, in Macedonia, and other places. I guess I am writing for readers in the United States in the future. If I told people things they expected to hear, or if I said nice things about my contemporaries, I might have a kind of reader I can visualize. I can visualize that reader very clearly, indeed.

The ordering of the poem was psychological. I wanted one feeling and image to lead naturally to another.

I wanted the poem to open at the end, onto infinity.

The persona in the poem is a part of myself. As though I were a character in a novel. I use techniques of prose fiction in writing my poems. I write narrative poems for the most part—or poetry in which there are elements of narrative—and I set out writing a poem in the way that Conrad or Chekhov would set about writing a story in prose.

Sometimes I'll use a cliché but I'm not conscious of having done so in this poem.

The poem is shaped in verse paragraphs so as not

to weary the eye with masses of words that just keep going.

"How would you describe the tone of this poem?" I'd rather not describe it. If the tone isn't obvious, then this poem has failed.

I would rather not paraphrase the poem for the same reason that I don't want to describe the tone. If a poet were sure of the exact meaning of his poem it would be a poem with a limited meaning. But I want my poetry to open on the unknown.

"The Hour of Feeling" is a continuation of work I have done before. It has the quality of my best writing. In its attempt to create the atmosphere of New York and its presentation of the woman's character the poem may mark an advance: at any rate, the material is presented in a new way and with greater understanding on my part. It is my understanding that gives the disparate elements their coherence. This is an important poem for me, one of the most important I have written.

A Race That Has Not Yet Arrived

An Interview with Beate Josephi

Louis Simpson, in so many of your poems, especially in your Pulitzer Prize winning volume At the End of the Open Road, *you strongly attack the American Dream—the dream as Walt Whitman announced it. Did you ever see America as a great promise that then turned sour?*

What I was attacking in Whitman there was one side of Whitman. There are two Whitmans as I see it. And the side I attacked was his expansionist, materialist, 1880s Gilded Age side in which Whitman was hailing the advance of the railroad, the advance of the American prosperity. That was a public Whitman used by other people and that was the side I was attacking in him and in America generally. Time has proved that I was perfectly right in that the expansionist idea had to stop, was stopped

---

Interviews are usually corrected before they go into print, in order to remove awkwardnesses of thought and speech. In this interview, however, no improvements were made by an editor, and I have made only a few for this reprinting. Though incoherent in places, it has the authentic sound of speech.

The interview took place in Adelaide, Australia. It first appeared in *Opinion* 8, no. 2 (May 1979).

as of the 1950s and 1960s. America then had come to the end of the great materialistic explosion, the idea of the materialistic frontier was at an end. What I was asking for in that book, in fact said very explicitly, was that there would have to be a turning away from sheer materialist life to an inner life.

Yes. I was disillusioned with American materialism as Americans will be, if they are not already. But I was not dissillusioned with the future of America if it expanded in terms of a spiritual, intellectual, or emotional life, or whatever you want to call it.

In your poem "Walt Whitman at Bear Mountain" you say "Where are you, Walt?/The open road goes to the used-car lot." I think this describes very much your disillusionment. Yet is it not amazing that California to so many poets and people, especially in the sixties when your book was published, appeared as a kind of paradise—and to you it appeared as "the end of the open road?"

Well, it was logical and inevitable. I mean poets—with all due modesty—poets are supposed to see things that other people do not see. And it was obvious to me that, although it looked like paradise, given the conditions of American life, the productivity of American life, the expanding population, that this paradise would soon start to choke up. By the time I left California, left San Francisco, they had already started to fill in the bay, et cetera.

What I actually meant was that your reaction seemed to have been so different from, let us say, people like Allen Ginsberg, Jack Kerouac or Lawrence Ferlinghetti to whom it seemed "the open road."

Yes, that is true. They were on the move and were seeing it as an explosion of freedom.

In a sense, when I came to America from Jamaica I had gone on the road myself. But mine is a different temperament from theirs. I am very much European in orientation. I believe with Baudelaire that poetry is melancholy, and that materialism is bound to disappoint you ultimately, and that you must find other values.

Probably the first thing America ever wanted of you was to go to war.

Yes, that's right. Well, it wanted that of everybody at the time. It didn't want it of anybody, actually. You must remember that America didn't go to war. America didn't start the war with Japan. America was attacked. That's just a basic fact.

Was this the feeling when you went to war?

Definitely. It is very hard to explain to other people, especially to younger people. There are a couple of things they really don't understand. One is that they think of World War II and Vietnam and Korea as one war of the same kind. They are as different as the sun and the moon. In World War II there was no alternative for an American, unless you were a thoroughgoing pacifist, which I was not and never will be. But I was against the war in Vietnam. This was a completely different thing. Apart from it being absolutely stupid and ignorant to be there, uninformed about the nature of Vietnam, China, and

Cambodia and all those places, we simply had no business there at all.

To a different matter: in your poem "In the Suburbs"—if I may quote it in full:

In the Suburbs

There's no way out.
You were born to waste your life.
You were born to this middle class of life

As others before you
Were born to walk in procession
To the temple, singing.

The last line stands as an ambiguous comparison to ancient times. Do you see it as a negative or a positive analogy?

That's a good question, because most people who read that poem think it is just being satirical, comparing the poor present with a wonderful past. This is not how I meant it. What I really meant was you have to see in your lives, even though they are middle class and in the suburbs, a pattern which is just as important and religious and holy as that of the people walking to the temple, singing: if you can see it.

But then, there is the beginning stanza of "Sacred Objects":

I am taking part in a great experiment—
whether a writer can live peacefully in the suburbs
and not be bored to death . . .

See, I think it is somehow inevitable that if you write about the suburbs you are going to be satirical. All I am saying is that you must be other things as well. Of course, there are so many things about suburbia which are limiting. It is the middle-class nuclear family and—I am a little down on that—the way parents hang on to their children to provide them with a direction or an incentive for living. They are really electing their children to solve their own problems. It is the timidity of suburban life that is so limiting.

Of course, they have the comfortable life, the kidney-shaped swimming pools, et cetera. That is kind of ridiculous to me. But that is California. Culturally pretentious and unexperimental. The mindless, affluent, good life. The reason I left California was I don't want "the good life." I really can't stand it.

You mentioned the William Carlos Williams saying—I approximate it now—to "take the ordinary and lift it up on a poetic level" was what you once found very relevant when formulating your own direction of poetry.

Yes, Williams makes it more complicated than that. He has a whole theory of locality which doesn't mean just writing about where you live, but writing out of your own experience. Everything you write must somehow be connected to your own experience. This quite often includes locality. But the general aim of his writing is to begin with particulars of place and experience, and to transform them into something significant. Incidentally, this is not only Williams but William James and the American positivists with whom Williams was in sympathy. And also Count Hermann Keyserling, who wrote *America Set Free.*

I felt the emphasis was also on "the ordinary"—that it doesn't have to be an exotic or exquisite moment in your life.

No, preferably you should not take an exotic or extraordinary moment, because that would not be very significant really.

But isn't it so much harder to write about the ordinary experience?

It is difficult, it requires a kind of concentration I would describe as Buddhist. It means concentrating on the ordinary and removing distraction, which leads to the question of metaphor. When you concentrate on the thing in front of you, you don't compare it to anything else because it distracts you from the moment of concentration.

You actually see your style of poetry very much as a turning away from "the gorgeous English poetics," brimful with metaphors.

Yes, for the same reason. There is a constant process of comparison, simile, and metaphor, going on in traditional English poetry, and this actually distracts you from dealing with everyday life.

To what extent did your mother being of Russian-Jewish origin influence your attitude towards America? Did you ever feel like a migrant, or part of a minority?

Very much so. I have always felt like a migrant, an outsider in America. And I used to worry about it. But then I realized so many Americans do in one way or another. I used to feel if I only had been born in Ohio, or something, I wouldn't have had all these terrible problems of identity. Also, I could have written more easily because I would have been more consistent. I wouldn't have had all these mixtures. But then I came to know people from Ohio, and found, when they went to New York, they felt completely out of it, too. Everybody shifts in America, is out of it somehow. And the people who are in, the old-fashioned WASP families, some of their children are the most lost of all. They feel that they are privileged and they don't want to be. They feel that they have been cut out of vital minority experience. That's very common in the sixties and seventies.

So, my mother was a Jew, I was a Jamaican, my father was Jamaican. And then I gave up my own culture and came to America. I was a very displaced person when I was seventeen. This is why I went, why I had to go into the war—or go back to Jamaica, that was the choice—because I felt, apart from ethical or political reasons, going into the army I would be assimilated as fast as possible. Also, I made myself get jobs in America, jobs that were the job of the common man. I waited on tables, worked in a packing firm packing, and so on. I wanted to know very fast what it is like to be an American.

In one of your poems you say "I feel part of a race that has not yet arrived in America."

That's right. I do. But that's not just a race. That's a question of being a poet. I feel all the poets in America are part of a race that has not yet arrived, but that we are doing something right now that is terribly important. There is in America in the last fifteen, twenty years a feeling amongst poets that they are working out a body of poetry that is for the future. I think they are conscious of this development. If you were a young person, a young poet or a literary person, thirty years from now, you would have a terrific richness to choose from. There are lots of good poets, and they all have this feeling that what they are doing is very important—not necessarily great, that concept has gone out of our generation, with a couple of exceptions I won't name because I think it is despicable in them, cultivating their own greatness—but in general I think a lot of very fine American poets are conscious of this ongoing thing that they all share which is that we are writing poems for other people in the future. But they have not yet arrived—that is what I meant.

There are some poems or lines that ring familiar in Australian ears, for example your sentence in "Lines Written Near San Francisco": "Do Americans always have to be second rate," reminds me strongly of A. D. Hope's dictum that Australia is the place "where secondhand European pullulate/timidly on alien shores." Isn't this actually a sign of a culture still in colonial bonds?

Yes it is. Of course, in America it is much less strong than here. But I am particularly conscious of it in America because I came from a colony like Australia. I was very anti-English when I was seventeen years old. I was actually distributing a revolutionary newspaper in the streets of Jamaica, called *Public Opinion,* and I was really part of a group that was trying to get the English out. And I have never been back in this atmosphere until I came here. It reminds me again of this English overlay. In America we've pretty much broken away from that. But not entirely by any means.

Also another poem entitled "American Poetry":

> Whatever it is, it must have
> A stomach that can digest
> Rubber, coal, uranium, moons, poems.
>
> Like the shark, it contains a shoe.
> It must swim for miles through the desert
> Uttering cries that are almost human.

All the images used in this poem could easily sum up to a poem called "Australian Poetry." Do you think the necessities you mention in your poem for American poetry are in fact universal?

No, not universal, but for any culture that is comparatively new, yes, certainly. Any culture where you are in a state of not having fully formulated your own culture the poem would apply. I wouldn't think that a Frenchman would understand that poem—actually I do know a Frenchman who understands it, but he is a rare kind of Frenchman.

In one of your poems you call your generation "The Silent Generation" where heroic acts cannot be performed anymore. Do you think this judgment also holds for the following generations?

No. That poem was written in the very late 1950s and I would not have been able to write this poem five years later, because then it wasn't silent. I was talking about my own generation. I am a different generation from Allen Ginsberg for example. Our age difference is not that great, but it was the war experience that made the difference. They spoke out directly. I still came from a generation that did not. Even now, I don't speak directly like Allen

Ginsberg and never will. Because I don't want to. But there was that phrase "The Silent Generation" which was very common of the 1950s people. They were not silent in the long run, as you can see with Saul Bellow or Norman Mailer, who were people of my age. Only for a while after the Second World War not many voices were raised.

What made the change, Vietnam?

No, no. The speaking out began before Vietnam. It began in poetry in the late fifties. By the time Ginsberg read "Howl" in 1956. "The Silent Generation" lasted from the end of the war, 1946, to 1956. Ten years of what seemed like a kind of exhausted period. But in this exhausted period people were gathering themselves to speak out in the sixties. I would say for poetry the turning point was Ginsberg's performance of "Howl" and for prose, well, I don't know, perhaps Bellow's publishing of *The Adventures of Augie March.*

Your own poetry is very accessible without being flat. However you pointed out how dangerous a path it is, how easily one could fall into flat prose.

Yes, you can. The only thing that can save you from doing that is intensity of concentration, and selectivity. The secret is selecting the right detail and concentrating on that. And what you get is actually a transformation of the everyday by winnowing out the irrelevant things. That means you must have a concept in your mind. You do have a concept and you remove from it things that are distracting. But again, the danger is very great of being just flat and prosaic.

Which you try to avoid in your own poetry . . .

Which I try to avoid in my own, naturally. One way of avoiding it is if you do have a narrative of some kind with something happening actually in the poem: what the reader is carried by is a structure of events in the poem or movement from point to point or a feeling or emotion, and the poem is not allowed to bog down. It does not depend on the kind of language you use, but on the structure of the poem and what you say.

William Carlos Williams's
Idea of Poetry

Thirty years ago William Carlos Williams was an obscure author, his work known only to a few hundred readers of modern poetry. In the 1950s his reputation began to grow, and today he is as famous as a poet can hope to be, but he is still obscure, for his ideas are misunderstood, not least by people who think that they understand them. They believe that Williams's ideas are straightforward and that there is no need to look up what he actually said. They believe that he stood for two principles: that American poets must write about their own lives, in their immediate environment, and that they should write in the language of ordinary, everyday speech.

For these people the matter is perfectly simple; looked at from their point of view, Williams is reduced to a know-nothing, provincial writer, the kind of person that hostile critics—T. S. Eliot, for example—have taken him to be. But this view of Williams is mistaken. He was a far more generous thinker than his followers would have us believe, and

---

This article first appeared in *Poetry Society of America Bulletin* 68, no. 4 (May 1978).

his poetry is more subtle than the kind of writing, of a plain, everyday, confessional kind, that is ascribed to his influence.

In the 1920s Williams made a choice: he would live in Rutherford, make his life there as a doctor and a poet. He was not willing to give his life entirely to art, as had his friend Ezra Pound. Perhaps he was not so sure of his talent . . . and besides, he liked people who came to him with their ailments. They were material for poems . . . more than he could have found in a rootless, bohemian existence.

The decision cost him a great deal, however, for Rutherford is not London or Paris. While he was doing his hospital rounds, or visiting some sick woman in a dank basement, Pound, Eliot, and a dozen other American writers were meeting exciting people, listening to the newest ideas, and being exposed to art. The industrial landscape of New Jersey had little of the kind to offer. Williams would drive in to Manhattan and meet with painters and poets, but still he felt that his life was dull, for an artist.

So he searched about in the writings of other men for a justification. John Dewey had said, "The local is the only universal, upon that all art builds." Keyserling said much the same: "Every autochthonous culture in the world began as a local culture. Culture is always a daughter of spirit, married to earth. A man who is not yet the native son of a soil can conquer matter spiritually only on a small scale."

From reading such as this, and out of the need to make a life where he was, Williams developed his theory of "locality." In poem after poem he wrote about things he had seen or heard in Rutherford. He wrote about "The odor of the poor farmer's fried supper . . . mixing with the smell of the hemlocks." Williams is the poet of the place where he lived—no question of it.

If this were all, then the common idea of Williams would be true. But Williams's locality does not stop at the local—it includes it, then goes on to other things. This is the point that many readers have not seen. If we turn to Williams's poetry it is clear that he was not only the poet of Rutherford. Consider, for example, the following lines from *Paterson.*

> A flight of birds, all together,
> seeking their nests in the season
> a flock before dawn, small birds
> "That slepen al the night with open ye,"
> moved by desire, passionately, they
> have come a long way . . .

Far from being limited to New Jersey, this passage, with its line from Chaucer, positively evokes another landscape and another time. Williams locality was able to include this too—it was able to include anything that came into the poet's mind.

There is one commandment, however, and like most commandments it begins with Thou Shalt Not. The poet must not try to be universal without first being particular. It would be foolish for a poet living in New Jersey to attempt to deny this and write as though he were living in Chaucer's England. The poet must respond to his environment. He must put everything he knows into his writing, his own life included. From there he may proceed to write about anything, as Williams did when he wrote about a unicorn and about paintings by Breughel. But it is the life of the poet that gives life to his verse.

The commandment is inclusive rather than the reverse, and poets who have taken Williams's writing about ordinary, everyday things as meaning that poetry must limit itself to this, or that the poet must remain fixed within the circumference of his own, personal experience, have narrowed the idea of poetry in a way that Williams never intended. He wanted every man to fulfill himself in his own way, and to proceed from there. Let him fulfill himself, however—that was essential. One can only arrive at the universal by going through the particular. Mere abstractions are of no use. What kind of universal would it be if, when we got there, we found that it included nothing we had known for ourselves . . . none of the sights, and sounds, and smells of earth?

This assumes that life, at the bottom, is good . . . that nature is good. And, indeed, Williams is romantic, in the line that descends from Rousseau. This is especially admirable when one considers that Williams was a doctor whose practice lay among the poor. Experience did not make him disillusioned—if anything, it made him a more feeling man as time went by.

The poet of *Paterson* and *Pictures from Breughel* has a passionate faith in nature and the intelligence of the people. If you immerse yourself in the life of the people and penetrate beneath the surface of their language, you will discover poetry. "The underlying meaning of all they want to tell us and have always failed to communicate is the poem, the poem which their lives are being lived to realize. No one will believe it. And it is the actual words, as we hear them spoken under all circumstances, which contain it."

Note that Williams says that the actual words contain poetry—he does not say that they are poetry. For Williams, as for Wordsworth, poetry is a *selection* of the language really used by men.

Allen Ginsberg tells of going to hear Williams read his poems at the Museum of Modern Art, and of discovering that Williams wrote just as he talked. Williams read one poem that ended with an unfinished sentence. It just trailed off, the way one might let a sentence trail off if one were speaking, unable to find the right word. For Ginsberg this was a complete overturning of his previously held ideas. It wasn't necessary to put one's thoughts in rhyme and meter—one just wrote them down as they came. The thought would find its own shape.

For Ginsberg perhaps, and all who have followed him, but certainly not for Williams. It is true that Williams took phrases and rhythms from American speech and incorporated them in his writing. When Ginsberg visited Williams he found him thinking about a phrase he had heard a workman use, "I'll kick yuh eye." It had a syncopation, he told Ginsberg, that could not be reproduced in traditional English meters. But though he used patterns of speech in his poetry, Williams's poems do not sound like speech. Consider, for example, the following lines from "Asphodel, That Greeny Flower."

> I saw another man
> yesterday
>   in the subway.
> I was on my way uptown
>   to a meeting.
>   He kept looking at me
> and I at him:
>   He had a worn knobbed stick
>   between his knees
> suitable
>   to keep off dogs,
>   a man of perhaps forty . . .
>   His trousers

were striped
　　and a lively
　　　reddish brown. His shoes
which were good
　　if somewhat worn
　　　had been recently polished.
His brown socks
　　were about his ankles.
　　　In his breast pocket
he carried
　　a gold fountain pen
　　and a mechanical
pencil. For some reason
　　which I could not fathom
　　　I was unable
to keep my eyes off him.
　　A worn leather zipper case
　　　bulging with its contents
lay between his ankles
　　on the floor.
　　　Then I remembered:
When my father was a young man—
　　it came to me
　　　from an old photograph—
he wore such a beard.
　　This man
　　　reminds me of my father.
I am looking
　　into my father's
　　　face!

No one could possibly think that this is the language of speech. It is a selection of language, shaped to produce a certain effect. It is the sound of a man thinking.

Most of Williams's poetry has this sound. So that the idea that Williams's poetry is taken directly from common speech is a misrepresentation. Hearing Williams read his poems may have freed Ginsberg from dependence on literary English and conventional verse forms, but his conclusion is false, that Williams wrote just as he talked. A glance at Williams's poetry will show that it is not so: it took a great deal of art to produce these effects of effortless simplicity.

The point is important because nowadays, especially among younger poets, there is a belief that Williams stood for writing out your thoughts just as they arise, in the language of conversation, and that this is enough to make poetry. The belief is due to what has been said about Williams by other poets who did hold a belief in instantaneous composition, notably Kerouac and Ginsberg, though Ginsberg is by no means as instantaneous as his statements would lead one to believe. But for Williams writing was an act that required all possible thought—he had no intention of sinking himself in the vernacular. It is true that he kept an ear cocked for American talk, and included it on occasion in his poetry. But, again, his idea of language, like his idea of locality, was to include, not to exclude. The language of his poetry, as I have said, is that of a man thinking, and finding the words that are right for the poem.

Williams did write an "American language," and in an "American measure," because his life was American. The measure, however, cannot be measured—it is up to every man to find it for himself.

Williams's language was the echo of his thought, and as his thinking was determined by his way of life, and as all his life he was engaged with the people around him, his poetry is indeed American—not because it is narrow, but because it is deep.

Reflections on Narrative Poetry

Why tell stories in lines of verse? Isn't prose a more suitable medium?

It would be, if poets only had ideas and wished to convey them. But feeling is more urgent, and their feelings are expressed by the movement of lines. In poetry the form, more than the idea, creates the emotion we feel when we read the poem.

In everything else poets share the concerns of the writer of prose, and may indeed learn more about writing narrative poems from the novelist than from other poets, for in the past two hundred years it has been the novelist whose labor it was to imitate life, while the poet prided himself on his originality, his remoteness from the everyday. "Life" was the business of the middle class and the novelists who entertained it.

As a result, poetry has been impoverished. In the theory of poetry held by Poe and his French translators, poetry is lyrical and intense, the reflection of an unearthly beauty. Many people believe that poetry is a language we do not speak, and that the best poetry is that which we are least able to understand.

I wish to discuss another kind of poetry, that which undertakes to be an imitation of life. The aim of the narrative poet is the same as for the writer of prose fiction: to interpret experience, with the difference I have mentioned: his writing will move in measure. And this measure evokes a harmony that seems apart from life. I say "seems" because it would be impossible to prove that it exists. Readers of poetry, however, feel it. This harmony is what poetry is, as distinct from prose.

Let us learn from the novelist, however, how to deal with the world, for it is his specialty. We may learn from Chekhov, and Conrad, and Joyce . . . and a hundred other writers of fiction. I see no reason that a poet should not take notes, as prose writers do, or write out his story first in prose. I believe that Yeats sometimes worked in this way.

I once read an interview with a poet in which she spoke contemptuously of "subject-seeking" poets. It was Charles Olson's teaching, I believe, that the poet should not have a subject but should put himself into a dynamic relationship with the environment, and poetry would rise out of this. But when I read the books of the poet who was so down on subject-seekers, I found that her own poems always had a subject. In fact, she could be all too explicit, writing about her family or writing poems with a political message. Either she was deceived about the nature of her writing or felt that she could dispense with the rule she had made for others.

There are kinds of poetry that seem visionary, having little resemblance to life. But even these rely on images, and the images, however farfetched, have points of contact with our experience. The room envisioned by Rimbaud at the bottom of a lake is still a room. But I shall not insist on the point. Let us admit that there are kinds of poetry that are not representations of life. This does not concern us: we are speaking of narrative poetry. This has to do with actions and scenes. The action may be subtle, the scene barely sketched, but the aim is to move the reader, and to increase understanding, by touching the springs of nature.

But it is not enough to hold a mirror up to nature. As Henry James says in the preface to *The Spoils of Poynton*, "Life has no direct sense whatever for the subject and is capable, luckily for us, of nothing but splendid waste. Hence the opportunity for the sublime economy of art."

So you take what you need and rearrange it, and you invent. Invention is supposed to be the sine qua non of the so-called creative arts. It is what people usually mean when they use the word "imagination." The poet, says Longinus, thinks that he sees what he describes, and so is able to place it before the eyes of the reader.

Yes, of course. But I wonder how useful this description is to the man who does the job? It may actually do more harm than good, by urging the writer to strain his powers of invention. Rather than try to work himself up to a pitch of imagination, the poet would do well to discover what is there, in the subject. Let him immerse himself in the scene and wait for something to happen . . . the right, true thing.

"There can be," says James, "evidently, only one logic for these things; there can be for [the writer] only one truth and one direction—the quarter in which his subject most completely expresses itself."

So you choose the direction that has most to offer. Some writers, however, are unwilling to go so far. It is instructive to take up a book of poems and see, with every poem, which direction the poet has chosen to take. Some poets take the easiest direction, an ending that will please most people. The sad thing about these poets is that they don't please anyone very much: for all their attempts to be good-natured the public will desert them for some poet whose writing is obscure and who seems to despise them. The mob does not admire those who flatter it—at any rate, not for long. They know they are only a mob and reserve their admiration for those who tell them so.

One day you were stopped on a street corner by an old panhandler. While the lights were changing and people hurrying by, he told you his story.

He served in Mexico with "Black Jack" Pershing, over forty years ago. He had a wife who was unfaithful. One day he followed her and confronted her with it. "Baby," he said, "I'm wise to you and the lieutenant."

A few days later you wrote a poem about it, trying to describe a Mexican landscape and evoke the atmosphere. But something was missing.

It was not until you asked yourself why you were interested that the story began to move. The account of his following touched upon some unease in your soul. The rest was merely scaffolding: you were not interested in the landscape or the history of the time. But the tale of jealousy affected you . . . you could imagine yourself in his shoes.

But though poetry rises out of feeling, the poem is not just personal. You could put yourself in the old man's shoes . . . you saw yourself following the woman through a lane in the dust and heat. But, and this is my point, you *saw* . . . you were a character in the story. Your feelings had been separated from yourself. You were therefore able to make them move in one direction or another. You were writing a poem to be read by others, not just getting a feeling out of your system.

Storytelling is an impersonal kind of art, even when the story appears to be about oneself. The "I" who appears in the poem is a dramatic character. "Je est un *autre*."

In recent years there was talk of "confessional poetry." Robert Lowell and Sylvia Plath, among others, were said to be confessional poets—that is, to be writing directly about their lives. But when we read the poems in *Life Studies* and *Ariel* we find that the incidents they relate have been shaped so as to make a point. The protagonist is seen as on a stage. In confessional poetry, on the other hand, there is no drama. The drama is not in the poem but outside it, in a life we cannot share.

I would advise the poet to be as objective about himself as possible. In this way you will not be locked into the treadmill of your own personal history, treading the same stairs again and again.

For twenty years there has been an outpouring of subjective art. There was a generation that believed that poetry should be nothing more than an expression of the poet's feelings. "Why talk about art? Be sincere and tell it like it is."

That was an unhappy generation. They could never advance beyond themselves. It is ironic that, at the same time that they were abolishing art, they complained of a lack of understanding. For art is a key to understanding.

Everyone has feelings—indeed it is impossible not to feel. But we need to understand one another.

Scripture tells us that all the ways of a man are right in his own eyes but the Lord pondereth the hearts. The ways of the poet James Merrill must surely be right in his own eyes, and I cannot explain my aversion to his style except as an aversion to the personality it presents. The style is the man.

> Tap on the door and in strolls Robert Morse,
> Closest of summer friends in Stonington.
> (The others are his Isabel, of course,
>
> And Grace and Eleanor—to think what fun
> We've had throughout the years on Water Street . . .)
> He, if no more the youthful fifty-one
>
> Of that first season, is no less the complete
> Amateur. Fugue by fugue Bach's honeycomb
> Drips from his wrist—then, whoops! the Dolly Suite.

What else can one possibly say on this subject? There is one thing: one can say, as an absolute rule, that poets must not use words loosely.

When I was a young man I wrote a poem in which I said that poetry had made me "nearly poor." I showed this to a friend, himself a writer, and he advised me to change "nearly poor" to "poor"—it would be more striking. I kept the line as it was, and never again did I pay attention to anything this critic had to say. A man who does not know the difference between being nearly poor and being poor, or who is willing to disregard it in order to make a better-sounding line, is not to be trusted. A man like that would say anything.

Since we have moved away from standard forms, the movement of the line, also, depends on the movement of the poet's soul, how he feels, and thinks, and breathes. As late as the 1950s American poets were expected to write in meter and rhyme. And a few years ago there was talk of songwriters' bringing about a renaissance of rhyme. But there has been no talk of this lately. Most American poets write free verse. This may fall into groups of lines that make a repeating pattern, but the pattern is still irregular. I do not know of any poet who writes in regular forms—meter, stanza, and rhyme—with the assurance of Robert Lowell and Richard Wilbur thirty years ago.

I believe that we shall continue to write free verse of one kind and another, and that it is possible to write a sustained narrative in free verse just as effectively as though it were written in hexameters or the meters used by Walter Scott. The long narrative poem by Patrick Kavanagh titled "The Great Hunger" is a case in point. It moves just as well as writing in rhyme and meter, and, moreover, echoes the speech of a modern world, which meter and rhyme cannot.

I can see no reason for writing in the old forms of verse. Finding the form for the poem as one writes is half the joy of poetry.

Poets try to think of new images. But it does not matter whether the image be new or old—what matters is that it be true. Poets who think that by producing farfetched images they are changing our consciousness are doing nothing of the kind. One comes to expect the unexpected.

As the painter Magritte points out, everyone is familiar with the bird in a cage. Anyone can visualize a fish in a cage, or a shoe. But these images, though they are curious, are, unfortunately, arbitrary and accidental. If you wish to surprise, alarm, and alert the reader on the deeper levels of consciousness, visualize a large egg in the cage.

"There exists a secret affinity between certain images; it holds equally for the objects represented by these images."

One writes, refusing temptations, sailing past the siren voices. Are the lines about morphology really necessary? What worked for another may not work for you. All sorts of ideas come into a writer's head, but only some are in keeping with his nature, his way of saying a thing.

Imagine that you are reading your poem aloud, and that two or three people whose intelligence you respect are sitting in the audience. If you say something banal, or try to conceal a poverty of thought in a cloud of verbiage, you will see them yawn, their eyes beginning to close.

If you visualize an audience you won't go in for merely descriptive writing. It was description that killed the narrative poem in the nineteenth century. Think of the long poems of Tennyson or Swinburne. What was it the Victorians found in all that scenery? Perhaps it had something to do with sex. The shopkeepers who ruled Western Europe and, later, the United States, couldn't tolerate talk of sex in their houses. But the woods were loaded with naked bums and flying feet.

Since movies were invented we have had no time for descriptions of scenery and for long drawn-out transitions. Nor for the working-out of an obvious plot. And still this kind of poetry continues to be written. The history of the conquistadors and wagon trains are favorite subjects. Sometimes these volumes are handsomely bound—American publishers are incurable optimists, they hope for another *John Brown's Body,* but what they are more likely to get is the equivalent of the Thanksgiving play, with scenes of the Pilgrim Fathers—the parts being taken by members of the town council—Red Indians, the minister and the minister's wife, and the farmhand and his girl. It ends with bringing on a cow and baskets heaped with corn and pumpkins. Perhaps this is what people have in mind when they warn us of the danger of having a subject.

I have been reading an article on prose fiction in which the writer says that, without anyone's noticing, we have entered upon a new period of realism. I believe this to be true, and true of poetry as well.

"Most artists and critics," said Susan Sontag, writing in the sixties, "have discarded the theory of art as representation of an outer reality in favor of art as subjective expression."

Critics define movements in art just as they come to an end. For twenty years we have been reading poetry that expressed the personal feelings and opinions of the poet. The movement is exhausted— this is apparent in the visual arts as well as poetry and fiction. People long for understanding and a community of some kind.

The word "realism" can be misleading. I do not mean reporting, but writing that penetrates beneath the surface to currents of feeling and thought. Not Champfleury but Flaubert.

I do not know a better way to explain my ideas than by showing how I have applied them. I shall therefore end with a poem.

The images have the affinities Magritte speaks of, though I do not think I should point them out—to do so would take away the pleasure of reading, for myself as well as the reader. I may point out, however, that realism allows for fantastic images and ideas . . . but they have a reason for being. The landscape that suddenly appears in the poem . . . the old man sitting with his back to the wall, the woman who appears in a doorway . . . are in the mind of one of the characters.

The Man She Loved

In the dusk
men with sidelocks, wearing hats
and long black coats walked side by side,
hands clasped behind their backs,
talking Yiddish. It was like being in a foreign
    country.

The members of the family
arrived one by one . . .
his aunts, his uncle, and his mother
talking about her business
in Venezuela. She had moved to a new building
with enough space and an excellent location.

To their simple, affectionate questions
he returned simple answers.
For how could he explain what it meant to be a
    writer . . .
a world that was entirely different,
and yet it would include the sofa
and the smell of chicken cooking.

Little did they know as they spoke
that one day they would be immortal
in a novel that commanded the sweep
of Tolstoy, a magnificent creation
that would bring within its compass
offices in Manhattan and jungles
of the Amazon. A grasp of psychology
and sense of the passing of time
that can only be compared to,
without exaggerating, Proust.

The path wound through undergrowth.
Palms rose at an angle from the humid plain.
He passed a hut with chickens and goats . . .
an old man who sat with his back to a wall,
not seeing. A woman came out of a door
and stared after him.
                    In the distance
the purple mountains shone, fading
as the heat increased.

"Let me take a look at it,"
said Joey. He took the watch
from Beth, pried open the back,
and laid it on the table before him.
He reached in his jacket
and produced a jeweler's loupe . . .
screwed it into his eye,
and examined the works.
"I can fix it. It only needs an adjustment."

"Are you sure?" said his sister.
"I wouldn't want anything to happen to it.
Jack gave it to me."

The used-car tycoon. But they never married.
"I've got," he said, "a tiger by the tail,"
meaning the used-car business.

Joey stared at her.
"Don't you think I know my business?"

Siblings. Members of the one family,
tied by affection, and doubt . . .
right down to the funeral

when, looking at the face in the box,
you can be sure. "That's real enough."

Spreading her wings at the piano . . .
"The Man I Love." A pleasant voice
but thin.

She travelled to Central America
on the Grace Line, singing with a band.
White boats on a deep blue sea . . .
at night a trail of fireflies.
"Sitting at the Captain's table,"
"Teeing off at the Liguanea Club."

This picture was taken much earlier . . .
three flappers with knee-high skirts.
1921.
They were still living in Delancey Street.

The songs that year were "Say It with Music"
and "If You Would Care for Me."